THE LIFE BEYOND THE VEIL

SPIRIT MESSAGES RECEIVED AND
WRITTEN DOWN
BY THE REV. GEORGE VALE OWEN {1860-1931}
VICAR OF ORFORD, LANCASHIRE

WITH AN APPRECIATION BY
LORD NORTHCLIFFE

AND AN INTRODUCTION BY
SIR ARTHUR CONAN DOYLE, M.D., LL.D.

EDITED BY H. W. ENGHOLM

BOOK I: THE LOWLANDS OF HEAVEN
BOOK II: THE HIGHLANDS OF HEAVEN

A Red Pill Press classic reprint

Visit us at redpillpress.com

Printed in Canada

AN APPRECIATION BY LORD NORTHCLIFFE

I have not had an opportunity of reading the whole of The Life Beyond the Veil, but among the passages I have perused are many of great beauty.

It seems to me that the personality of the Rev. G. Vale Owen is a matter of deep importance and to be considered in connection with these very remarkable documents. During the brief interview that I had with him I felt that I was in the presence of a man of sincerity and conviction. He laid no claims to any particular psychic gift. He expressed a desire for as little publicity as possible, and declined any of the great emoluments that could easily have come to him as the result of the enormous interest felt by the public all over the world in these scripts.

TABLE OF CONTENTS

On the borderland—An initiation—"From strength to strength"—Sorrow and joy—Trees and flowers—The Chasm and the Bridge—"There is a great Gulf fixed"—The Cross of Light—"One Sinner who repenteth".

The Home of Music—"They stand, those Halls of Sion, all Jubilant with song, and bright with many an Angel"—The Halls of Colour—The heavenly life—A story with a moral—After death, realization and first experiences—A parting and a meeting—A children's school, progressive botany—A Manifestation—The child and the globe of light—All creation one—Creative thinking.

At the Home of Arnol—A lesson in wisdom—Evolution, inverted and progressive—The science of creation—The entity the "Name"— Chasm and the Bridge—"Send out Thy light" to "lead me"— From darkness into light—Angels can suffer—Angelic ministry.

BOOK I: THE LOWLANDS OF HEAVEN

PREFACE

THIS volume contains the first of a series of communications from beyond the veil, received and written down by the Rev. G. Vale Owen, Vicar of Orford, Lancashire.

It should be clearly understood that these messages, while complete in themselves, deal chiefly with the "Sphere of Light" nearest to the earth in which the Vicar's mother, who is the principal communicator, states that she dwells, and that her impressions are chiefly individual to herself and are thus those of a newcomer and learner whose experiences are limited to a restricted area. Wider regions and greater heights and depths are explored, the inter-relation of this and the after-life is more fully explained, and both narrative and exposition of aims and principles are more vigorous, clear and comprehensive in succeeding messages, contained in other volumes of the series which follow this.

That said, however, the high importance and far-reaching significance of this volume must be affirmed. It gives the most complete and most detailed statement of conditions in the after-life yet published. It must be read and studied in order to gain an understanding of the further messages.

The narrative brings one face to face with a Spiritual Universe of unimaginable immensity and grandeur, with sphere upon sphere of the realms of light which stretch away into infinity. We are told that those who have passed from our earth life inhabit the nearer spheres, amid surroundings not wholly dissimilar from those they have known in this world; that at death we shall enter the sphere for which our spiritual development fits us. There is to be no sudden change in our personality. We shall not be plunged into forgetfulness. A human being is not transformed into another being.

In the first sphere of light we find trees and flowers like those that grow in earthly gardens; but more beautiful, immune from decay and death, and endowed with qualities that make them more completely a part of our lives. Around us are birds and animals, still the friends of man, but nearer, more intelligent, and freed from the fears and the cruelties they suffer here. We find houses and gardens, but of substance, colour and atmosphere more responsive to our presence; water whose playing is music; wide ranging harmonies of colour. We find everything more radiant, more joyous, more exquisitely complex, and while our activities are multiplied, our life is more restful.

Differences in age disappear. There, are no "old" in the Spheres of Light; there are only the graceful and strong.

Spirits from a higher sphere may descend to the lower, may even be sent on a mission to earth. But ere they can reach us they must first accustom themselves to the dimmer light and heavier "air" of the lower spheres. They must undergo a change ere they can penetrate the dense and murky atmosphere in which our world is enfolded.

That is why the spirit voices so often reach us in broken fragments which our dull intelligence can hardly piece together. That is why we can so rarely hear the words and feel the presence of those who are longing to reach and to comfort their friends.

So small a thing is the change which we call death, the narrative tells us, that many do not realize it. They have to be taught that they are in another world, the world of reunion. "She fell asleep", says one of the messages which describe the passing of such a spirit.

"She fell asleep, and the cord of life was severed by our watching friends, and then softly they awoke her, and she looked up and smiled very sweetly into the face of one who leaned over her. [...] She began to wonder why these strange faces were around her in place of the friends and nurses she had last seen.

"She inquired where she was. When she was told, a look of wonder and yearning came over her face, and she asked to be allowed to see the friends she had left. This was granted her, and she looked on them through the veil, and lowered her head sadly. 'If only they could know', she said, 'how free from pain I am now and comfortable! Can you not tell them?' We tried to do so, but only one of them heard, I think, and he only imperfectly, and soon put it away as a fancy."

11

To many, indeed, these spirit messages will seem to shed new illumination upon passages in the Bible whose interpretation they have hitherto regarded as obscure. Others, whose faith may have wavered beneath the impact of modern criticism or under the trials of sorrow and bereavement, may well find in this new revelation the answer that will resolve their doubts and deepen into certainty their hope of ultimate reunion after death.

Here is a document which is placed before the reader as an authentic communication from the world beyond. No man can say what the limits of its influence will be, or how far-reaching an effect it may have upon the minds and lives of the men and women by whom it will be read. But one thing is certain. A manuscript of such a character, coming from such a source, demands the most careful study—so tremendous are the claims made for these revelations, so rich in human interest is the actual narrative, so undoubted is Mr. Vale Owen's sincerity.

G.V.O.

"WHAT MANNER OF MAN IS HE?"

The Rev. G. Vale Owen is a typical clergyman of the Church of England, devoted to his parish and completely absorbed in his work. Nothing was further from his thoughts, a few years ago, than that he should be made a medium for "spirit" communications. His career has been uneventful. Born in Birmingham in 1869, and educated at the Midland Institute and Queen's College in that city, he was ordained by the Bishop of Liverpool to the curacy of Seaforth in 1893; then was curate successively of Fairfield, 1895, and of Matthew's, Scotland Road, 1897—both of Liverpool.

It was in 1900 that he went to Orford, Warrington, as curate-in-charge. Orford Church was built in 1908, when a new parish was formed and he became the first vicar. His vicarage was built so recently as 1915.

Though he feared that the quietude of his life in his parish would be disturbed, Mr. Vale Owen felt that the importance of the revelations which were sent through him did not permit him to follow his own wishes and withhold his name, and regarding himself as only an instrument for the transmission of the messages, he refused to accept any money payment for the publication of the scripts, great as had been the labour they had thrown upon him.

Though his personality was much discussed on the first appearance of the messages, that circumstance did not affect his absorption in the work of his parish. He felt that that parish was peculiarly his own, since his was the only church in the village, and he had become intimately bound up with every family in it during his twenty years' service.

Villagers speak of him as "G.V.O."—an abbreviation of his name which in itself is a sign of affection. One of them recounted an incident typical of the means by which he has won and retained their close friendship.

"Coming home late one night", he said, "I was startled to see a tall, dark figure dash past me at a run. It was our Vicar. I learnt afterwards that one of his young parishioners, who was ill, had become restless through pain, and had asked that Mr. Owen should come and talk to her and pray at her bedside. Her brother had at once cycled to the vicarage, and Mr. Owen, who had retired for the night, had dressed at top speed and hurried to the house.

"He is always available at any hour, and such is his influence that invalids belonging to all denominations ask for him. Can you wonder why he is a welcome guest in every house?"

When Mr. Vale Owen went first to Orford his congregation worshipped in a large room of the village schoolroom. He told them they were "getting their religion too cheaply" and did not appreciate it enough. Then, obtaining donations from prosperous friends of the village, he called the parishioners together and organized a system of weekly collections, to which every family subscribed according to its means. In this way he succeeded in getting a church bat and an excellent organ installed. When the War came, about 200 Orford men served in the Forces. All of them regarded "G.V.O." as their chief "home pal" and wrote to him regularly of their adventures. All were "his lads", and he always wrote encouraging them to "play the game".

In appearance, the Rev. G. Vale Owen is tall, spare, and a little bent. One might at first judge him to be the shy recluse. But his deeply-lined face lights up readily with a smile and, most unassuming and approachable of men, he has a genius for friendship. There is no trace of the aloofness of the dreamer in his relations with anyone with whom he comes in contact. He is above all practical. The building of his new church at a time which many thought premature, is one of the standing evidences of that quality. To know him is to realize that he is a fitting instrument indeed to receive such communications as are set forth in these pages. His life has been one of strenuous endeavour to help his fellows to understand the reality of sacred things, to lighten their hearts and strengthen their courage; his first thought and his last have been for others. But G.V.O.'s point of view may perhaps best be shown by the following illustration.

Amongst many thousands of letters received at the vicarage at Orford during the early days of the publication of the script in The Weekly Dispatch was this:

"Rev. Sir,— Pray for the writer of this note who is in great trouble concerning a little child who is afflicted. I have read about

BOOK I: THE LOWLANDS OF HEAVEN

you and I feel you must be very near to God, and if you were to say, 'Dear Father, help your child', He would hear. Please do not fail to pray. The Lord understands. This is a cry for help from a mother's aching heart. God bless you."

Mr. Vale Owen's comment in speaking of this to a friend was: "...And yet The Weekly Dispatch says I am receiving no payment."It was in this spirit that the Vicar of Orford gave permission for these communications to be placed before the world. He hoped that by so doing he would be instrumental in bringing light into many dark places, strengthening the faith of the people and doing his humble duty to those fair angel friends, who, as he himself often remarked, "have been so gentle and patient with me during those precious hours I spent at their bidding in the vestry of the little Parish Church at Orford".

H. W. ENGHOLM.   LONDON, May, 1920.

GENERAL NOTES

HOW THE MESSAGES CAME

In the typewritten copies of the original manuscript, Mr. Vale Owen gave a description of how it came about that he acted as amanuensis for his mother and the spirit beings who in turn took her place at the sittings in the vestry of the church at Orford. He said:

"There is an opinion abroad that the clergy are very credulous beings. But our training in the exercise of the critical faculty places us among the most hard-to-convince when any new truth is in question. It took a quarter of a century to convince me—ten years that spirit communication was a fact, and fifteen that the fact was legitimate and good.

"From the moment I had taken this decision, the answer began to appear. First my wife developed the power of automatic writing. Then through her I received requests that I would sit quietly, pencil in hand, and take down any thoughts which seem to come into my mind projected there by some external personality and not consequent on the exercise of my own mentality. Reluctance lasted a long time, but at last I felt that friends were at hand who wished very earnestly to speak with me. They did not overrule or compel my will in any way—that would have settled the matter at once, so far as I was concerned—but their wishes were made ever more plain.

"I felt at last that I ought to give them an opportunity, for I was impressed with the feeling that the influence was a good one, so, at last, very doubtfully I decided to sit in my cassock in the vestry after Evensong.

"The first four or five messages wandered aimlessly from one subject to another. But gradually the sentences began to take consecutive form, and at last I got some which were understandable. From that time, development kept pace with practice. When the whole series of messages was finished I reckoned up and found that the speed had been maintained at an average rate of twenty-four words a minute. On two occasions only had I any idea what subject was to be treated. That was when the message had obviously been left uncompleted. At other times I had fully expected a certain subject to be taken, but on taking up my pencil the stream of thought went off in an altogether different direction."

G. V. O.

HOW THE COMMUNICATORS OPERATED ON THE OTHER SIDE

It is particularly interesting to note the explanations given by his mother and others of their methods of impressing the mind of Mr. Vale Owen with the words they wished his hand to write. We select the following illustrative passages, which, however, do not appear in this, the first, volume of communications.

It transpired from a later script that when Mr. Vale Owen's mother was communicating, the girl Kathleen, mentioned below, acted for her on the other side as an amanuensis, and controlled the actual writing down of the messages for all the communicators. In the case of Mr. Vale Owen's mother the difficulties of getting through antique words and expressions that were not modern did not, of course, arise in her case, but there seems no doubt from the character of many of her messages that she was not alone in giving them.

(Extract from a later script.)

"Only in part are we able to make in anywise clear to you the method we are employing in this particular case. And that we will so far as we be able.

"First, then, here we stand a group to-night of seven—sometimes more, at others less. We have already broadly settled what we will say to you, but leave the precise wording till we sight you and sense your disposition of mind.

"Then, we take our stand a little distance away lest our influence, the emanations of our several minds, reach you in detail, and not as one stream but as many, and so confuse you. But from the little distance at which we stand they merge and mingle, and are focused into one, so that by the time our thoughts reach you there is unity and not multiplicity of diction.

17

THE LIFE BEYOND THE VEIL

"When you sometimes hesitate, doubtful of a word or phrase, that is when our thoughts, mingling in one, are not quite perfected into the special word required. You pause: and, continuing their blending together, our thoughts at last assume unity, and then you get our idea and at once continue on your way. You have noticed this, doubtless?"

"Yes, but I did not know the cause."[1]

"No. Well, now, to continue. We think our thoughts to you, and sometimes they are in such words as are too antique, as you say, for you to grasp them readily. This is remedied by filtering them through a more modern[2] instrument, and it is of this we now would speak. That instrument is your little friend Kathleen,[3] who is good enough to come between you and us, and so render our thoughts available for you. This in more ways than one.[4]

"First, because she is nearer to you in status than we, who, having been longer here, have become somewhat removed from earth. She is of more recent transplanting, and not yet so far away that when she speaks you cannot hear.

"For a like reason also she comes between. That is, by the words that form her present store. She can still think in her old

---

[1] Question by G.V.O.

[2] On the opposite page is a reproduction of a sheet {Illustrations were not acquired in time to include in this edition} from the actual script written down by the Rev. G. Vale Owen at the sitting of October 6, 1913. It will be noticed how the words and sentences have flowed from the pencil in a swift and steady stream. They are joined together as if the writer were striving to keep pace with the communication which was being impressed upon his mind.

This page of the MS. is particularly interesting, for it shows a question written down by Mr. Vale Owen, and the answer to it immediately following in a steady flow of words.

Mr. Vale Owen always numbered a quantity of sheets of paper before he began to write. He placed these in a block before him on the table in the vestry. Then, using shaded candlelight to illuminate the sheet of paper and with his pencil in his hand, he would wait until he felt the influence to write. When once he started the influence was maintained without a stop until the message for the evening was concluded by the communicator.

H. W. E.

[3] See notes on Kathleen on p. 23

[4] The text of the above MS. will be found on page 67, commencing "Our onward way..."

18

tongue of earth, and it is more modern than our own—though we like it not so well, since it seems to us more composite and less precise.

"But we must not find fault with what is still beautiful. We have, no doubt, still our prejudices and insularity; when we come down here we cannot but take on anew some of those traits we once had but gradually have cast aside.

"The little lady Kathleen is nearer you than we in these respects, and the stream of our impelling we direct on you through her for that reason.

"However, we stand a little apart from you, because the presence of us combined would overmatch you. You could not write down what we would give, and our purpose in coming is to give you such narrative of words as you and others may read with intelligence.

"You glance at the dial of your timekeeper. You call it a watch. Why? That is one little instance of our preference for our older way of speaking. Timekeeper seems to us more explicit than the other word. The meaning of your glance is clear, whatever we call the thing on which it fall. So we bid you good night, good friend....

"We find sometimes, when we read what message we have given, that much which we tried to impress is not apparent there, and some lesser quantity of what we had not in mind appears.

"This is but a natural consequence of the intervention.

of so thick a veil between the sphere from which we speak and that in which the recorder [i.e. Mr. Vale Owen] lives his life.

"The atmosphere of the two spheres is so diverse in quality that, in passing from one to the other, there is always a diminution of speed, so sudden and so marked that a shock is given to the stream of our thoughts, and there is produced, just on the border line, some inevitable confusion. This is one of the many difficulties we find.

"Here is another. The human brain is a very wonderful instrument, but it is of material substance, and, even when the stream of our thoughts reaches and impinges upon it, yet, because of its density, the penetration is impeded and sometimes altogether brought to a stop. For the vibrations, as they leave us, are of high intensity, and the fineness of their quality is a hindrance to their effecting a correspondence in the human brain, which is, gross by comparison.

"Once again: there are many things here for which there are no words in any of the earth languages to express their meaning.

"There are colours which your eyes do not see, but are present in your spectrum; there are more colours which are of higher sublimity than could be reproduced by the medium, which shows both the earth colours to you and registers those invisible to you, but present withal.

"There are also notes and tones of sound of like nature, and too fine for registration by the atmosphere of earth.

"There are forces also, not available with you, not able, to be expressed to you....

"These and other matters are interpenetrating all our life and forming our environment. And when we come to speak of our life here, or of the causes we see in operation, of which you behold the effects alone, we are much perplexed and strive continually to find just how to say it so that it shall be both understood of you and also not too wide of a target as known to us.

"So you will see that we have a task to do in speaking into your sphere from this of ours which is by no means easy. Still, it is worth the doing of it, and so we essay our best and try to rest content."

MR. VALE OWEN'S COMMENTS

In view of the above description, it is interesting to have the following remarks from Mr. Vale Owen, descriptive of his mental and physical condition during the time he was actually receiving the communications. In a letter to the Editor of this volume, Mr. Vale Owen wrote:

"You point out to me the fact that, while in the script itself my communicators give not a little information as to the methods employed in the transmission of messages from their side to ours, yet, on my own part, I have never given you any definite description of the effect produced upon myself.

"The effect of what, perhaps, we might term the more mechanical operations, as these impinge upon the organism of the human brain, the transmitters themselves describe in some detail. Vibrations, initiated by them and projected through the Veil, find their target in the mentality of the human instrument and are reproduced, on this side, in what is, in effect, a kind of inner clairvoyance and clairaudience. Viewed inversely, from the standpoint of the instrument himself, it assumes an aspect something like this: the scenes they describe seem to come along a kind of X-ray stream of vibrations and are received by means of the faculty of visualization. That is, he sees these scenes in his imagination as he, by a similar process, is able to visualize his garden or house, or other well known place, when at a distance.

"The words of the messages seem to travel on a celestial-mundane telephonic current. He can hear them interiorly in much the same manner as he is able to hum over a well-remembered tune, or to reproduce a speech he has heard with all its inflections and cadences, pathetic or uplifting—all this also interiorly, and without himself uttering a sound.

"In addition, however, there is a deeper content in the operation. It is that effect upon the human instrument produced by the more or less intimate contact of spirit with spirit. This is actual 'Spiritual Communion', and is recognized in the Creed of Christendom in the article 'The Communion of Saints'.

"Here enters in an essentially spiritual element which, as our spirit communicators repeatedly tell us, it is not possible adequately to contain in any earthly form of words. It is uplifting to the boundaries, and on occasion, into the very domain, of ecstasy.

"At times such as these earth and earth's affairs retreat into the background, and glimpses are had of what eternity and infinity mean, and of the Presence of God.

"Then Christendom assumes an enlarged aspect and occupies a broader room. It is seen that the whole Church on earth is but a small portion of the Divine Kingdom, which includes within itself, not alone all races and all systems of religion here below, but also that realm of interstellar glories and powers in the mere contemplation of which the human heart grows faint and the reaches of human imagination fade into the boundless infinities pulsating with the heart-love of the One Ineffable Light.

THE LIFE BEYOND THE VEIL

"It is almost needless to add that any one who has ever experienced such contact as this has no room in his heart any more for any paltry sentiment of self-exaltation, or of spiritual pride. I know of no better teacher of humility than this realization of the smallness of the individual earthdweller amid the myriads of those so much brighter ones who, with himself, form the one family of the Creator.

"On the other hand, the sense of security, of comrade ship, of oneness with them, and of the sweet intimacy of their love, is a sure warrant of protection to us lesser ones to whom our angel friends bend down for our uplifting. Be a man prayerful, clean-living and of a humble mind, and no danger of 'devils' can enter in between him and them."

Sincerely your friend,

G. VALE OWEN.

"P.S.—For all this, yet so intimate and so perfect must be the sympathy of aim and affection existing between transmitter and receiver, that whenever any thought comes through which seems to be at variance with what is true, immediately a shock is felt and the instrument faces about, as it were, with a query in his mind, which on the part of the communicator is as immediately observed and noted.

"This sympathy is quite apart from the difference in status, both in mental and spiritual capacity, between the spirit-communicator and the human instrument, and is not affected by it. As I have said above, they 'bend down' to us, and thus bridge over any such inequality."

G. V. O.

ABOUT THOSE WHO COMMUNICATED

Mrs. Owen, the Vicar's mother, from whom the major portion of the messages in this volume came, died on June 8, 1909 at the age of 63. She had not during her life shown any interest in the question of spirit communication.

BOOK I: THE LOWLANDS OF HEAVEN

Her life was spent at Birmingham, where her husband, at first practicing as an architect and surveyor, was compelled by a breakdown in health to change his occupation to that of a chemist. She visited Orford little, and was never during her lifetime on earth in the vestry of the church where the messages were received.

KATHLEEN AND RUBY

Kathleen was first heard of on July 28, 1917, when, as Mrs. Vale Owen, the Vicar's wife, was using the planchette, the following interchange took place, the words written being shown in ordinary, and the questions asked in italic, type:

"Kathleen."

"Who is Kathleen?"

"A friend of Ruby's. Would you like to make my acquaintance?"

"Very much, if you are Ruby's friend."

"Ruby told me to come. She said she was sure you would welcome me for her sake."

("Ruby", it should be explained, was the daughter of the Rev. G. Vale Owen. She was born at Fairfield, Liverpool, on August 26, 1895, and died at the same address on November 21, 1896.)

Kathleen, in answer to questions, said she had been a seamstress, living in Walton Breck Road, Anfield, Liverpool, and had "passed over" at the age of 28, about three years before Ruby. Ruby, she said, was taken to a home where Kathleen looked after, or "mothered" her.

According to her story, the child subsequently brought her frequently to visit Mr. Vale Owen's home, under the care of a guardian. Kathleen from that time constantly came with friends when Mrs. Vale Owen was using the planchette.

ASTRIEL

Intermingled with the messages from Mr. Vale Owen's mother, given in this volume, came others from Astriel, who had been headmaster of a school at Warwick in mid-eighteenth century. His messages touch upon religious faith, philosophical and scientific matters. They have been separated from those of Mrs. Owen and placed in their proper order at the end of this volume.

PRESENCE FORM

The meaning of the term "Presence Form", which appears in various places in this volume and for the first time in the message dated Monday, September 29, 1913 (page 63), is explained in the following communication received by Mr. Vale Owen, in answer to his request that the term be defined:

"A presence form is the form in which a person becomes localized and visible in form at a distance from himself essentially. The form is not an empty sign or symbol, but is alive with the life of the person it so manifests, action and expression being responsive to the thought, will, action and spiritual state of its original. The personality is projected and becomes visible in any place where God (or those of His angels who are so authorized) wills the manifestation to take place.

"By this method the wishes, prayers, thoughts and the whole spiritual state of any one in the earth life, or in any of the regions of the spiritual world, may be manifested in any place or sphere at any moment whets those to whom this high gift is entrusted shall will that it be so.

"A person is not always so manifested in the same presence form, which, from time to time, may be given a different aspect and take a different shape, Under whatever aspect he manifested, however, that form is, for the time being, his real self projected."[5]

---

[5] Initials only are used throughout this volume when reference is made to any person outside Mr. Vale Owen's own family. The name Rose refers to Mr. Vale Owen's wife, and Rene is their daughter.

H. W. E.

24

INTRODUCTION BY SIR ARTHUR CONAN DOYLE

THE long battle is nearly won. The future may be chequered. It may hold many a setback and many a disappointment, but the end is sure.

It has always seemed certain to those who were in touch with truth, that if any inspired document of the new revelation could get really into the hands of the mass of the public, it would be sure by its innate beauty and reasonableness to sweep away every doubt and every prejudice.

Now world-wide publicity is being given to the very one of all others which one would have selected, the purest, the highest, the most complete, the most exalted in its source. Verily the hand of the Lord is here! The narrative is before you and ready to speak for itself. Do not judge it merely by the opening, lofty as that may be, but mark the ever ascending beauty of the narrative, rising steadily until it reaches a level of sustained grandeur.

Do not carp about minute details, but judge it by the general impression.

Do not be unduly humorous because it is new and strange.

Remember that there is no narrative upon earth, not even the most sacred of all, which could not be turned to ridicule by the extraction of passages from their context and by over accentuation of what is immaterial. The total effect upon your mind and soul is the only standard by which to judge the sweep and power of this revelation.

Why should God have scaled up the founts of inspiration two thousand years ago? What warrant have we anywhere for so unnatural a belief? Is it not infinitely more reasonable that a living God should continue to show living force, and that fresh help and knowledge should be poured out from Him to meet the evolution and increased power of comprehension of a more receptive human nature, now purified by suffering.

All these marvels and wonders, these preternatural happenings during the last seventy years, so obvious and notorious that only shut eyes have failed to see them, are trivial in themselves, but are the signals which have called our material minds to attention, and have directed them towards those messages of which this particular script may be said to be the most complete example.

THE LIFE BEYOND THE VEIL

There are many others, varying in detail according to the sphere described or the opacity of the transmitter, for each tinges the light to greater or less extent as it passes through. Only with pure spirit will absolutely pure teaching be received, and yet this story of Heaven must, one would think, be as near to it as mortal conditions allow.

And is it subversive of old beliefs? A thousand times No. It broadens them, it defines them, it beautifies them, it fills in the empty voids which have bewildered us, but save to narrow pedants of the exact word who have lost touch with the spirit, it is infinitely reassuring and illuminating.

How many fleeting phrases of the old Scriptures now take visible shape and meaning?

Do we not begin to understand that "House with many mansions", and realize Paul's "House not made with hands", even as we catch some fleeting glance of that glory which the mind of man has not conceived, neither has his tongue spoken.

It all ceases to be a far-off elusive vision and it becomes real, solid, assured, a bright light ahead as we sail the dark waters of Time, adding a deeper joy to our hours of gladness and wiping away the tear of sorrow by assuring us that if we are only true to God's law and our own higher instincts there are no words to express the happiness which awaits us. Those who mistake words for things will say that Mr. Vale Owen got all this from his subconscious self. Can they then explain why so many others have had the same experience, if in a less exalted degree? I have myself epitomized in two small volumes the general account of the other world, drawn from a great number of sources. It was done as independently of Mr. Vale Owen as his account was independent of mine. Neither had possible access to the other. And yet as I read this far grander and more detailed conception I do not find one single point of importance in which I have erred.

How, then, is this agreement possible if the general scheme is not resting upon inspired truth?

The world needs some stronger driving force. It has been running on old inspiration as a train runs when the engine is removed. New impulse is needed If religion had been a real compelling thing, then it would show itself in the greatest affairs of all—the affairs of nations, and the late war would have been impossible. What church is there which came well out of that supreme test? Is it not manifest that the things of the spirit need to be restated and to be recoupled with the things of life?

A new era is beginning. Those who have worked for it may be excused if they feel some sense of reverent satisfaction as they see the truths for which they laboured and testified gaining wider attention from the world. It is not an occasion for self-assertion, for every man and woman who has been honoured by being allowed to work in such a cause is well aware that he or she is but in agent in the hands of unseen but very real, wise, and dominating forces. And yet one would not be human if one were not relieved when one sees fresh sources of strength, and realizes the all-precious ship is held more firmly than ever upon her course.

Arthur Conan Doyle.

INTO THE LIGHT

The good God is, and God is good,
And when to us 'tis dimly seen
'Tis but the mists that come between
Like darkness round the Holy Rood,
Or Sinai Mount where they adored
The Rising Glory of the Lord.
He giveth life, so life is good,
As all is good that He has given.
Earth is the vestibule of Heaven;
And so He feeds with angel's food
Those in His likeness He has made,
That death may find us unafraid.
Death is no wraith, of visage pale,
Out of this darkened womb of earth,
But waits attendant on our birth
To lead us gently through the Veil,
To realms of radiance, broad and free,
To Christ and immortality.
September, 1915[6]

---

[6] Subsequent to the reception of the portion of the script which is included in this volume, I received at three separate sittings the verses printed above. It was intimated to me, at that time, that the purpose for which this hymn was transmitted was that it should be regarded as a keynote to the messages received some years previously from my mother and her fellow-workers. G. V. O.

CHAPTER I

**On the borderland—An initiation—"From strength to
strength"—Sorrow and joy—Trees and flowers—The Chasm and
the Bridge—"There is a great Gulf fixed"—The Cross of
Light—"One Sinner who repenteth".**

Tuesday, September 23, 1911

WHO is here?

Mother and other friends who have come to help. We are
progressing very well, but are not able to give you all the words
we would like to yet, as your mind is not so quiet and passive as
we would wish.

Tell me something about your home and occupation.

Our occupation varies according to the needs of those to whom
we minister. It is very various, but directed to the uplifting of those
who are still in earth life. For instance, it is we who suggested to
Rose the creation of a band of people to come to her aid in case of
her feeling any danger when she was in the room writing as we
moved her hand, and that band is at present in charge of her case.
Does she not feel their presence at times near her? She should do
so, for they are ever near at call.

About our home. It is very bright and beautiful, and our
companions from the higher spheres are continually coming to us
to cheer us on our upward way.

A thought here came into my mind. Could they see these
beings from the higher realms, or was it with them as with us? I
may say that here and there throughout these records the reader
will come upon passages which are quite obviously answers to my
unspoken thoughts, usually beginning "Yes" or "No". This being
understood, there will be no need for me to indicate them unless
any particular instance seems to require it.

Yes, we can see them when they wish that we should do so, but
that depends on the state of our advancement and their own power
of service to us.

Now will you please describe your home scenery, etc.?

Earth made perfect. But of course what you call a fourth
dimension does exist here, in a way, and that hinders us in

describing it adequately. We have hills and rivers and beautiful forests, and houses, too, and all the work of those who have come before us to make ready. We are at present at work, in our turn, building and ordering for those who must still for a little while continue their battle on earth, and when they come they will find all things ready and the feast prepared.

We will tell you of a scene which we witnessed not long ago. Yes, a scene in this land of ours. We were told that a ceremony was about to take place in a certain wide plain not far from our home, at which we might be present. It was the ceremony of initiation of one who had passed the gate of what we will call prejudice, that is, of prejudice against those who were not of his own particular way of learning, and who was about to go forth into a wider and fuller sphere of usefulness.

We went, as we were bidden, and found a great many people arriving from many quarters. Some came in... why do you hesitate? We are describing quite literally what we saw—chariots; call them otherwise, if you will. They were drawn by horses, and their drivers seemed to know just what to say to them, for they were not driven with reins like they are on earth, but seemed to go where the drivers willed. Some came on foot and some through space by aerial flight. No, not wings, which are not necessary.

When they had all gathered, a circle was made, and one stepped out, the one who was to be initiated, and he wore a robe of orange colour, but bright, not like the colour as you know it; none of our colours are; but we have to speak to you in our old tongue. The one who had had him in his care then took him by the hand and placed him on a green knoll near the Middle of the clear space, and prayed. And then a very beautiful thing occurred.

The sky seemed to intensify in colour—blue and gold mostly—and out of it descended a veil-like cloud, but which seemed to be made up of fine lace-work, and the figures dominating were birds and flowers—not white, but all golden and radiant. This slowly expanded and settled on the two, and then they seemed to become part of it, and it of them, and, as it slowly faded away, it left both more beautiful than before—permanently beautiful, for both had been advanced into a higher sphere of light.

BOOK I: THE LOWLANDS OF HEAVEN

Then we began to sing, and, although I could see no instrument, yet instrumental music blended with our singing and became one with it. It was very beautiful, and served both as a reward to those who had earned it and a spur to those who had still to tread the path they two had trodden. The music, as I found out later by inquiry, proceeded from a temple grove outside the circle, but indeed it did not seem to come from any one point. That is a faculty of music here. It seems very often to be part of the atmosphere.

Nor was the jewel lacking. When the cloud cleared, or dissolved, we saw it on the brow of the initiate, gold and red, and his guide, who had one already, wore his on his shoulder—left shoulder—and we noticed it had increased in size and brightness. I do not know how this happens, but have an idea, not definite enough to tell you, however, and it is difficult to explain what we ourselves understand. When the ceremony was over we all separated to our own work again. It was longer than I have described and had a very heartening effect on the rest of us.

Over the hill on the farther side of the plain to that where we stood I noticed a light grow up and it seemed to us a beautiful form in human shape. I do not think it was an appearance of our Lord, but some great Angel Master who came to give power, and to do His will. No doubt some there could see more clearly than I, because we are able to see, and also to understand, in proportion to our stage of advancement.

Now, my boy, just think for a moment. Is this from your mind or through it, as you say? When you sat down to write as you know, nothing was farther from your thoughts, for we had carefully refrained from impressing you, and yet you went off at once on the account as we influenced you. Is that not so?

Yes. I admit that frankly.

Quite right. And now we will leave—not you, for we are always with you in a way you do not understand—but we will leave this writing, with our prayer and blessing on you and yours. Good night and good-bye till to-morrow.[7]

---

[7] When the whole series of messages was finished I reckoned up and found that the speed had been maintained at an average rate of twenty

31

THE LIFE BEYOND THE VEIL

Wednesday, September 24, 1913.

Suppose we were to ask you to look forward a little space and try to imagine the effect of our communications as viewed in relation to the ultimate outcome of your present state of mind. What then, think you, should have been the issue of events as we see them from our own sphere in the spirit world? It would be something like the effect of sunlight when it is projected into a sea-mist, which mist gradually vanishes away, and the scene it enveloped becomes clearer to the vision, and more beautiful than when dimly discerned through the enveloping mist.

So do we view your minds and, if the sun for awhile dazzles and perplexes rather than clarifies the sight, you know that the end is light, and the end of all that Light in whom there is no darkness at all. Yet light is not conducive to peace always, but, in its passage, often creates a series of vibrations which bring destruction to those species of living creatures which are not fashioned to survive in the light of the sun. Let them go, and, for yourself, go onward, and as you go your eyes will become used to the greater light, the greater beauty of the Love of God, the very intensity of which, blended as it is with infinite Wisdom, is perplexing to those who are not altogether of the light.

And now, dear son, listen while we tell you of one more scene which has gladdened us here in these regions of God's own light.

We were wandering a short time ago in a beautiful woodland place, and as we went we talked a little, but not more than a little because of the sense of music which seemed to absorb all else into its own holy silence. Then, standing in the pathway in front of us, whom should we see but an angel from a higher sphere. He stood and looked on us with a smile, but did not speak, and we became aware that he had a message for one of us especially. It was so,

---

four words a minute. On two occasions only had I any idea what subject was to be treated. That was when the message had obviously been left uncompleted. At other times I had fully expected a certain subject to be taken, but on taking up my pencil the stream of thought went off in an altogether different direction.

for, as we halted and stood in expectation, he came forward and, lifting the cloak he wore—amber it was in colour—he placed his arm and it round my shoulder and, laying his cheek on my hair—for he was much taller than I am—he said softly, "My child, I am sent to you from the Master Whom you have learned to trust, and the way before you is seen by Him but not by you. You will be given strength for whatever you have to do; and you have been chosen for a mission which is new to you in your service here. You will be able, of course, to visit these your friends at will, but now you must leave them for a time and I will show you your new home and duties."

Then the others gathered round me and kissed me and held my hands in theirs. They were as glad as I—only that is not quite the word to use in my case, it is not peaceful enough. After awhile, when he had let us talk and wonder what his message meant, he came forward once more and this time took me by the hand and led me away.

We walked for a little time and then I felt my feet leave the ground and we went through the air. I was not afraid, for his strength was given to me. We passed over a high mountain range where many palaces were, and at last, after a fairly long journey, we descended in a city where I had not been before.

The light was not unkind, but my eyes were not used to such a degree of brightness. However, I soon made out that we were in a garden surrounding a large building, with steps up to it all along the front, at the top of which was a kind of terrace. The building seemed all of one piece of material of different hues—pink and blue and red and yellow—which shone like gold, but softly. Up these we went, and at the great doorway, without any door to it, we met a very beautiful lady, stately but not proud. She was the Angel of the House of Sorrow. You wonder at the word used in this connection. What it means is this:

The sorrow is not of those who dwell there, but is the lot of those to whom they minister. The sorrowful ones are those on earth, and it is the business of the residents in this House to send to them vibrations which have the effect of neutralizing the vibrations of sorrowful hearts on earth. You must understand that here we have to get at the bottom of things, and learn the cause of

33

things, and that is a very deep study, only learned in gradual stages bit by bit. I therefore speak of the causes of things when I use the word "vibrations", as one you will understand best.

She received me very kindly and took me within, where she showed me over part of the place. It was quite unlike anything on earth, so it is hard to describe. But I may say that the whole house seemed to vibrate with life, and to respond to our own will and vitality.

This, then, is my present and latest phase of service, and a very happy one it promises to be. But I have only just begun to understand the prayers which are brought to us there and registered, and the sighs of those in trouble we hear—or rather, they are also registered, and we see or feel them, as it were, and send out our own vibrations in answer. This in time becomes involuntary, but is a great effort at first, I find it so. But even the effort has a reflex blessing on those who work so.

There are many such places here, as I learn, all in touch with earth, which at present would seem impossible to me except that, as the effects are also registered back again to us, I know the amount of comfort and help we send. I only am on duty for a short space at one time, and then go out and see the sights of this city and its neighbourhood. And very glorious it all is, even more beautiful than my old sphere, which I also revisit to see my friends. So you can imagine the talks we have when we do meet. That is almost as great a joy as the work itself. Peace in Jesus our Lord is the atmosphere all around us. And this is the land where there is no darkness and, when those mists are of the past, dear, you will come here, and I will show you all—until you are perhaps able to take me by the hand, as he did, and lead me to see the work in your own sphere. You think I am ambitious for you, dear lad. Well, so I am, and that is a mother's—shall I say weakness, or rather blessing?

Good-bye, dear. Your own heart at this moment is a witness that this is all real, for I can see it glowing happy and bright, and that is gladness also to me your mother, dear son. Good night, then, and God will keep you and yours in His peace.

Thursday, September 25, 1913.

34

BOOK I: THE LOWLANDS OF HEAVEN

What we want most to say to you to-night is to be understood as a very imperfect attempt to tell you what is the meaning of that passage of which you have often thought where our Lord tells St. Peter that he is an adversary to Him. He, as you will remember, was on the way to the Holy City, and had been telling His Apostles that He would be killed there. Now, what He evidently wished to impress on them was the fact that, although to men His mission might seem to have ended in failure, yet to eyes which were enabled to see as He would theirs might see, His end was only the beginning of a much more powerful and glorious development of the life-giving mission which He had undertaken on behalf of the Father and for the uplifting of the world.

Peter, by his attitude, showed that he did not understand this. Which is all plain and easy enough, so far, to understand. But what is usually lost sight of is the fact that the Christ was pursuing one straight line of progress, and that His death was but an incident in the way of His onward path, and that sorrow, as the world understands it, is not the antithesis of joy, but may be a part of it, because, if rightly used, it becomes the fulcrum on which the lever may rest which may lift a weight off the heart of the one who understands that all is part of God's plan for our good. It is only by knowing the real "value" of sorrow that we understand how limited it is in effect, so far as making us unhappy goes. Now, He was about to inflict the heaviest sorrow He possibly could on the Apostles and, unless they understood this, they would be unable to use that sorrow to lift themselves above the turmoil of the world, and so, unable to do the work he had in hand for them to do. "Your sorrow shall be converted into joy", He told them, and so it came to pass, but not until they had learned the scientific value of sorrow—in a limited measure indeed, but in a measure nevertheless.

All this sounds very simple when it is written down thus, and no doubt it is simple, in a way, because all the fundamentals of God's economy are simple. But to us, and to me at the present time, it has an importance which may not be apparent to you. For the problem which is the chief study of the new House in which I spend so much of my time is this same subject, namely, the turning, or converting, of the vibrations of sorrow into the vibrations which produce joy in the human heart. It is a very beautiful study, but many perplexities enter into it because of the restrictions imposed on us by the sacredness of freewill. We may not overrule the will of any, but have so to work through their wills as to produce the desired effect and yet leave them free all the time, and so, deserving, in a way and in a measure at least, of the blessing received.

I get tired sometimes, but that will pass away as I become stronger in the work.—What is your question? I think you wish to ask one.

No, thank you, I have no particular question in mind.

Wasn't there something you wished to ask about something to do with the method by which we impress you?

I did think of asking you that this morning. But I had forgotten it. I suppose there is nothing much to explain, is there? should call it mental impression.

Yes, that is correct, as far as it goes, but it does not go far. Mental impression is a phrase which covers up a great deal which is not understood. We impress you by means of these same vibrations, some of a different nature from others all directed on your will. But I see you are not much interested in that matter at the present moment. We will return to it, if you wish, at another time. I want to speak of those things which are of present interest to you.

Then tell me something more about that home of yours and your new work.

Very well, then, I will try to do so as well as I can.

It is beautifully appointed within and without. Within are baths and a music room and apparatus to aid us in registering our work. It is a very large place. I called it a house, but it is really a series of houses, each house allotted to a certain class of work, and progressive as a series. We pass from one to another as we learn all we can from any particular house. But it is all so wonderful that people would neither understand nor believe; so I would rather tell you of the simpler things.

The grounds are very extensive, and all have a kind of relation to the buildings, a kind of responsiveness. For instance, the trees are true trees and grow much as trees do on earth, but they have a kind of responsiveness to the buildings, and different kinds of trees respond more to one house than to the others, and help the effect and the work for which that particular house was raised. So it is with the grouping of trees in the groves, and the bordering flower-beds of the paths, and the arrangement of the streams and falls which are found in different parts of the grounds. All these things have been thought out with marvellous wisdom, and the effect produced is very beautiful.

The same thing obtains on earth, but the vibrations there are so heavy, comparatively, both those sent out and those which respond, that the effect is almost unseen. Nevertheless, it is so. For instance, you know that some people can plant flowers and trees more successfully than others, and that flowers will last longer in some houses—that is families—than others; cut flowers, we mean. All that is the same thing in grosser state.

Here these influences are more potent in action, and also the recipients more sensitive in perception. And that, by the way, is one of the things which help us to accurate diagnosis of cases which are registered here for us to deal with.

The atmosphere also is naturally affected by vegetation and by buildings, for, let me repeat, those houses have not been raised merely mechanically, but are the outcome—growth, if you will—of the action of the will of those high in rank in these realms, and so of very powerful creative wills.

The atmosphere also has an effect on our clothing, and enters into the influence of our own personalities in its effect on texture and colour. So that while, if we were all of the same quality spiritually our clothing would be of the same tint and texture, by reason of the atmospheric influence, this is in fact modified by the degree in which our own characters differ one from another.

Also the tint of our robes changes according to the part of the grounds in which we happen to be. It is very interesting and instructive, and also very beautiful, to see them change as one turns down a side walk where different vegetation flourishes, or where the arrangement of the various species of plants is different.

The water also is very beautiful. You hear of water-nymphs and suchlike beings, in the earth life. Well, I may tell you that here, at any rate, these things are true. For the whole place is pervaded and interpenetrated with life, and that means with living creatures. I had some idea of this in the sphere from which I have lately come, but here, as I grow accustomed to the strangeness and newness of it, I see it all much more plainly and begin to wonder what it will be a few spheres onward. For the wonder of this place seems to be about as much as any place could hold.

But there, let it rest. He Who enables us in one part of His beautiful Kingdom will enable us in another.

Which is a word for you, my dear son, and which I will, leave with you now, and my blessing.[8]

Friday, September 26, 1913

Our last installment was given in answer to a request by one of our band that we should try to impress you in a rather deeper kind of way than heretofore, but we were only able to begin, as it were,

---

[8] While writing the first part of this message I could not see the drift of the argument, which seemed to me to be rather thin and muddled. On reading it over, however, I am by no means sure of my estimate.

Taking what is said of the vibrations of sorrow as merely a hint on "fundamentals", and applying to it some such reasoning as that by which the wave theory is applied to the radiation of light and heat, the result would be something like this:

In dealing with that combination of vibrations which cause sorrow, the method is not so much that of substitution as of readjustment. By directing on the sorrowful soul other classes of vibrations those of sorrow are, some of them, neutralized; and others are modified and converted into vibrations the effect of which is joy or peace.

Viewed thus the above message does seem to hold some significance, and may perhaps throw light on the way in which troubles are actually dealt with in life. It certainly does seem to be part of the divine method, not that the outer aspect and circumstances of sorrow should be remedied (except in extremely rare cases), but that other elements should be infused which should have the effect of converting that sorrow into joy. This is merely a matter of everyday observation. To the unscientific mind this will probably seem to be drawing a very long bow. To others it may not seem so unreasonable to suggest that these "other vibrations" are really vibrations of other classes or "values".

The passage referred to is John xvi. 20: [Greek] h luph umwn eiV caran genhsetai. —G.V.O.

and not to complete our explanation, If you wish it therefore, we will continue the subject now.

Thank you; yes.

Then you must, for a moment, try to think with us as from our side the Veil. Things, you must understand, take on a very different aspect here from what they did as viewed from the earth plane, and an aspect, I fear, which to those still on earth will, in many cases at least, wear a semblance of unreality and romance. And the least things here are fraught with so much wonder to those who are newly come over that until they have divested themselves of the habit of thinking in three dimensional terms, they are unable to progress very far. And that, believe me, is a matter of no little difficulty.

Now, the term "vibrations" is one which will have to serve, but it is far from adequate as understood of things material. For such vibrations as those of which we speak are not merely mechanical in movement and quality, but have an essence of vitality in themselves, and it is by that vitality that we are able to appropriate and use them. That is the connecting link between our wills and the outward manifestation in vibrations, for that is really all that these are. They are just phenomena of the deeper life which envelops us and all things. By them, as raw material, we are able to accomplish things, and build up things which have a durability which the term itself would seem to belie.

For instance, it is by this method that the bridge over the chasm[9] between the spheres of light and darkness is constructed, and that bridge is not all of one colour. On the farther side it is shrouded in darkness and, as it gradually emerges into, or towards, the region of light, it assumes an ever brighter hue and, where it lands on the heights where begin the brighter lands, it is of pink hue and glistens in the light enveloping it like some rare kind of silver, or alabaster rather.

Yes, of course there is a bridge over the chasm Otherwise how would those who have fought their way upward through the gloom get over.

---

[9] See p. 87.

True—and I had forgotten it—there are some who do proceed through the awful realm of darkness, and climb up the regions on this side the chasm. But these are few, and they are those obstinate ones who reject the help and guidance of those guardians of the way who are stationed on the farther side to show those who are qualified the way across.

Also, you must know, those guardians are only visible to those poor people, in proportion to the light that has been generated in their hearts; and so a certain amount of trust is needed if they would commit themselves to their keeping. This trust also is the outcome of a better mind by which they have become, in a measure, able to discern between light and darkness. Well, the complications of the human spirit are manifold and perplexing, and so let us get on to something easier of putting into words. I have called this a bridge, but—I ought to have referred you to the passage, "The light of the body is thine eye". Read that in this connection, and you will see that it bears on the case, not only of those on earth but those here also. I have called this a bridge, but, as a matter of fact, it has little likeness to a bridge, on earth.

For these regions are vast, and the bridge is more like a tract of country than anything else I can think of to call it to you. And remember I have only seen but a small part of these spheres, and so just tell you of that part which I know. Doubtless there are other chasms and bridges— probably numbers of them. Across the ridge, or bridge, then, those who seek the light make their journey, and that journey is but slow, and there are many rest-houses at which they stay, from time to time, on their progress across, and are handed on from one to another party of angel ministers, until the last stage lands them here on this side. Our work in the house, or colony, to which I now belong, is also directed to these progressive spirits, as well as to those on earth. But that is a different department from mine at present. I have not yet got that far in my study.

For it is more difficult, because the influences around those in the darkness here are much more evil than the influences on earth, where good influences are ever mingling with the bad. It is only when careless and wicked people get over here that they realize the awful task before them; and that is why so many of them remain for ages in a condition of hopelessness and despair.

When they are safely over the bridge they are welcomed by those on the slopes where grass and trees grow, and they are just stupefied with delight, in spite of the gradualness of their preparation. For they have not yet become used to love and its sweetness after their experience of the opposite down there.

I said this bridge landed on the heights; I speak comparatively. The landing place is highland as compared with those regions of darkness below. But, as a matter of fact, it is lowland, and the lowest land indeed, of the heavenly country.

You are thinking of the "great gulf", or chasm, "fixed", of the Parable. That is all quite in accord with what I have written, and you have already had this explained to you elsewhere. Also the reason why these who come over do so instead of attaining this side by aerial travel, or "flight", as you would perhaps call it, is because they are not able to make the journey so on account of their weakness spiritually. If they were to attempt it they would only fall into the dark valley, and then lose their way.

I have not been far into those dark regions, but I have been a little way; and the misery I saw was quite enough to suffice for some time to come. When I have progressed in my present work, and have for some time helped those poor souls from the vantage point of this house, I may be permitted, and probably shall be, to go farther among them. But that is not yet.

One thing more I may say—for it is time that you should cease. When they break away, and come to the other end of the bridge, I am told that the noises which are heard from behind them are horrible; and dull red flashes of fire are seen. How that is caused I am not able clearly to state, but we are told that both the yells and screeches and howls, and also the flashes, are made by those left behind who are enraged because of their powerlessness to recapture the fugitive, or to hold him as he is slipping away; for evil is ever powerless against good, be the good ever so small in amount. But I must not pursue this farther now, and what I am now saying is not what I have myself seen, but hearsay, that is, it is given to you at second-hand; but it is true, nevertheless.

THE LIFE BEYOND THE VEIL

Good night, then, dear son, and may the All Father shed His light and peace on you and yours...... In His light shall you see light; and the shining of that light is of the peaceful overbreaking dawn.

Saturday, September 27, 1913

I asked my friends to try to impress me more vividly.

It is scarcely necessary that we should be careful to impress you more vividly than we have already done, for we have managed to get through the messages as we intended them, to help you to realize somewhat of our life, and conditions prevailing here. Only we would add that what should be clear to you is that—when we come here we are not in our own proper element, but that what to you is a natural environment is to us as a mist, and through it we have to work as best we can.

Are you able to see me as I sit here writing?

We do see you, but with other eyes than yours. Our eyes are not accustomed to the effect of light as you have it on earth. Our light is of a different kind, a sort of interpenetrating element by which we are able to discern your inmost mind, and that is it to which we speak—to you yourself and not, of course, to your outward ears. So it is yourself we see, and not your material body, which is but an enveloping robe. When we touch you, therefore, you do not feel the touch physically but spiritually, and if you wish to apprehend our touch, you will have to keep this in mind and look deeper than the body and its mechanical brain.

You would wish to know something more of the way we work here and the conditions in which our life is spent, Not every one who comes over here is able to understand that one of the elementary truths which it is necessary to assimilate in order to progress is that God is no more visibly present here than He is in the earth life. They expect to see Him bodily, and are much disappointed when they are told that that is a quite mistaken idea of the way of His dealing with us. His life and beauty are quite apparent on earth to those who can look deeper than the externals of nature. And so it is here, with this modification: that life here is more tangible, and easier to lay hold of and use by those who study its nature, and it pulsates all around us, and we, being in a more sensitive state, are more able to feel it than when we, were in the earth life. Still, having said this on the general conditions, it is true to add that, from time to time, manifestations of the Divine Presence are given us, when some particular purpose necessitates; and of one of these I will tell you now.

We were called to a tract of country where many people were to forgather, of different creeds and faiths and countries. When we arrived we found that a band of missionary spirits had returned from their period of duty in one of the regions bordering on the earth sphere, where they had been working among souls just come over who did not realize that they had crossed the border-line between earth and the spirit land. Many had been enlightened, and these had been brought to the place in order that they might join with us in a service of thanksgiving before going to their own proper homes. They were of various ages, for the old had not progressed yet in becoming youthful and vigorous again, and the young had not progressed to complete stature. They were all agape with happy expectation, and, as one company after another of their new companions in this life arrived, they scanned their faces, and the different coloured robes worn by the different orders and estates in wonder.

By and by we were all assembled, and then we heard a burst of music which seemed to invade us all and unify the whole great multitude into one great family. Then we saw a great cross of light appear. It seemed to lie on the slope of the great mountain which bordered the plain and, as we watched it, it began to break up into specks of bright light, and we gradually became aware that it was a large company of angels of a higher sphere who stood on the mountain in the form of a cross; and all about them was a golden glow, which we could feel at that distance as a warm breath, of love.

Gradually they became more distinct to our vision as they emerged more perfectly into this, to them, lower environment, and then we saw, standing over the square where the arms of the cross joined the stem, a larger Being. We all seemed to know Him at once instinctively. It was a Manifestation of the Christ in what you have come to know as Presence Form.

THE LIFE BEYOND THE VEIL

He stood there silent and still for a long time, and then lifted His right hand on high, and we saw a column of light descend and rest upon it as He held it aloft. This column was a pathway, and on it we saw another company descending and, when they came to the uplifted hand, they paused and stood still with their hands folded on their breasts and heads bowed. Then slowly the hand moved out until it had swung round and down and the fingers pointed over the plain, and we saw the column stretch out towards us in mid-heaven until it bridged the space between the mountain and the plain, and the end of it rested over the multitude gathered there.

Along this column walked the company last become visible, and hovered above us. They spread out their hands then, and all slowly turned towards the mountain, and softly we heard their voices half speaking and half singing a hymn of devotion to Him Who stood there all so beautiful and so holy that at first we were awed into silence. But presently we also took up their words and sang, or chanted, with them, for that evidently was their purpose in coming to us. And as we sang there arose between us and the mountain a mist of bluish tint which had a very curious effect. It seemed to act like a telescopic lens, and brought the vision of Him nearer until we could see the expression on His face. It also acted similarly on the forms of those who stood just below Him. But we had no eyes for them only for His gracious face and form. I cannot describe the expression. It was a blend of things which words can only tell in small part. There were blended love and pity and joy and majesty, and I felt that life was a very sacred thing when it held Him and us in one bond. I think others felt something like this too, but we did not speak to one another, all our attention being taken up with the sight of Him.

Then slowly the mist melted into the atmosphere, and we saw the cross on the mountain and Him standing as before, only seen more dimly; and the angels who had come over to us had gone, and hovered above Him. And then all gradually faded away. But the effect was a very definite sense of His Presence remaining and perpetual. Perhaps that was the object of the vision being given to the new-comers who, although they could not see so clearly as we could who had been here longer, yet would be able to see enough to encourage them and give them peace.

We lingered some time longer, and then quietly went our ways, not speaking much, because we were so impressed with what we had witnessed. And also, in all these Manifestations there is always so much to think out after. It is so glorious that one is not able, while it is taking place, to take in all the meaning. That has to be thought out gradually; and we talk it over, together, and each gives his impressions, and then we add them up, and find that a revelation has been given of something we did not understand be fore so well. In this instance what seemed to impress us most was the power He had of speaking to us in silence. He did not utter a word and yet we seemed to be hearing His voice speaking to us whenever He made a movement, and we understood quite well what the voice said, although it did not actually speak.

That is all I can tell you now, so, good-bye, dear son, and may you, as you will, see for yourself one day what our Lord has in store for them who love Him.

Monday, September 29, 1913

The idea of viewing things from the standpoint of a higher sphere than yours is one which should be given due weight when you read what we have already written. Otherwise you will often be mystified at the seeming incongruity in the association of ideas as we have given them. To us it is perfectly natural to link together the coming of our Lord in Presence Form[10] and the other incident of the formation of that bridge which spans the great continent of the chasm. For what is there seen in the concrete— that is, of course, concrete to us here—is but a phenomenon of the same invisible power as that by which the Lord and His company of angel attendants bridged the gulf between the spheres in which we at present move and those from which these higher beings come.

You will understand that that Manifestation was to us very much what materialization is to you. It was the linking up of two estates in the Kingdom of the Father by bridging the space by

_____

[10] See page 18.

higher vibrations than those which we are able to use in these lower spheres. How it is done we can only surmise, but, having passed through from your earth sphere into this, the connection between this and the next does not seem strange.

We would wish you could be further enlightened in regard to some of the wonders of our land, for then it would seem more natural to you, both during your sojourn on earth, and also when you come over here it would be less unfamiliar to your mind. The former in that you would see that earth is heaven in embryo, and heaven is but earth cleansed and made perfect; and the latter for reasons quite obvious.

In order to help you in this matter, therefore, we will try to tell you of a system which we have here of separating and discerning between things that matter and those of lesser importance. Whenever we are perplexed about anything—and I speak just of our own immediate circle—we go up to the top of some building, or hill, or some high place where the surrounding country may be viewed from a distance. Then we state our difficulties, and when we have made the tale complete, we preserve silence for a time and endeavour to retreat into ourselves, as it were. After a time we begin to see and hear on a higher plane than ours, and those things which matter, we find, are those which are shown to us, by sight and hearing, as persisting on that higher plane, in those higher spheres. But the things which do not matter so greatly we do not see nor hear, and thus we are able to separate the one class from the other.

It seems all right, dear, but could you give me a specific instance by way of example?

I think we can. We had a case of doubt to deal with, and scarcely knew how to act for the best. It was that of a woman who had been over here for rather a long time, and who did not seem able to progress much. She was not a bad sort of person, but seemed to be uncertain of herself and everybody—round her. Her chief difficulty was about angels—whether they were all of light and goodness, or whether there were some of angelic estate and yet who were of the darkness. For some time we could not quite see why this should trouble her, as everything here seemed to be of love and brightness. But we found at last she had some relatives who had come over before her, and whom she had not seen, and could not find where they were. When we got at her real trouble we talked it over among ourselves, and then we went to the top of a hill and stated our wish to help her and asked to be shown the best way. A rather remarkable thing happened, as unexpected as helpful.

As we knelt there the whole summit of the hill seemed to become transparent and, as we were kneeling with bowed heads, we saw right through it, and a part of the regions below was brought out with distinctness. The scene we saw—and we all saw it, so there could be no delusion—was a dry and barren plain in semi-darkness and, standing leaning against a rock, was a man of large stature. Before him, kneeling on the ground, with face in hands, was another smaller form. It was that of a man, and he seemed to be pleading with the other, who stood with a look of doubt upon his face. Then at last, with a sudden impulse, he stooped down and caught the prostrate form to his breast, and strode with him over the plain towards that horizon where a faint light glimmered.

He went a long journey with that burden and, when they came to a place where the light was stronger, he set him down and pointed out the way to him; and we saw the smaller form thank him again and again, and then turn and run towards the light. We followed him with our eyes, and then saw that the other had directed him to the bridge, of which I have told you already—only that end of it which is on the other side of the chasm. Still we could not understand why this vision had been shown to us, and we continued to follow the man until he had reached the large building which stands at the entrance of the bridge—not to guard it, but to watch for those who come and who require refreshment and help.

We saw that the man had been sighted from the watchtower, for a flash of light signaled the fact to those below and to those on the next watchtower along the bridge.

And then the hill resumed its normal aspect again, and we saw no more.

We were more perplexed than ever now, and were descending the hill when our Chief Lady met us, and, in her company, one who seemed to be a high officer in some part of our spheres, but whom we had not met before. She said he had come to explain to us the instruction we had just received. The smaller man was the husband of the woman whom we were trying to help, and we must tell her to go to the bridge and she would be given a lodging there, where she could wait till her loved one arrived. The larger man whom we had seen was what the woman would call an angel of darkness, for he was one of the more powerful spirits in that dark land. But, as we had observed, he was capable of a good deed. Why then, we asked, was he still in the regions of darkness?

The officer smiled and said, "My dear friends, the Kingdom of God our Father is a very much more wonderful place than you seem to imagine. You never yet have met with a realm or sphere which was complete in itself, and independent and separate from all other spheres. Nor are there any such. That dark angel blends within his nature many spheres of knowledge and goodness and badness. He remains where he is first because of the badness remaining in him, and which unfits him for the regions of light. He remains also because, while he could progress if he would, yet he does not wish to do so at present, partly because of his obstinacy, and partly because he still hates the light, and thinks those who set out upon the awful uphill way fools because the pains and agonies are sharper then by reason of the contrast which they see between the light and the darkness. So he remains; and there are multitudes such as he whom a kind of dull and numb despair prevents coming over. Also in his time of hatred and frenzy he is cruel. He had tortured and ill-treated this same man whom you saw with him from time to time, and that with the cruelty of a cowardly bully. But, as you saw, that wore itself out, and, when the man pleaded this last time, some soft chord in the heart of the other vibrated just a little, and, on the impulse, fearing a reversal of his intention, he liberated the victim who wished to make the journey, and pointed out to him the way, no doubt thinking in his heart that he was a fool and yet, perhaps, a wiser fool than he, after all."

This was new to us. We had not realized that there was any goodness in those dark regions before; but now we saw that it was but natural that there should be, or, if every one were totally bad, no one would ever desire to come to us here.

BOOK I: THE LOWLANDS OF HEAVEN

But what bearing has all this on the discerning between the things which matter and those of lesser importance?

All that is of good is of God, and light and darkness, as applied to His children, are not, and cannot be, absolute. They are to be understood relatively. There are, as we now know, many "angels of darkness" who are in the darkness because of some twist in their natures, some obstinate trait which prevents the good in them having its effect. And these one day may pass us on the road of the ages, and become greater in the Kingdom of the Heavens than we who now are more blessed than they.

Good night, dear son. Think over what we have written. It has been a very wholesome lesson to us, and one which it were well if many in your present life could learn.

CHAPTER II: SCENES THAT ARE BRIGHTER

The Home of Music—"They stand, those Halls of Sion, all
Jubilant with song, and bright with many an Angel"—The Halls of
Colour—The heavenly life—A story with a moral—After death,
realization and first experiences—A parting and a meeting—A
children's school, progressive botany—A Manifestation—The child
and the globe of light—All creation one—Creative thinking.

Tuesday, September 30, 1913

YOU would scarcely realize all that we feel when we come to
earth in this way, and commune with one still wending his way
through the valley.

We feel that we are of those who are more than ordinarily
privileged, for, once we are able to convince people how much lies
to their hand that they might use for the uplifting of the race, there
seems to be no bounds to the possibilities of good and
enlightenment. Still, we are but able to do a little, and must rest
content until others will co-operate with us, as you have done,
fearlessly, knowing that no evil can come to those who love the
Father, and serve Him in His Son, our Saviour Lord.

Now, in order to help those who still doubt us and our mission
and message, let me say that we do not lightly leave our beautiful
home to come down into the mists which surround the earth
sphere. We have a mission and a work in hand which some one
must do, and there is joy in the doing of it.

A little time since—to speak in earth phrase—we were sent
into a region where the waters were collected into a large lake, or
basin, and round the lake, at some distance from each other, were
erected buildings in the form of large halls with towers. They were
of varied architecture and design, and not all builded of one
material. Spacious gardens and woods surrounded them, some of
them miles in extent, and full of beautiful fauna and flora, most of
the species known on earth, but also some which would be strange
to you now, although I think that at least a proportion of them
lived once on earth. That is a detail. What I wish to explain to you
is the purpose of these colonies.

BOOK I: THE LOWLANDS OF HEAVEN

They are for nothing else than the manufacture of music and musical instruments. Those who live there are engaged in the study of music and its combinations and effects, not only as to what you know as sound, but also in other connections. We visited several of the great houses and found bright and happy faces to welcome us and show us over the place; and also to explain what we were able to understand, and I frankly confess that was not much. Such as I personally did understand I will try to explain to you.

One house—or college, for they were more like colleges than manufactories, when I come to think of it—was devoted to the study of the best methods of conveying musical inspiration to those who had a talent for composition on earth; and another house gave attention rather to those who were clever at playing music, and others to singing, and still others made a special study of ecclesiastical music, and others concert music, and others operatic composition, and so on.

The results of their studies are tabulated, and there their duty ends. These results are studied again by another class, who consider the best method of communicating them to composers of music generally, and then another body do the actual work of transmission through the Veil into the earth sphere. Here are pointed out to them the objects of their endeavours, namely, those who are likely to prove most ready of response to their inspiration. These have been carefully selected by others who are trained in selection of such. All is in perfect order; from the colleges round the lake to the church or concert hall or opera house on earth there is a chain of trained workers who are constantly active in giving to earth some little gift of heavenly music. And that is how all your best music comes to you...

Yes, you are quite correct. Much of your music is not from us; and much is sullied in its passage. But that is not the fault of the workers from those spheres, but lies at the door of those on your side of the Veil, and those on this side who are of the gloomy regions and whom the character of the composer gives a foothold to tamper with that which comes from us here.

What were the towers for?

I was just going to explain that to you.

THE LIFE BEYOND THE VEIL

The lake is of vast extent, and the buildings at some little distance from it on all sides. But at certain times, previously arranged, the workers of some of these colleges, and now and again of all of them, send certain of their company to the towertop and, when all are assembled, then a concert, literally true to its name, is held. They all practise something they have previously agreed upon together. On one tower will be instrumentalists of one class, on another those of another class, and on the third vocalists; and on another, another class of vocalists; for there are many classes, not only four, as usually with you, but many toned voices. And other towers are devoted to other workers whose actual duties I could not understand. From what I could make out, some of these were expert in harmonizing the whole, or part, of the volume of sound combined from the different towers.

But I want to get on to the description of the thing itself—the concert or festival, or whatever you like to call it. We were taken to an island in the midst of the lake, and there, in a beautiful scene of trees and grass and flowers and terraces and arbours of trees and little nooks and seats of stone or wood, we heard the festival.

First there came a chord, long and sustained, growing louder and louder, until it seemed to invade the whole landscape and waterscape and every leaf of every tree. It was the key given to the musicians on the various towers. It died into silence and all seemed very still. Then gradually, we heard the orchestra. It came from many towers, but we could not tell any single contribution apart. It was perfect harmony, and the balance of tone was exquisite.

Then the singers took up their part, it is of no use for me to try to describe this music of the heavenly spheres in earth language, but I may perhaps be able to give you some idea of the effect. Briefly, it made everything more lovely—not only beautiful, but lovely, too—for there is a difference in meaning of these two words as I use them here. All our faces took on a more lovely hue and expression, the trees became deeper in colour, and the atmosphere gradually grew into a vapour of tints like a rainbow. But the vapour did not obscure anything; it seemed to bring everything nearer together rather. The water reflected the rainbow tints, and our clothing also became intensified in colour.

Moreover, the animals and birds about us also responded. One white bird I remember especially. Her beautiful milky feathers gradually grew brighter and, when I saw her last, before she flew into a grove, she shone like gold burnished and glowing, like transparent light or fire. Then, as the mists slowly faded away, we all became, and everything became, normal once again. But the effect remained, and if I could give it a name, I should say it was "peace".

That, then, is one little experience which I had in the Home of Music.

What we heard will be discussed again and again by meetings of experts, a little altered here, and a little there, and then some use will be made of it; perhaps at some great service of thanksgiving here, or some reception of spirits come over from the earth life, or some other function. For music enters into so many phases of our life here, and, indeed, all seems music in these spheres of light—music and blended colour and beauty, all breathing love among all, and to Him Who loves us as we are not able to love. But His love draws us onward, and, as we go, is all about us, and we must inbreathe it, as we do the beauty of His presence. This we cannot choose but do, for He is All in All here, and love is a delight which only you will understand when you stand where we have stood, and heard what we have heard, and seen the beauty of His presence, breathing and shimmering all around and above and beneath, as we learned some little more of His love.

Be strong and live the valiant life, for the end is worth the cost, as we ourselves have proved.

Good night, dear lad, and remember that sometimes in your sleep we are able to waft some faint echo of such music as this into your spiritual environment, and it is not without its effect on the aspect worn in your mind by your next day's life and work.

Wednesday, October 1, 1913

What we said last evening relative to the Home of Music was but an outline sketch of all that we heard and saw; and we only went over part of the place. We are informed, however, that it is of much larger extent even than we thought at the time, and extends far away from the lake into the mountainous country outlying the plain in which the lake lies. In those mountains there are other colleges, all linked up with those we saw by means of a kind of wireless telephony, and a co-operative work is continually going on.

On our way back to our own home we turned aside to see another new thing. It was a plantation of very large trees in which was built another tower, not a single column, but a series of chambers and halls, with pinnacles and turrets and domes of manifold colours. These were all in the one building, which was very high and also spacious. We were shown within very courteously and kindly by one of the dwellers there, and the first thing that struck us was the curious aspect of the walls. What had from the outside appeared opaque, from the inside were translucent, and, as we went from hall to hall, and chamber to chamber, we noticed that the light which filled each was slightly different in tint from the one which led to it—not of different colour, for the variance was not so marked as that, but just a slight degree deeper or lighter.

In most at least of the smaller compartments the light was of one definite and delicate hue, but every now and then, after passing through a more or less complete series of chambers, we came to a large hall, and in this hall were gathered all the component tints of the surrounding chambers. I am not quite sure whether I am exactly correct in saying that all the smaller laboratories only distilled one tint, but am telling you as nearly as I can remember. There was so much we saw that it is difficult to separate all into details; and it was my first visit. So I do not vouch for more than a true description of the general scheme.

One of these great halls was the Orange Hall, and in it were all the tints of that primary, from the faintest of light gold to the deepest of deep orange. Another was the Red Hall, where hues were ambient all about us, from the faintest rose-leaf pink to the deepest crimson of the rose or dahlia. Another, the Violet Hall, was radiant with hues ranging from the most delicate heliotrope, or amethyst, to the dark rich hue of the pansy. And now I must tell you that there were not only more but several more of these halls devoted to those tints which you do not know, but which you call the ultra-violet and the ultra-red, and most wonderful they are.

Now, these rays are not blended together in one hue, but each tint was distinct in its gradation, and yet A harmonized wonderfully and beautifully.

You are wondering to what purpose these buildings of crystal are put. They are for studying the effect of colours as applied to different departments of life, animal, vegetable and even mineral life, but the two former chiefly, together with clothing. For both the texture and the hue of our garments take their quality from the spiritual state and character of the wearer. Our environment is part of us, just as with you, and light is one component, and an important one, of our environment. Therefore it is very powerful in its application, under certain conditions, as we saw it in these halls.

I am told that the results of those studies are handed on to those who have charge of trees and other plant life on earth and other planets. But there are other results which are too rare in nature for such application to the grosser environment of earth and the other planets, so, of course, only a very small part of these studies is handed on in your direction.

I am sorry that I can tell you little more, partly because of these same limitations, and partly because it is rather scientific and out of my line. But this I may add, for I inquired while there. They do not gather the primary colours together in one hall in that colony. Why, I do not know. It may be, as some of my friends think, who understand these matters better than I do, that the force generated by such combination would collectively be too tremendous for that building and require a specially constructed one, and that, probably, away in some high mountain; as it is possible, they told me, that no vegetation would live within a long distance of such a place.

And they add that they doubt whether people of the degree we met could safely control such forces as would be so generated. They think it would require those of much higher state and skill. But away in another and higher sphere there may be, and probably is, a place where this is done, and that place in touch with the one we saw. Judging from the way things are ordered here, that much is almost certain.

We left the colony, or university, as it might be called, and when we were at some distance away on the plain where we could see the central dome above the trees, our guide, who had come with us to speed us on our way, told us to stop and see a little parting surprise which the Chief had promised to afford us. We watched and saw nothing, and, after a while, looked at our guide questioningly. He smiled, and we looked again.

Presently one of our party said, "What colour was that dome when we first paused here?" One said, "I believe it was red". But none could be sure. Anyway, it was then a golden tint, so we said we would watch it. Sure enough, presently it was green, and yet we had not seen it change, so gradually and evenly was the progress from one colour to the other made. This went on for some time, and it was extremely beautiful.

Then the dome disappeared utterly. Our guide told us it was still there in the same place, but the disappearance was one of the feats they had managed to accomplish by combining certain elements of light from the various halls. Then above the dome and the trees —the dome still being invisible—there appeared an enormous rose of pink, which slowly deepened into crimson, and all among its petals there were beautiful forms of children playing, and men and women standing or walking and talking together, handsome, beautiful and happy; and fawns and antelopes and birds, running or flitting or lying among the petals, whose shapes swelled like hills and mounds and landscapes. Over these swells ran children with the animals, playing very happily and prettily. And then it all slowly faded away, and all was blank. We were shown several of these displays as we stood there.

Another was a column of light which shot up vertically from where we knew the dome was, and stood erect in the heavens. It was of the purest white light, and so steady that it looked almost solid. Then came a ray from one of the halls obliquely and gently struck against the side of the column. Then came another from another hall, of a different colour—red, blue, green, violet, orange; light, middle and dark of all colours you know, and some which you do not know—and they all lodged against the white column about half way up.

Then we saw the oblique lines of light taking shape, and they slowly became each a highway with buildings, houses, castles, palaces, groves of trees, temples and all manner of such, all along the broadways. And up these ways came crowds of people, some on foot, some on horseback, and others driving in chariots. All on one shaft of light were of one colour, but manifold in hues. It was very lovely to see them. They approached the column and halted a little distance from it all round.

Then the top of the column opened out slowly, like a beautiful white lily, and the petals began to curl over, and lower, and ever lower, until they overspread the space between the people and the column. And then the base of the column began to do the same, until it formed a platform, circular in shape, between the different shafts of light, from the column to so far as the places on each causeway where the people halted.

Then they could move onward. But they mingled now, and their horses and conveyances, each retaining its own tint and colour, but mingling with the rest. And we became aware that what we were looking at was a great multitude of lovely and happy people, gathered as if for a feast or festival, in an enormous pavilion of varitinted light. For their hues were now reflected against and into the roof and the floor, or pavement, and most wonderful was the radiance of it all. Slowly they formed into groups, and then we noticed that the centre column was piped like a great organ, and we understood what to expect.

And it came very soon—a great burst of music, vocal and instrumental, a grand Gloria in excelsis to Him Who dwells in the light which is as darkness to His children, even as our darkness is as light when He sheds down on us a ray of His present power; for Omnipotent is the King Whose Light is life to all His children, and Whose glory is reflected in the light such as we are able to endure. Something like that they sang, and then all that, too, faded away. I expected they would retrace their steps along the causeways, but these were withdrawn, and apparently it was unnecessary.

Your time is up, dear lad, so we must stop regretfully, with our usual love to you, my dear one, and those who love you and us, as we love them. God be with you, Who is Light, and in Whom no darkness can find a place to rest.

Thursday, October 2, 1913

"Speak unto the children of Israel that they go forward." That is the message we would impress on you now. Do not lag behind in the way, for light is shed along it which will show you the path, and, if you hold fast to your faith in the All Father and His dear Son our Lord, you need have no fear of any beside.

We write this on account of certain lingering doubts still about you. You feel our presence, we know, but our messages have taken on such a complexion as to seem too fairy-like to be real. Know, then, that no fairy story ever written can equal the wonder of these Heavenly Realms, or the beauties of them. Moreover, much of the description you read in fairy books of scenery and buildings is not altogether unlike many things we have seen here in this beautiful land.

Only a little yet have we been able to learn, but, from that little, we are convinced that nothing which can enter into the creative imagination of a man while in the earth life can equal the glories which await his wondering intellect when he puts off the earth body, with its limitations, and stands free in the light of the Heavenly Land.

Now, what we wish to try to tell you tonight is of a rather different order from our former messages, and has regard rather to the essential nature of things than to the phenomena of life as displayed for our instruction and joy.

If a man could take his stand here on some one of the high summits with which this landscape is crowned, he would behold some rather strange and unfamiliar sights. For instance, he would probably first observe that the air was clear, and that distance had a different aspect from that it wears on earth. It would not seem far away in the same sense, for, if he wished to leave the summit on which he stood and go to some point near the horizon, or even beyond, he would do so by means of his will, and it would depend on the quality of that will, and his own nature, whether he went fast or slow; and also how far he could penetrate into the regions which lie beyond the various mountain ranges and whose—I suppose we shall have to use the word—atmosphere is of rarer quality than that in which his present lot is cast.

It is on account of this that we do not always see those messengers who come to us from the higher spheres. They are seen by some better than by others, and are only truly and definitely visible when they so condition their bodies as to emerge into visibility. Now, if we go too far in their direction—that is, in the direction of their home—we feel an exhaustion which disables us to penetrate farther, although some are able to go farther than others.

Again, standing on that summit, the observer would notice that the firmament was not exactly opaque to the vision, but rather in the nature of light, but light of a quality which intensifies as the distance from the surface of the landscape increases. And some are able to look farther into that light than others, and to see there beings and scenes enacting which others less developed are not able to see.

Also, he would see all around him dwellings and buildings of various kinds, some of which I have described. But those buildings would not be merely houses and work-places and colleges to him. From each structure he would read not its character so much as the character of those who built it and those who inhabit it. Permanent they are, but not of the same dull permanency as those of earth. They can be developed and modified and adapted, in colour, shape and material, according as the need should require. They would not have to be pulled down, and then the material used in rebuilding. The material would be dealt with as the building stood. Time has no effect on our buildings. They do not crumble or decay. Their durability depends simply on the wills of their masters, and, so long as these will, the building stands, and then is altered as they will.

Another thing he would notice would be flights of birds coming from out the distance and going, with perfect precision, to some particular spot. Now there are messenger birds trained on earth, but not as these are trained. In the first place, as they are never killed or ill-used, they have no fear of us. These birds are one of the means we use to send messages from one colony to another. They are not really necessary, as we have other quicker and more business-like ways of communication. We use them more as pretty fancies, just as we use colours and ornaments for beauty's sake sometimes. These birds are always making flights, and are dear loving creatures. They seem to know what their business is, and love to do it.

There is a tale here that once one of these birds, in his eagerness to outstrip his fellows, overshot the others and projected himself into the earth sphere. There he was seen by a clairvoyant man, who shot at him, and so astonished was the wanderer—not at the shooting, but at the sensation which he felt coming from the man's thoughts—that he realized that he was not in his right element somehow, and as soon as he realized that, he was back again here. What he had felt coming from the man's brain was the resolution and desire to kill, and, although he knew it was something uncanny, when he came to try to tell his other bird friends he was at a loss, because nothing of the kind is known here, and he could no more describe it than a bird from this realm could describe his life to one of the earth sphere. So the other birds said that, as he had a tale to tell which he could not, he was to return and find the man and ask him what word he should use.

He did so, and the man, who was a farmer, said "Pigeon-pie" would best describe his idea. The bird returned and, as they could not translate the term into their language, or make any meaning of it, they passed a resolution to the effect that whoever should wish to visit earth in future should place himself under guard until inquiries had been made as to whether he was in his own proper sphere or no.

And the moral of it all is this: Keep to your own appointed task which you will understand, and where you will be understood by those who are your fellow-servants in the work: and do not be too eager to shoot ahead before you are sure of your ground, or "atmosphere", or, thinking you are going forward, you may find yourself in a sphere which is below the one from which you started, and where the highest beings of that sphere are less progressed, in many ways, than the lowest of your own, and much less pleasant as company.

BOOK I: THE LOWLANDS OF HEAVEN

Well, that is a light story as a little interlude, and will serve to show you that we can laugh here, and be foolish wisely, and wise foolishly, on occasion, and that we are not grown-up much in some things since we left your earth and came over here.

Good-bye, dear; keep up a merry heart.

Friday, October 3, 1913

When you are in any doubt as to the reality of spirit communion think of the messages you have already received and you will find that in all we have written we have preserved a clear purpose throughout. It is that we may help you, and through you others also, to understand how natural all is here, if wonderful also. Sometimes, when we look back upon our earth life, we feel a wistful longing to make the way of those still there a little clearer and brighter than was our own in our forward glances into the future life. We did not understand, and so we went on in uncertainty as to what really awaited us. Many, as we know, say that this is good, and yet, as we view things from our present vantage ground, we cannot agree that uncertainty is good when a definite goal is to be won. Certainty, on the other hand, gives decision and conduces to courageous action, and if we may be given to implant in just a few of earth's sojourners the certainty of life and brightness here for those who fight the good fight well, we shall be amply repaid for our journeys hither from our own bright home in light.

Now let us see if we can impress you to write a few words of the conditions which we found when we arrived here—the conditions, that is, of those who pass over here when they first arrive. They are not all of an equal degree of spiritual development, of course, and therefore require different treatment. Many, as you know, do not realize for some time the fact that they are what they would call dead, because they find themselves alive and with a body, and their previous vague notions of the after-death state are not, by any means, lightly thrown away.

The first thing to do, then, with such as those is to help them to realize the fact that they are no more in the earth life, and, to do this, we employ many methods.

THE LIFE BEYOND THE VEIL

One is to ask them whether they remember some friend or relative, and, when they reply that they do so but that he is dead, we try to enable them to see this particular spirit, who, appearing alive, should convince the doubter that he is really passed over. This is not always the case, for the ingrained fallacies are obstinate, and so we try another method.

We take him to some scene on earth with which he is familiar, and show him those whom he has left behind, and the difference in his state and theirs. If this should fail, then we bring to his recollection the last experiences he underwent before passing, and gradually lead up to the time when he fell asleep, and then try to connect up that moment with his awakening here.

All these endeavours often fail—more often than you would imagine— for character is builded up year by year, and the ideas which go to help in this building become very firmly imbedded in his character. Also we have to be very careful not to overtax him, or it would delay his enlightenment. Sometimes, however, in the case of those who are more enlightened, they realize immediately that they are passed into the spirit land, and then our work is easy.

We once were sent to a large town where we were to meet with other helpers at a hospital to receive the spirit of a woman who was coming over. These others had been watching by her during her illness, and were to hand her over to us to bring away. We found a number of friends round the bed in the ward, and they all wore long dismal faces, as if some dire disaster was about to happen to their sick friend. It seemed so strange, for she was a good woman, and was about to be ushered into the light out of a life of toil and sorrow and, lately, of much bodily suffering.

She fell asleep, and the cord of life was severed by our watching friends, and then, softly, they awoke her, and she looked up and smiled very sweetly at the kind face of one who leaned over her. She lay there perfectly happy and content until she began to wonder why these strange faces were around her in place of the nurses and friends she had last seen. She inquired where she was, and, when she was told, a look of wonder and of yearning came over her face, and she asked to be allowed to see the friends she had left.

This was granted her, and she looked on them through the Veil and shook her head sadly. "If only they could know", she said, "how free from pain I am now, and comfortable. Can you not tell them"? We tried to do so, but only one of them heard, I think, and he only imperfectly, and soon put it away as a fancy.

We took her from that scene, and, after she had somewhat gained strength, to a children's school, where her little boy was, and, when she saw him, her joy was too great for words. He had passed over some few years before, and had been placed in this school where he had lived ever since. Then the child became instructor to his mother, and this sight was a pretty one to see. He led her about the school and the grounds and showed her the different places, and his schoolmates, and, all the while, his face beamed with delight; and so did the mother's.

We left her awhile, and then, when we returned, we found those two sitting in an arbour, and she was telling him about those she had left behind, and he was telling her of those who had come on before, and whom he had met, and of his life in the school, and it was as much as we could do to tear her away, with a promise that she should return soon and often to her boy.

That is one of the better cases, and there are many such, but others are otherwise.

Now, while we waited for the mother who was talking with her son, we wandered over the grounds and looked at the various appliances for teaching children. One especially engaged my attention. It was a large globe of glass, about six or seven feet in diameter. It stood at the crossing of two paths, and reflected them. But as you looked into the globe you could see not only the flowers and trees and plants which grew there, but also the different orders from which they had been derived in time past. It was very much like a lesson in progressive botany, such as might be given on earth and deduced from the fossil plants of geology. But here we saw the same plants alive and growing, and all the species of them from the original parent down to the present representative of the same family.

We learned that the task set for the children was: to consider this progression up to this particular plant or tree or flower actually growing in that garden and reflected in the globe, and then to try to construct in their minds the further and future development of that same species. This is excellent training for their mental faculties, but the results are usually amusing. It is the same study which full-grown students are also at work upon in other departments here, and is put by them to a practical end. One of them thought it would be a useful method to help the children to use their own minds, and so constructed the ball for their especial use. When they have thought out their conclusion, they have to make a model of the plant as it will appear after another period of evolution, and fearful and wonderful some of those models are, and as impossible as they are strange.

Well, I must not keep you longer, so we will continue when you are able to write again. God bless you and yours. Good night.

Monday, October 6, 1913

Well, dear, you have had a very happy Harvest Thanksgiving, and we were with you although you did not see us, and were too busy to think about us very much. We love to come and join with our fellow-worshippers still incarnate, and also to give what we are able to help in their worship. It may surprise you to know that here in these Realms of Light, we too, from time to time, hold such services as yours, and join in thanking our Father for harvest plenty. We do this by way of supplementing the thanksgiving of our brethren on earth, and also for our own uplifting. We have here no such harvests as yours, but still we have services of thanksgiving for other blessings which are to us what harvest is to you.

For instance, we thank Him for the beauty all around us and all the glories of light and love which sustain us in vigour for our work and progress, and have services of thanksgiving for such blessings as these. At such times we usually are given some Manifestation from the Higher Spheres, one of which I will tell you about now.

We were holding our Eucharist in a valley, where two lofty hills stood some little distance apart, one on each side, but at one end of the vale. We had offered up our praises and worship, and stood with heads bowed down awaiting, in that silent peace, which always fills us at such times, for the word of Benediction from him who had been the chief minister. He stood a little way up the hillside, but he did not speak, and we wondered why.

After awhile we all slowly raised our heads, as if by one consent and impelled thereto by some inner voice, and we saw that the hill on which he stood was covered with a golden light which seemed to rest upon it like a veil. This slowly drew together and concentrated around the form of the Priest, who stood as if oblivious of anything about him. Then he seemed to come to himself again, and, stepping out of the cloud, he advanced towards us and told us that we were to wait awhile until we were able to see into the higher sphere from which certain angels of that sphere had descended and were present. So we waited, well content; for we have learned that when such an injunction is given it will presently be justified.

The cloud then lifted and spread out over the valley, farther and farther, until it covered the whole sky above us, and then it gradually descended and enveloped us, and we were in a sea of light far brighter than the light of our own sphere, but yet not dazzling to our eyes, but soft and mellow. By and by we were able to see by means of it, and then we saw the vision prepared for us.

The two high hills at the end of the valley glowed with fire, and each was the side, or arm, of a Throne, and about that Throne all colours of the rainbow played, much like that scene of which you read in the Book of Isaiah and of the Revelation. But we did not see the One Who sat on the Throne, at least not in bodily form. What we did see was a Manifestation of Him as to His Fatherhood. On the terrace, which was instead of the seat of the Throne, we saw a great company of Angels, and they were all bending in worship and love over a cradle. In the cradle we saw a child who smiled at them, and at length raised his hands towards the open space above him, where a light seemed to stream down from above.

Then into his arms there descended a golden globe, and he stood up and held it on his left hand. It seemed alive with the light of life and sparkled and glowed and became brighter and brighter until we scarcely noticed anything else but that ball itself and the child who held it, and whose body seemed to be irradiated through and through by its living light. Then he took it in his two hands and opened it in two halves, and held it aloft, turning the open circles towards us. One was filled with a pink radiance, and the other with blue. In the latter we saw the heavenly realms set in concentric circles, and each circle full of glorious and beautiful beings of those realms. But the outer circles were not so bright as the inner ones, and yet we could see the inhabitants more plainly because they were more nearly of our own estate than those others. As the innermost circles were neared, the light became too intense to see clearly what they held. But the very outermost circle we recognized as that of our own order.

The other bowl of pink light was different. There were no circles apparent in it. But yet, in perfect order, we beheld all the different species of animal and vegetable life as they are on the planets, including Earth. But we saw them not as they are with you, but in perfection, from man to the lowest form of sea-animal, and from the largest tree and most luscious fruit to the tiniest weed which grows. When we had viewed these awhile the child gently brought the two halves together, the glorious Heavens and the perfect Material Creation, and, when he had joined them, we could see no mark of the joining, nor tell which was one half and which the other.

But as we looked on the reunited ball, we saw that it was enlarging, and, at last, it slowly floated up from the hand of the child and rose into the space above him, and stood there poised, a beautiful ball of light. Then there gradually emerged into view, standing on the great sphere, the figure of the Christ, Who in His left arm held a cross, the base of which rested on the globe and the top was some little space above His shoulder. In His right hand He held the child, on whose forehead we now noticed a single circle of gold worn, as a fillet on his head, and over his heart a jewel like a great ruby. Then the globe began slowly to ascend into the heaven above, and the higher it went the smaller it grew to our sight, until it melted into the distance over the space between the two hills.

Then we were in our normal state again, and all sat down to wonder at what we had seen, and the meaning of it. But although some seemed to have some glimmerings as to the meaning of it, nobody was very illuminative. Then we thought of our minister, who had first received the baptism of the cloud, and, as it seemed to us, in a more intense degree than the rest of us. We found him sitting there by himself on a rock, with a quiet smile on his face, as if he knew we should come to him at last, and was waiting till we remembered him. He bade us sit down again, and, still sitting on the rock where he could be seen by all, he told us of the Vision.

It had been explained to him as to its more obvious meanings, and these he was able to hand on to us, leaving us to think it over and work out the higher and inner teaching for ourselves, each according to his own phase of mind. This is what is usually done, I find, when teaching is given to us by such means as this.

The pink hemisphere represented the Creation which was inferior to our Sphere, and the blue one our own and that superior to us. But these were not two Creations, but one; and there was no break between these two hemispheres or any of their sub-departments. The child was the embodiment of the beginning, progress and end, which has no ending—our onward way. The ruby stood for sacrifice, and the crown for achievement, and the ascension of the globe and the Christ and the child led our aspirations into those realms which are at present beyond our attainment.

But of course, there is much more than this mere outline in it, and we are, as I said, left to work it out for ourselves. This, according to our custom, we shall do, and, at future gatherings, give our conclusions from time to time, and discuss them.

Thank you. May I now ask you a question which I have been requested to put to you?

No need to put it into words. We can see it in your mind, and knew it before you wrote.[11] The dove which Miss E. saw above the altar of your church was a Manifestation, in presence form, such as that I have just related. It was for your invisible congregation, and symbolized, in a way they would readily understand, the gentleness of the presences about the altar, that they were there

---

[11] A member of the congregation of All Hallows, Oxford, had told me a few days previously that she had seen clairvoyantly a dove hovering over the altar during the celebration of the Holy Communion—G.V.O.

indeed in love, and ready to help those who were willing to receive their help, and, in token of their gentleness, a dove was seen hovering near them and unafraid; a state of mind which those who are not progressed are not always able to maintain in the presence of those from the higher realms whose bright holiness sometimes, in the minds of those who are not able to judge proportionately, by reason of their still lingering imperfections, eclipse their other virtues and make the poor doubting ones afraid.

Wednesday, October 8, 1913.

Because of certain matters which are of importance to those who would understand our meaning in its inner sense, we have decided to endeavour to-night to give you some instruction which will be of help and guidance when dealing with those things which lie beneath the surface of things, and which are usually not taken into account by the ordinary mind. One of these is the aspect which thoughts wear when projected from your sphere into ours. Thoughts which are good appear with a luminance which is absent from those of a less holy kind. This luminance appears to issue from the form of the thinker, and, by means of its manifold rays of divided colours, we are able to come at some knowledge as to his spiritual state, not alone as to whether his state is of the light or of the darkness, and of what degree in light, but also of the points in which he excels or comes short in any direction. It is by this that we are able to allot to him the guardians who will best be able to help him in the fostering of that which is good in him, and in the cleansing away of that which is not good or desirable. By means of a kind of prismatic system we divide up his character, and so reach our conclusions, which are based on the result.

In this life such a method is unnecessary, for it is a matter concerning the spiritual body, and here, of course, that body is patent to all, and, being a perfect index of the spirit, shows forth his characteristics. Only I may say that the colours of which I have spoken are here communicated, in a degree, to our clothing, and those which are dominant over the others serve to classify us into our various spheres and grades. But thoughts which are the effect of spirit action, are seen in the effect they, in their turn, produce on the environment of the thinker, and not only are seen, but felt, or sensed, by us in a more accurate and intense way than with you.

Following on this line of reasoning, you will naturally see that when we think anything very intensely our wills are able to produce an outward manifestation which is really objective to those who behold it. Thus are many beautiful effects produced.

Can you give me a particular instance, by way of illustration?

Yes, it will help you to see what we mean.

A company of my friends and myself, who were being instructed in this knowledge, met together in order to see how far we had progressed, and resolved on an experiment to that end. We selected a glade in the midst of a beautiful wood, and, as a test, we resolved all to will one particular thing, and see if we were successful. What we selected was the producing of a phenomenon in the open space which should be so solid and permanent as to allow of us examining it after-wards. And that was to be a statue of an animal something like an elephant, but rather different; an animal which we have here, but which has ceased to inhabit your earth.

We all sat round the open space and concentrated our wills on the object to be produced. Very quickly it appeared and stood there before us. We were much surprised at the quickness of the result. But, from our point of view, there were two defects. It was much too large, for we had failed to regulate the combination of our wills in due proportion. And it was much more like a live animal than a statue, for many had thought in their minds of the live animal itself, and also of its colouring, and so the result was a mixture between stone and flesh. Also many points were disproportionate—the head too large and the body too small, and so on, showing that more power had been concentrated on some parts than on others. It is thus we learn our imperfections, and how to remedy them, in all our studies. We experiment, and then examine the result, and try again. We did so now.

Taking our minds off the statue so produced, and talking together, it gradually faded away. And then we were fresh and ready for our next trial. We decided not to select the same model as before, or our minds would probably run into more or less the same grooves. So we, this time, chose a tree with fruit on it—something like an orange tree, but not quite the same.

We were more successful this time. The chief points of failure were that some of the fruit was ripe and some unripe. And the leaves were not correct in colour, nor the branches rightly proportioned. And so we tried one thing after another, and found ourselves a little more successful each time. You can imagine somewhat of the joy of such schooling as this, and the laughter and happy humour which result from our mistakes. Those among you who think that in this life we never make jokes, and never even laugh, will have to revise their ideas some day or they will find us strange company—or perhaps we shall find them so. But they soon learn what the love of this land is, where we can be perfectly natural and unrestrained, and indeed are compelled to be so if we wish to be accepted into respectable company, as you would phrase it. I fear the obverse is rather true on earth, is it not? Ah well, live and learn, and those who live in this life—and not merely exist, or worse—learn very quickly. And the more we learn, the more we marvel at the forces at our command.

Astriel,[12] who came yesterday—is he here now!

Not to-night. But he will, no doubt, come again, as you wish it.

Thank you. But I hope you will come and, smile, too.

Oh yes, we will do so, for it is practice both for you and for us also, for, in thus impressing you, we are learning to use our wills and powers in a similar way to that I have been describing. Do you not see the image of the things we are telling you in your mind?

Yes, very vividly sometimes; but I had not thought of it in that way.

Ah well, my boy, you see now, do you not, that we had an object in writing what we have above? All the time you were thinking it was rather thin (and perhaps it was—we do not say to the contrary), and you were wondering whither it all was tending,

---

[12] Astriel's messages were given on various dates which, however, were not consecutive. Why they were given in this way is not apparent. The effect, however, was to cut into the communications given by Mr. Vale Owen's mother in such a way as rather to break the continuity of her messages as well as to destroy the sequence of those of Astriel himself. I have deemed it advisable, therefore, to collect them into a separate chapter. See page 199.—H.W.E.

and, in your mind, you were just a very wee bit disgusted. Now, were you not, dear? Well, we were smiling all the time; and now you understand that you were interpreting our thoughts, more or less, as we sent them forth, and the object we had was to explain to you how those scenes appeared before you so vivid and so real, as you described them.

Good-bye, dear lad, and God bless you and your dear ones now and always.

CHAPTER III: FROM DARKNESS INTO LIGHT

At the Home of Arnol—A lesson in wisdom—Evolution, inverted and progressive—The science of creation—The entity the "Name"—Chasm and the Bridge—"Send out Thy light" to "lead me"— From darkness into light—Angels can suffer—Angelic ministry.

Friday, October 10, 1913

WERE we to impress you to write on matters which to us are of everyday concern, you would perhaps be able to compare them with your own daily life, and you would see then that we and you are both at school, and that the school is a very large one, with many classes, and many instructors, —but with one scheme running throughout the course of instruction, and that scheme a unity of progress from the simple to the complex, and that complexity does not mean perplexity, for, as we learn more of the wisdom of the Divine Author of all, we see how beautifully composite is the realm in which He exerts His Loving Will to the end we may, by our very joy of knowledge, give homage to the Glory of Him Who holds all things in the hollow of His Hand.

And so, dear lad, we will once again take up our theme, and tell you of our doings here in these bright realms, and of how the Father's love encompasses us all around as a radiant cloud in which all things appear to us more plainly, —as we progress in humility and in love.

One of those things which matter here is that due proportion be meted out between wisdom and love. These are not contrary the one from the other, but are two great phases of one great principle. For love is to wisdom as the tree is to the leaves, and if love actuate and wisdom breathe, then the fruit is healthy and sound. By way of illustrating this we will give you a concrete instance of how we are taught to consider duly both love and wisdom in our dealings with ourselves and others to whom we are permitted to minister.

We were given a task to perform a short time ago in which a party of us, to the number of five, were to go to a colony in a rather distant part of this land, and inquire of them by what means could best be given help to those on earth who were in doubt and perplexity as to God's Love. For we were often hampered by our lack of experience in dealing with such cases, and these cases, as you know, are many.

The Principal of the College was a man who in earth-life had been a statesman of no little ability, but his fame was not so great, and it was only when he came over here that he found play for his powers, and understood that the earth is not the only field in which earth's training may be put to use and effect in the Kingdom of God.

We stated to him the object of our mission, and he was very courteous and kind, for all his high office.

I suppose you would call him a great angel, and indeed, if he could come to earth and assume visibility, his brightness would be somewhat awe-inspiring.

He is very beautiful, both of form and countenance; radiant and beaming and glowing would perhaps describe him best. He listened and encouraged us, now and then, with a quiet word, to state our difficulties, and we forgot that he was so high in estate, and talked without fear or restraint. And then he said, "Well, my dear pupils—for so you are good enough to become for a little time—what you have told me is very interesting, and also very general in the work in which you are now engaged. Now, if I were to solve your perplexities you would go back to your work with light hearts, but you would probably find that the solution, when it came to work out, would not be without many flaws in the working, for just those points which are most necessary to remember are those little things which can best be learned by experience; and experience is the only thing which can show you how great these little things are. Come, therefore, with me, and I will teach you what is necessary for you to learn in a better way."

So we went with him, and he led us into the grounds which surrounded his house, and there we found there were gardeners at work tending the flowers and fruit trees, and doing the general work of a garden. He took us some distance along the walks, winding here and there, and through plantations of tree s and shrubs, where birds were singing and small pretty furry animals played here and there. At length we came to a stream and by it stood a stone arbour, which reminded me of a miniature temple of Egypt, and led us within. Then we sat on a seat under a network of flowering plants of different colours, and he sat on another bench at right angles to us.

Drawn on the floor, in indented lines, was a plan, and he pointed to it and said, "Now, this is a plan of my house and these grounds through which I have led you. Here is marked this little place in which we sit. We have come, as you will see, a considerable distance from the gate where I met you, and you were all talking so much of the pretty things you saw as you came that not one of you gave heed to the direction in which you came. It will be good practice, therefore, and not altogether lacking in pleasure, for you to find your way back again to me, and, when you arrive, I shall perhaps be able to give you some help by way of instruction on the difficulties you have stated to me."

With that he left us, and we all looked at one another, and then burst out laughing at ourselves for being so foolish as not to guess his object in leading us to this place by so circuitous a route. We then examined the plan again and again, but it was all lines and triangles and squares and circles, and we could make little of it at first.

Gradually, however, we began to understand. It was a map of the estate, and the arbour was in the centre, or nearly so, but the entrance was not shown, and, as there were four paths leading up to it, we did not know which to take to get back again. We, however reasoned that it did not matter much, for all seemed to lead to the outer circle; because there were so many paths between us and that, which crossed and recrossed each other. I must not tell you of all our endeavours to solve the problem, as it would take much too long.

At last I had a thought which I considered, and then, thinking it might perhaps help, told the others. They said it was the very thing they had been waiting for, and would very likely prove the key to the riddle. It was nothing more wonderful than just to go out and take whatever path led in the most direct line onwards from any we were forced to leave. That is awkward —what I mean is this: to go by those paths which would lead us in the straightest line from the arbour in any direction whatever. Then, when we had reached the boundary, which we saw by the plan was a perfect circle, we could skirt that and must inevitably reach the gate sooner or later.

So we set off, and a long and very pleasant journey it was, and not without adventure, for the place was extensive, with hills and valleys and woods and streams, and all so beautiful that we had to keep our object very firmly before our minds or we should have forgotten to choose the correct path when we came to two ways.

We reached the outermost boundary, however, although we did not, I think, take quite the best and most direct route. This boundary, I may say in passing, was composed of a wide stretch of grassland, and we saw, by the shape of its border, that it was circular, although we could not see much of it. So we turned to the left and then, as we went on, the bend of the circular estate seemed endless. Still we followed it and eventually came to the gate where first we had met our instructor.

He greeted us encouragingly, and we went up on to a terrace before the house, and then told him all our adventures — much more than I have narrated to you — and he listened as before, and then said, "Well, you have not done so badly, for you have gained your object, you have returned to the gate. And now let me tell you the lesson you have learned.

"First of all, the thing is to make sure of the direction you wish to go; and then the next thing is to take, not the path which seems shortest, but the one which seems surest to lead you right in the end. That path will not always be the quickest, and may lead you to the borderland where infinity shades off from the realm you know. Still, beyond the border line you are the better able to see both the extent and also the limitation of the estate you are negotiating, and it is only a matter of steadfastness and patience, and the goal you desire is quite sure to be won.

"Also, from just beyond the boundary between the local and the infinite, you are able to see that, although it contains within itself paths winding and many, and valleys and groves from which you cannot see very far away, yet that, viewed as a whole, it is perfectly symmetrical — a true circle in fact, which, for all the seeming maze and medley within, yet, as a circle, contains within itself a perfect geometrical entity, simple in itself, considered as a unit from the larger, wider point of view; perplexing when passing through its paths inside the boundary line.

"Also, you noted that, as you followed that curve on its outer side, you were able only to see a little portion of it at one time. Still, knowing that, from its shape, it would lead to the place you sought, you were content to follow on in faith based on reasoned conclusions, and, true enough, here you are and prove by your presence that your reasoning was, at least in the main, sound.

"Now, I could pursue this subject considerably further, but I will hand you over now to some of my friends who are with me here and help me in the work, and they will show you more of our home and its surroundings, and, if you wish, will be glad to accompany you farther afield, for there is much of interest to show you. Also you will be able to talk over with them the lessons I have been happy enough to be able to give you, and among you will, no doubt, have something more to tell and to ask me when we meet a little later."

So he bade us good-bye, and a band of happy people came from the house and led us within. But, as the time is up for you to go to other duties, we must cease now, with our love and assurance to you of our delight in coming thus to commune with you, if only for this little while.

God bless you, dear lad, and all our loved ones. Mother and friends.

Saturday, October 11, 1913

We were able to give you only a very brief account last evening of our visit to the home of our instructor on account of the shortness of time. We will now continue, and relate some of our experiences in that region. It is a region where there are many such institutions, and they are mostly devoted to the study of the best way of helping those on earth who are in doubt and perplexity as to the problems which stretch out into the realms beyond.

You will be able, by meditation, to amplify our own instruction if you view the place and our experience there in the light of a parable. So we pass on to other scenes, and will describe them as well as we can.

BOOK I: THE LOWLANDS OF HEAVEN

Our guides led us to a place outside the boundary of the estate of which we have already spoken, and we found that the grassland was very extensive. It is one of those plains of Heaven where manifestations from the higher Heavens are sometimes given. The call goes forth and vast multitudes assemble, and then some of the glories of the higher spheres are manifested, as well as is possible in these lower realms.

We passed over this tract until we at length began to ascend, and presently found ourselves on a tableland, where there were several buildings scattered about, some larger than others. In the centre was a large structure, and this we entered and found ourselves in a large and spacious hall, the only compartment in the place. It was circular in shape, and round the walls were carvings of a curious kind.

We examined them and found that they were representations of the heavenly bodies; and one was the earth. But they were not fixed, but turned on pivots, half in and half out of the wall. There were also models of animals and trees and human beings, but they were all movable, and mostly stood on pedestals in niches or alcoves. We inquired the meaning and were told that this was a purely scientific institution.

We were taken up to a balcony on one side of the circular space. It projected somewhat, and so we could see the whole at once. Then we were told that a small demonstration would be made for our benefit in order that we might get some idea of the use to which these things were put.

We sat there waiting, and at length a blue mist began to fill the central space. Then a ray of light swept round the hall and rested on the globe which represented the earth. As it hovered about it the sphere appeared to absorb the ray and became luminous, and after a time, the ray being withdrawn, we saw the earth globe was shining as from within. Then another ray was sent on to it of a deeper and different kind, and the globe slowly left the pedestal, or pivot, or whatever it rested on, and began to float out from the wall.

As it approached the centre of the space it entered the blue mist and immediately on contact began to enlarge until it became a great sphere glowing with its own light and floating in the blue space. It was exceedingly beautiful. Slowly, very slowly, it revolved on its axis, evidently in the same way the earth does, and we were able to see the oceans and continents. These were flat patterns, like those on the terrestrial globes used on earth. But as it revolved they began to assume a different aspect.

The mountains and hills began to stand out, and the waters to sway and ripple; and presently we saw minute models of the cities, and even details of the buildings. And still more detailed grew the model of earth, till we could see the people themselves, first the crowds and at last the individuals. This will be hard for you to understand, that on a globe of some, perhaps, eighty to a hundred feet in diameter we were able to see individual men and animals. But that is part of the science of this institution—the enabling of these details being seen individually.

Still more distinct grew these wonderful scenes, and, as the globe revolved, we saw men hurrying about the cities and working in the fields. We saw the wide spaces of prairie and desert and forest and the animals roaming in them. And as the globe slowly circled we saw the oceans and seas, some placid and others tossing and roaring, and here and there a ship. And all the life of earth passed before our eyes.

We looked at this a long time, and our friend who belonged to this settlement spoke to us from below where we sat. He told us that what we were looking at was the earth as it was at that moment. If we wished he would now show us the retroprogress of the ages from the present time to the beginning of man as an intelligent being. We replied that we would indeed be glad to see more of this wonderful and beautiful phenomenon, and he left us to go, I suppose, to the apparatus by which these things were controlled.

I may here pause to explain a matter which I see is in your mind. The place was not dark, it was light everywhere. But the globe itself shone with such extra intensity that, without any unpleasant sensation whatever, it obscured everything which was outside the blue cloud, which cloud seemed to be the circumference of the radiating beams shed by the globe.

Soon, then, the scenes began to change on the revolving sphere, and we were taken back through the thousands of years of the life of the earth and the generations of men and animals and plant life which had been from the present to the ages when men were just emerging from the forest to settle in colonies on the plains.

Now, I must explain here that history was not followed as historians follow it. These phenomena were not of nations and centuries, but of aeons and species. The geologic periods passed before us, and it was intensely interesting to watch what men called the iron age and the stone age, the ice age, the floods, and so on. And those of us who understood enough to follow it noticed that these ages were rather arbitrarily named. For the ice age, for example, might correctly describe the state of things in one or two regions of the earth, but there was by no means ice everywhere, as we saw as the sphere revolved. Also we noticed that very frequently one continent was in one age and another continent in another age at the same time. The exhibition ended, however, when the earth was well progressed, and, as I have said, the advent of man was already an accomplished fact.

When we had satisfied our eyes for awhile looking on the beauty of this many-coloured and ever-changing jewel, and had realized that this was indeed no other than the old earth we thought we knew so well, and found we knew so little, the globe gradually became smaller and floated back to the niche in the wall, and then the light faded out from it and it looked like an alabaster carving, just as we had seen it at first set there as an ornament.

We were so interested in what we had seen that we questioned our kind guide, and he told us many things about this hall. The earth sphere which had just been used could be made to serve other purposes than the one we had seen. But that had been selected because its picturesqueness was suited to us who were not scientifically trained. Among other uses was that of illustrating the relation of the heavenly bodies one to another, and their evolution into their present state. In this, of course, the globe we had just seen played its appropriate part.

The animals about the walls were also used for a like purpose. One would be vivified by these powerful rays and brought forth into the centre of the hall. When so treated it could walk of itself like a live animal, which it was temporarily, and in a certain restricted way. When it had ascended a platform in the centre space, then it was treated with the enlarging rays—as I may call them, not knowing their scientific name—and then with others which rendered it transparent, and all the internal organism of the animal became plainly visible to the students assembled. Those who were of that settlement said that it was 9 very beautiful sight to see the whole economy of the system of animal or man at work so displayed.

Then it was possible to bring over the living model a change, so that it began to evolve backward—or should I say "involve"?—towards its simpler and primal state as a mammal, and so on. The whole structural history of the animal was shown in that life-like process. And often when the first period of its separate existence as a separate creature was reached, the process was reversed, and it passed through the different stages of development, this time in their correct order and direction, until it became again as it is to-day. Also it was possible for any student to take charge and continue the development according to his own idea, and this not of the animals alone, but of the heavenly bodies, and also of nations and peoples, which are dealt with in another hall, however, specially adapted to that study.

It was a student from one of these establishments, in this same region, who erected the globe in the children's garden, of which I told you.[13] But that is, of course, a much simpler affair, or so it appeared to us after visiting this colony of beauties and wonders.

That will have to suffice for this time, although there is a lot more we saw while there. But I must not start off again, or I shall be keeping you too long.

You have a question. Yes, I was present on Monday at your Study Circle.[14] I knew she saw me, but could not make her hear me.

---

[13] See Chapter II, p. 38.

[14] The reference to the Study Circle needs a note of explanation. It was on the previous Monday. I sat in the Sanctuary between the rails, and the members were facing each other in the choir stalls, Miss E. sat on my right at the Sanctuary end of the stall. She afterwards told me that, when I was summing up the debate, she saw my mother step forth from the altar and come forward behind me with outstretched arms and a look of intense yearning and love on her face. She was exceedingly bright and beautiful, and her body looked as substantial as that of

BOOK I: THE LOWLANDS OF HEAVEN
Good night, dear. We shall be with you to-morrow.

Monday, October 13, 1913

One more experience we had in that colony which you would like to hear about. It was one which was new to me and very interesting. We were being shown over the different establishments which formed a complete group, when we came to a kind of open-air pavilion. It was principally composed of a huge circular dome resting on tall pillars, and the interior space so enclosed was open to the air. In the centre of the platform to which we ascended by a flight of steps which were all round the building, was a kind of square altar some four feet high and three feet square. On this stood a bronze tablet, something like a sundial, marked with lines and symbols and different geometrical figures.

Above it in the centre of the dome was an opening which led, as we were told, into a chamber where the instruments used here were controlled. We were told to stand round the dial (as I will call it) and our guide left us, and, going without, ascended to the roof of the dome, and so entered the chamber above us. We did not know what was going to happen, and so stood gazing at the disc.

Presently the place took on a different aspect, the air seemed to be changing in colour and intensity. And when we looked about us we saw that the landscape had disappeared, and between the pillars there stretched what appeared to be gossamer threads in the form of curtains. They were of various tints all interwoven, and, as we looked round, these seemed to separate into their own colours and then to take on more definite forms. This continued until we found ourselves standing in a glade with the circular belt of trees gently waving in the breeze.

Then birds began to sing, and we saw their bright plumage as they flew from one tree to another. Gradually we saw the distance

---

any of the others present. Miss E. thought she was going to clasp me in her arms, and it was so vivid that she forgot, for the moment, that the form was not of flesh and blood, and, therefore, could not be seen by the others. She was on the point of crying out when she suddenly recollected herself, but had to look away in order to suppress her exclamation. It was about this I wished to ask the question. G.V.O.

deepen between the trees and could see far into a beautiful forest. The dome also was gone and the sky was above us, except where the trees stretched aloft like a canopy.

We turned again to the altar and the disc. These were still in place, but the figures and signs on the latter were now shining with a light which seemed to come from within the altar.

Now we heard the voice of our guide from above telling us to watch and try to read the tablet. We could make little of it at first, but at length one of our party more clever than the rest said that the signs were really representations of the various elements which went to make up the vegetable and animal bodies of the spiritual realms. It is difficult to explain the way in which the connection between the two was apparent to us. But when once pointed out it became quite clear that this was so.

Now our guide joined us once more and explained the use of the building. It seems that before the students are able to progress much in the science of creation as studied in this region, they have to get a thorough knowledge of the fundamental elements with which they have to deal. This is, of course, quite natural. This building is one of the first where they come to study, and the table, or dial, is a kind of register of these elements on which the student above in the chamber where the controlling instruments are can see the combination of elements he has brought about and also the proportion of each element entering into the combination.

Our guide was somewhat advanced in the science, and had contrived the forest scene by means of this same skill. As the learners progress they are able gradually to achieve the result they wish without the scientific apparatus which at first is necessary. One instrument after another is left out until at length they are able to depend solely on their will.

We asked our guide to what practical purpose the knowledge was put when acquired. He replied that the first use was the training of the mind and will of the student. That training was very excellent and very strenuous. When the student had become proficient he moved on to another college in this region where another branch of the science was learned, and then had to pass through many more stages of training. The actual use of his knowledge did not fall to his lot until he had passed through many spheres of progress. In the higher of these he was allowed to accompany some great Master, or Archangel, or Power (I do not know the exact and correct title) on one of his missions of service in the Infinite Creation of the One Father, and there witness the sublime process at work.

It was thought that this might be the creation of some new cosmos or system, either material or spiritual. But that is so high above this state in which we are at present that we have only a general idea of the duties of those High Beings, and it is a matter of a few ages of progress from here to there, if our ways lie in the direction of that particular system of Heavens.

And the chances are that, for us five women who visited the place I have been describing, our onward path will lead us somewhere else.

But we love to know all about the different spheres of service, even if we be destined never to be chosen for them. We cannot all be creators of cosmoi, I suppose, and there are other things as necessary, great and glorious, no doubt, in those far reaches beyond us nearer to the Throne and Dwelling of Him Who is all in all to all.

As we returned across the wide grass-lands we were met by a party of these same students who had been to another college to study a different branch of science. They were not all men; some were women. I inquired if their studies were all on the same lines as that of their brothers, and they replied in the affirmative, but added that while the men students mostly looked after the purely creative part, they were permitted to add to and round off the work with their genius of motherhood, and that the two aspects blending enhanced the beauty of the finished work—finished, that is, so far as it was possible as conditioned by the limitations of their present spheres. For here were not so much spheres of perfect accomplishment as of progress towards those higher spheres.

By the time we had returned to the first colony where we had met our instructor of the circular estate.

Why do you not give me his name?

THE LIFE BEYOND THE VEIL

His name was Arnol,[15] but these names sound so strange to earth ears, and people are always trying to find out their meaning, that we are rather shy of giving them. The meanings are mostly incomprehensible to you, so we will just say the name in future, as you wish it, and leave it there.

Well, it saves a lot of roundabout wording, doesn't it?

Yes: and yet if you understood the conditions under which we give you these narratives you would probably say that the longer was the more sure route. Remember our experience and teaching on Arnol's estate.

What makes it so difficult for you to give names? I have heard of this difficulty more than once.

There is also a difficulty in explaining the difficulty —from your point of view so apparently simple a matter. Let us put it in this way. You know that with the old Egyptians the name of a god or goddess was much more than a name as understood by the hardy materialistic Anglo-Saxon from whose race came the question: "What's in a name?" Well, from our point of view, and that also of the ancient wisdom of Egypt, based on data obtained from this side the Veil, there is a great deal in a name. Even in the mere repetition of some names there is actual power, and sometimes peril. That we know now as we did not when on earth. And so we here acquire a reverence for the entity "the Name", which to you would probably seem foolish. Nevertheless, it is partly for this reason that names do not come through to you so plentifully as many rather feeble investigators would wish.

Also the mere utterance and transmission of some of these names is, when we are in this earth region, a matter of more difficulty than you would perhaps deem. It is a subject, however, which is hard to explain to you, and only one which you will be able to understand when you have become more familiar with the fourth dimension which obtains here—which term, also, we use for want of a better. We will just refer you to two or three instances and there leave the matter.

---

[15] Arnol here referred to, for the first time, eventually communicated through the Rev. G. V. Owen a series of messages of a very high order, which are published in Volumes 3 and 4 . H.W.E.

BOOK I: THE LOWLANDS OF HEAVEN

One is the giving to Moses of the Name of the great Officer of the Supreme Who visited him. Moses asked for that Name, and got it—and neither he nor any one else to this day has been able to say what it means.

Then the lesser Angel who came to Jacob, Jacob asked for his name, and it was refused him. The Angels who came to Abraham and to others in the Old Testament very seldom gave their names. Likewise in the New Testament, most of the Angels who come to minister to earth's denizens are simply so called; and where the name is given, as in the case of Gabriel, it is little understood as to its inner significance. Of the new name which no man—that is, man on earth—knoweth, we have already spoken.

What is your name, mother—I mean your new name? Is it permissible for you to give it?

Permissible, yes, but not wise, dear. You know I would give it if it were so. But this for the present I must withhold even from you, knowing that you will understand my love even if my motive is not very clear.

Yes, dear, you know what is best.

Some day you, too, will know, and then you will see what glory awaits those whose names are written in the Book of the Life of the Lamb, a phrase also which is worth thinking over, for in it is a glorious and living truth which those who use that Name so lightly surely apprehend little or not at all.

God bless you, dear, and Rose and the children. Ruby once more bids me in her pretty way, to say she is coming to see you soon, and hopes you will be able to take down her commands—that is the word she used, bless her, who is graceful humility itself, and loved by all who know her. God bless you, dear. Good-bye.

Wednesday, October 15, 1913

How would you begin to explain to one who had little idea of a spirit world about him the truth of survival beyond the grave and the reality of this life and all its love and beauty? First you would probably endeavour to bring home to him the fact of his present actual existence as an immortal being. And then, when he had

85

really grasped the significance of that, as it affects his future, he would perhaps be open to a few words of description as to that life which be will find himself possessed of, and in touch with, when he puts aside the Veil and emerges into the greater light of the Beyond.

So we feel that if men could but understand that the life they now live is life indeed, and not merely an ephemeral existence, they would then be more inclined to count worthy of consideration the words of those who have proved for themselves both the reality of this persistence of life and individuality, and also the blessedness of the lot awaiting those who on earth are able to strive and to prevail.

Now, it is no small matter that men should so live their lives on earth that when they step over the threshold into the larger, freer sphere they should take up and continue their service in the Kingdom without a more or less protracted hiatus in their progress. We have seen the effect of the career of so many, as it is viewed in extension into this land, that we feel we cannot too much emphasize the importance of preparation and self-training while opportunity offers. For so many do put off the serious consideration of this, with the idea of starting afresh here, and when they come over they find that they had very little realized what that starting afresh really implied.

Who is this writing?

Still your mother and her friends. Astriel is not here to-night, but will be with us on another occasion. We will let you know when it is he and his party communicating.

Well, to proceed then. We have already told you of the Bridge and the Chasm.

Yes. But what of your further experience in Arnol's domain, and of your return to your own proper sphere? Have you nothing more to tell me of that episode?

No more than that we learned much, made many friends, saw a great deal more than we here set down, and shall visit the place again soon. Now let us get on to what we wished to say, and which will perhaps be as useful as if we were to continue our description of the Colony in that other region.

BOOK I: THE LOWLANDS OF HEAVEN

The Chasm and the Bridge[16]—bring back your mind to what we told you of them. We wish to relate an episode which we witnessed at the place where the Bridge—as I will continue to name it—emerges on to the uplands of life and light.

We were sent thither to receive a woman who was expected to arrive, having fought her way through those dreadful, dark regions which lie below the Bridge. She had not come over the great causeway, but through the horrors of the darkness and gloom in the region below. With us went a strong Angel from a sphere above us, who was specially commissioned for the task. This was one of the Sister Angels who organize our homes where the rescued are taken.

Can you give me her name?

Beam—no, we cannot get it through. Leave it, and we may be able to do so as we proceed.

When we arrived there we found that a light was glimmering some way down the rocky way which went down into the valley, and knew that some angel was there on the watch. Presently it grew more dim, and we noticed that it was moving away from us into the distance below. Then after a time we saw a flash far out over the valley, and this was immediately answered by a stream of light from one of the towers on the Bridge. It was not unlike what you know as a searchlight, and indeed answered a purpose somewhat similar. It shot out downward into the gloom and remained steady. Then Bea—our Angel Sister told us to abide where we were for a time, and she went quickly through the air to the tower top.

Then we lost her in the light, but one of my companions said she thought she saw her speeding along the ray of light which slanted downwards towards the depths. I did not; but afterwards we found that she had seen correctly.

I ought to pause here to explain that that light was not so much to enable the spirits to see (which they could do of their own power), but to give strength for the work and protection against the hurtful influences which held sway in the region below. It was for that reason that the first angel had sent out his signal, and it was

---

[16] See p. 26.

understood by the constant watchers on the Bridge and answered in the way I have told. The ray of light is, in some way I do not understand yet, impregnated with power of life and strength—the best description I am able to give—and it was sent to help him whose strength was in want of succour.

By and by we saw the two return. He was a strong Angel, but looked fatigued, and we learned later that he had encountered a band of very malignant spirits who did their best to get the woman back again amongst them. That is why he needed help. He walked on one side and she walked on the other side of the poor torn and tortured soul who was more than half in a swoon. They went very slowly for her sake now, walking in the ray of light towards the tower on the Bridge. We had never seen anything like this before, except once, and that I have recounted to you. I mean the Pavilion of light and the assembling of the people of many coloured dresses. But this was, in a way, much more solemn; for here was anguish in the midst of joy, and there joy alone. They reached the Bridge, and the rescued one was taken into one of the houses and tended, and there remained until she had sufficiently recovered to be handed over to our care.

Now, there are several points in this narrative which held new knowledge for us, and some which confirmed what had been mere surmises up to the time of that experience. Some of these I will name.

It is a mistake to think that Angels, even of such estate as those two who went and rescued that poor woman, are unable to suffer. They do suffer, and that frequently. And it is possible for the malicious ones to hurt them when they venture into their regions. Theoretically I cannot see why the evil ones should not now and then prevail so as to get them into their power. So well, however, are the powers of light and good organized, and so watchful, that I have not heard that this catastrophe has ever been known actually to happen. But their fight is a real fight, and fatiguing also.

That is the second point. Even these high Angels can become fatigued. But neither their suffering nor their fatigue do they mind. It may sound a paradox, but it is nevertheless true, that it is a joy to them to suffer so when some poor struggling soul is to be helped.

Also that light-ray—or perhaps I should say "ray of power and vitality"—was so strong that, had they not protected the woman by surrounding her with a certain negative influence, it would have harmed her, because it would have been too great a shock to one so unprepared as she.

Another point is this. That ray was seen far out in the region of gloom, and we heard a murmur coming, as it seemed, from hundreds of miles away, down across the valley. It was a strange experience, for the sound was that of many voices, and some were of rage and hate, and others of despair, and others cries for help and mercy. And these and other different cries seemed to be gathered each in its own particular locality, and to come from different directions. We could understand but little, but afterwards, while we waited for the rescued one, we asked Beanix—(I am afraid I cannot do better than that, so it will have to stand. We will call her Beanix, but it does not look quite correct when written down)—we asked her about those cries and where they came from. She said she did not know, but that there was provision for their registration, both collectively and individually, for their analysis, and that they would be scientifically treated in this science of love, and that then help would be sent out according to the merit of those who cried, and also in such form as would best be of service. Each cry was an evidence either of good or bad in some human soul in that region, and would receive its appropriate answer.

When the woman was handed over to us we first let her rest and surrounded her with a quiet restful influence, and then, when she was strong enough, led her away to a home where she is being cared for and tended.

We did not ask her any questions, but let her ask the few she was able to put to us. But I found that the poor thing had been in that dark land for more than twenty years past. Her life history on earth I have partly learned, but not enough to make a connected narrative. And it is not well to remind them too vividly at first of the earth they have left so long ago.

They usually have to work back from the present through their experience in the spirit life, in order to understand it and the relation of the whole— cause and effect, sowing and reaping—all explained.

That must serve for this time. Good-bye, dear, and God's blessing and our prayers shall be with and for you. May He keep you in His peace.

Amen.

CHAPTER IV: THE CITY AND REALM OF CASTREL

To the City and Realm of Castrel—The House of Castrel—Still-born children, not lost but gone before—Waters of life Death and beyond death, no gap—Earth made perfect—The Manifestation in the old Council Chamber—Jolly Hooper interrupted— Traversing the spheres—The "Stars are the Angels"—The harp of light—The Summerland of God: its atmosphere—Departure from the City of Castrel—Wilfulness.

Friday, October 17, 1913

BY the time we had reached the Horne where we were charged to leave our poor sister, now so blessed, we were aware of another mission allotted to us. We were bidden to go to another district farther to the East.... You again hesitate, but that is the word we want. By the East we mean the direction from which the Brighter Light is seen over the mountains which border the plain where the Vision of the Christ and the Cross had been given to us. We often speak of that direction as the East because it reminds us of the Sunrise.

We set off, the five of us, all women, and kept before us the description we had received of the place we were to seek. We were to look for a great city among the mountains, with a golden dome in the midst of it, and the City itself surrounded by a colonnade on a terrace which ran round the City on all sides.

We walked over the plain, and then went through the air, which requires more exertion, but is more speedy, and, in a case like ours, more convenient in enabling us to get a view of the country.

We sighted the City and descended before the principal gateway, by which we entered the main thoroughfare. It ran straight through the City and emerged through another gateway on the other side. On each side of this broad street there were large houses, or palaces, in spacious grounds, the residences of the principal officials of that district of which the City itself was the Capital.

As we came towards the City we had seen people working in the fields, and also many buildings, evidently not residences, but erected for some useful purpose. And now that we were within the City walls we saw the perfection of both buildings and horticulture. For each building had a typical garden to match it both in colour and design. We passed on, waiting for some sign as to our destination and mission, for on such occasions as this a message is always sent on ahead, so that the visitors are expected.

When we had gone some way we entered a large square, where beautiful trees grew on lawns of the greenest of green grass, and fountains played a harmony together; that is to say, there were perhaps a dozen fountains, and each had a tone of its own, and each was composed of many smaller jets of water, each being a note. These are manipulated, on occasion, so that a fairly complicated piece of music can he played, with an effect such as that produced by an organ with many stops. At such times there are large numbers of people assembled in the square, or park, as I might call it, both of the citizens and also those who dwell outside among the hills and pastures. But when we came to it the fountains were playing a simple series of chords, in perfect harmony, and with most pleasing effect.

Here we lingered for awhile, for it is exceedingly restful and beautiful.

We sat and lay upon the grass, and presently there came towards us a man who, by the smile on his face as he approached, we knew was the one who had been expecting us. We arose and stood before him in silence, for we did not feel inclined to begin the conversation, as we saw he was an angel of some degree considerably above us.

Please describe him, and give me his name if possible.

All in good time, dear. We learn to eliminate impatience here as a thing which confuses without adding impetus to the matter in hand.

He was tall—much taller than the average man on earth I should say he would be some seven and a half feet high in earth measurement. I am considerably taller than I was when with you, and he was much taller than I am. He wore a cream-coloured tunic, almost to his knees, bare arms and legs, and no sandals. You see I am answering what you are questioning in your mind. No, he had nothing on his head, but a beautiful veil of soft brown hair, parted in the middle and curling round his face and neck.

One broad fillet of gold he wore, and in the centre and at the sides were set three large blue stones. He wore a belt of silver and some pink metal mingled, and his limbs shone with a soft glow. And these points, together with others, told us of his high degree.

There was also a calm benevolence and power in his firm but kindly countenance which gave both peace and trustfulness to us, as we stood before him, but also induced a reverence which we were glad to pay to one of such real worth as he.

He spoke at last, quietly, modulating his voice, as we instinctively knew, to our case. We could, nevertheless, detect the reverberating power in the tone of it. He said, "My name is Cast—". I am sorry. These names seem to be one of my weaknesses. They always perplex me when I try to reproduce them down here. But never mind his name for the moment. "I am C.", he said. "You have already heard of me from your own Superior, and now we meet in person. Now, my sisters five, come with me, and I will tell you why you have been sent to this City and to me." So we followed him, and on the way he chatted pleasantly, and we were quite at ease in his presence.

He led us down an avenue at right angles to the square, and then we emerged into another square; but we saw at once that this was a private square, and that the great palace, which lay away across the parklands before and around it, was the residence of some great Lord. We were guided through the park until we approached the great building, which stood, like some Greek temple, on a plateau which had a flight of steps on all sides of it.

The building was immense, and stretched before us, to right and left, and had high arches and entrances and porticoes, and surmounting it was a great dome. It was the landmark we had seen when approaching the City, only we found that it was not all gold, but gold and blue. We inquired who lived here, and he answered, "Oh, this is my home; that is, it is my city home; but I have also other houses out there in the country parts where I go from time to time to visit my friends whose duties lie in those districts. Come within and you shall be given the welcome which is your due, who have come so far to see us."

93

He spoke quite simply. I have come to know that here simplicity is one of the marks of great power. One might have thought that the proper way to usher one into the presence of a great noble would be to send servants to lead us to the Palace, and then that be should receive us in state. But they look at things differently here. No purpose would have served in this case by such ceremony, and so it was dispensed with. In cases where ceremony is helpful or desirable it is observed and sometimes with much grandeur. When it has no use it is not observed.

And that is how we came to the House of Castrel, —now you have his name as well as I am able to give it; of whom more another evening. You have to go now, so good night, dear, and all blessing to you and yours from these glowing and beautiful realms. Dear lad, good night.

Saturday, October 18, 1913

So he led us within, and we found that the interior of the house was lofty and very magnificent. The entrance-hall in which we stood was circular in shape, and open right up to the great dome above, which did not stand over the centre of the building, but receded a little from the portico over this entrance. The rotunda was richly embellished with stones of many colours, and hangings of silk-like texture, mostly of deep crimson.

Doorways led off down long passages in front and on either side of us. Doves flitted about the dome itself, and evidently had means of ingress and egress. The material of which the arching roof of this dome was builded was a kind of semi-opaque stone, and permitted the light to filter through in a softened glow. When we had looked about us for a time we found that we were alone, for Castrel had left us.

By and by, from down a passage on our right, we heard laughter and happy voices, and there presently emerged a party of women, with a few children among them. They numbered about twenty in all, and came to us, and took our hands in welcome, and kissed us on the cheek, and smiled on us, so that we were happier, if possible, than before. Then they drew away, and stood at a little distance, except one who had remained in the rear. She came forward and led us to a recess in the wall, where she bade us be seated.

Then, standing before us, she addressed each of us by name in greeting, and said, "You will wonder why you have tome here, and what this City and place is to which you have been sent. This house in which you now are is the Palace of Castrel, as, no doubt, you already know. He is ruler of this wide district, where many occupations are followed, and many studies are pursued. I hear you have already been to the Colony of Music, and farther on to other settlements, where different branches of science are carried on. Now, we are in touch with all of these, and are constantly receiving their reports as to progress in this or that branch. These are considered and dealt with by Castrel and his officers, from the harmony point of view, as I will call it. Co-ordination, however, would express what I mean.

"For instance, a report will arrive from the College of Music, and another from that of Light, and another from the settlement where the Creative faculty is studied, and from other branches of service. These are all very carefully examined and analysed and tabulated, and, where necessity requires, the results are tested here, in one or other of the laboratories attached to this City. You will have seen some of these as you approached. They are scattered over the country to a great distance. They are not quite so complete in detail as those you have visited elsewhere, but, when any new apparatus is required, a mission is dispatched to inquire as to the construction, and these return and erect it in the spot most fitting in relation to the other establishments in this district; or perhaps it is added to the other apparatus already in existence in one or other of the buildings.

"You will understand, therefore, that an Overlord such as he who controls so varied a combination of knowledge must be well advanced in wisdom, and also is kept very busy at his work. It is this work you have been sent to see, and, while you remain with us, you will have ample opportunity of visiting some of the outlying stations. You will not, of course, understand all, or perhaps very much, of the scientific side of the work, but enough will be shown you to help you in your future work.

Now come, and I will show you over this house, if you would care to see it."

We replied that we would, and thanked her for her kindness. So we went all over the principal parts of that magnificent dwelling. That is the only word I can find for it. Everywhere was colour blended with colour, bold but harmonious, and in such a way that, instead of being glaring, it had sometimes an exhilarating and sometimes a soothing and restful effect.

Jewels and precious metals and beautiful ornaments, vases and pedestals and pillars—some standing alone as an ornament, each by itself, some in groups—hangings of glittering material which, as we passed through some doorway, swung into place again with a musical murmur, fountains with fish, courtyards open to the sky, in which grass and most beautiful trees and flowering shrubs grew, of such colours as are not known on earth.

Then we ascended to the roof, and here again was a roof garden, but one of large extent, with grass and arbours and shrubs and fountains once again. It was mostly from this garden that messages and messengers were sighted; and also there were appliances by which correspondence could be carried on with distant regions by a kind of what you would perhaps call wireless telegraphy, but it was really different from that, inasmuch as the messages arrived in visible form mostly, and not in words.

In this mansion we stayed for a considerable period, and visited both the City and also the district around, a district which in earth measure would be reckoned in thousands of miles across, but all in constant touch with the City and its communicating stations, and with this central Palace itself.

Time would fail to tell you all. So I will just give you a few details, and leave you to imagine the rest, which, however, I know you will fail to do.

The first thing which puzzled me was the presence of children, for I had thought that all children were reared in special Homes by themselves. The lady who had received us was the Mother of the place, and those who had attended her were some of her helpers. I asked one of these about these children who looked so happy and beautiful, and so perfectly at ease in this grand place. She explained that these were stillborn children, who had never breathed the atmosphere of earth. For this reason they were of different character from others who had been born alive, even from those who had only lived a few minutes. They also required different treatment, and were able much sooner to imbibe the knowledge of these spheres. So they were sent to some such home as this, and were trained until they had progressed in mind and stature to such a degree that they were able to begin their new course of knowledge. Then, strong in heavenly purity and wisdom, they were taken in hand by those teachers who were in touch with the earth itself, and were taught what they had not been able to learn before.

This was interesting to me, and presently I began to see that one reason I had been sent here was to learn this very thing, in order that there might be awakened in me by that knowledge the desire to know my own who had so passed into this land, and of whom I had not hoped to be called mother. O, the great and sweetest yearning which came to me when I realized this.

I will not dwell upon it, but confess that for a time tears of unutterable joy dimmed my eyes at this one more blessing added to my already abundant store. I sat down on the grass beneath a tree, and hid my face in my hands, and bowed my head upon my knees, and there I remained helpless, from the too exquisite rapture, which filled and vibrated through my being till I shook all over. My kind friend did not speak to me, but sat down by my side, and put her arms around my shoulders, and let me sob out my joy. Then, when I had somewhat recovered, she said very gently, "Dear, I also am a mother, the mother of one such as you will find here all your own. So I know what is in your heart at this moment, for I have experienced your present joy also".

Then I raised my eyes to her face, and she saw the question I could not ask her, and, taking my hand, she raised me, and, with her arm round my shoulder still, she led me towards a grove, where we heard children playing, their happy shouts and laughter coming through the trees—for I was very faint from all that great joy that filled me, and how should I sustain the greater joy to come?

Dear, that was not very long ago, and it is still so fresh to me that I find it hard to write for you clearly as I could wish. But you

97

must forgive me if I seem to be too profuse, or too disjointed in my words. I had not known this truth, and when it was revealed to me so suddenly, and all the—to me—tremendous significance of it—well, I must leave you to try to understand. Suffice to say, I found in that glade what I did not know I possessed, and such a gift as this is more readily bestowed in this land than one is able with due self-control to receive.

I must add, be fore I cease, what I ought to have said before, but was carried on in spite of myself by the recollection of that sweet hour. It is this: When young children come over here they are first schooled in this life and then have to learn what experience they have lacked on earth. The more training they have acquired in the earth life, the sooner they are sent to complete it. Those who are stillborn have had no earth training at all.

Nevertheless, they are children of the earth and, as such, they must return and acquire it. Not until it is safe for them to do so, however, and then under proper guardianship until they are competent to go alone. Their return to the neighbourhood of the earth sphere is consequently longer delayed, and one who has lived a long and busy life on earth has less to learn of earth life when he comes over here, and so can pass on to other and higher studies.

Of course, these are only the broad governing principles, and, in application to individuals, account has to be taken of personal characteristics, and the rule modified and adapted as the particular case requires or merits.

But all is well for all who live and love, and those who love best live the loveliest sufficiently recovered to be handed over to our rare life. That sounds rather too alliterative, but let it stand, for it is true. God bless you, dear. Good night.

Monday, October 20, 1913

We were walking down the principal street of that beautiful city on a tour of inspection. We wanted to understand why it was laid out in so many squares, and what was the use of some of the buildings we had noticed on both sides of that broad way. When we had arrived at the farther gateway, we saw that the City stood very high above the surrounding plains. Our guide explained that the reason for this was that those on the towers might see as far as possible, and also might be seen by those in the distant settlements of this district. This was the Capital City of the region, and all business going on found its focus here.

On our way back we visited several of the buildings, and were everywhere kindly received. We found few children, other than those in Castrel's Home. Here and there, however, there were groups in the squares, where the fountains played and were surrounded by basins into which their waters fell. These were all connected with one broad stream which issued forth from one side of the City, and fell into the plain below, a brilliant waterfall of many tints and of sparkling brightness. It took its way across the plain, a fairly broad stream flowing gently over the sands, and we saw, here and there, some children bathing in it, and throwing it over their beautiful bodies in great enjoyment.

I did not think much of this until my guide remarked that these children were encouraged to bathe in the waters, as they were electrically charged, and gave strength to them, for many came here very weak and required such nourishment.

I expressed my surprise at this, and she replied, "But what would you have? You know that, although not of material flesh and blood, yet our bodies here are solid and real as those we have laid aside. And you know that these bodies of our present state correspond to the spirit within much more accurately than those others used to do. Now these little spirits are, most of them, only beginning to develop and need bodily nourishment to help them on the way. Why not?"

Why not, indeed! Surely I was slow to learn all that that phrase I have already given you implied, "Earth made perfect". I fear many of you when you come over here will be much shocked to see how very natural all things are, even if more beautiful than on the earth. So many expect to find a vague shadowy world over here, totally diverse from earth in every possible way. And yet, come to think of it, and with common sense, what good would such a world be to us? It would not mean a gradual progress for us, but a vast leap, and that is not the way of God.

THE LIFE BEYOND THE VEIL

Things here when first we arrive are certainly different from those of the old life, but not so different as to make us feel dumbfounded by their strangeness. Indeed, those who come over after living an unprogressive life on earth, find themselves in spheres of so gross a character as to be, to them, indistinguishable from earth itself. That is one of the reasons why they are not able to realize that they have changed their state. As you progress through the lower spheres into the higher, this grossness gradually gives place to more rare conditions, and the higher you go the more sublimated is the environment. But few, if any, pass into those spheres where no trace of earth is seen, or no likeness to the earth life. I doubt if, as a rule, any do. But of this I must not speak dogmatically, for I have not myself reached, or even visited, a sphere where there is absolutely no likeness to God's beautiful earth. For it is beautiful, and we have to learn its beauties and wonders here, as part of our training. And, learning so, we find that earth is but one further manifestation outward from our own spheres, and in tune with us and our present environment in many very intimate ways. Were it not thus we could not be communing with you at this moment.

Also—and I merely say this as it appears to me who am not very wise in these things—I do not see how people passing over from the earth life into this could possibly get here were there a great gap between us, a gigantic void. How could they cross it? But that is simply my own thought, and there may be nothing in it at all. Only of this I am fairly certain: if people would but keep in mind the Oneness of God and His Kingdom, and the gradual progression which, in His wisdom, He has ordained for us, then they would much better understand what death is and what is beyond. It would probably be utterly absurd to many to be told that here we have real solid houses and streets and mountains and trees and animals and birds; and that animals are not here for ornament alone, but also for use; and that horses and oxen and other animals are put to use. But they enjoy their work in a way which makes one glad to watch them. I noticed a horse and rider coming along the street once, and I wondered which was enjoying the canter the more of the two. But I fear this will not be accepted by many, so I will get on to another theme.

One of the buildings in the broad street was a library where records were kept of reports from the outlying stations. Another was a laboratory where some of the reports could be tested by actual experiment. Another was a lecture hall where professors gave their results to those of their own and other branches of science. Another had a somewhat curious history.

It stood well back from the street and was builded of wood. It looked like polished mahogany, with streaks of gold in the grain. It was erected long ago as a Council Chamber for the Chief of that time, long before Castrel took over the work. Here he used to assemble the students in order that they might each give an exhibition of their knowledge in practical form.

A young man arose on one occasion, and, going to the centre of the auditorium, stood there and stretched out his hands, and remained facing the President. As he stood there his form seemed to change and become more radiant and translucent, until at last he was surrounded by a large halo of light, and there were seen about him many Angels from the higher spheres. His smile had some enigma in it which the Prince was trying to read, but could not. Just as he (the Prince or Chief) was about to speak, there came through the open door a little boy-child, and looked round in surprise at all the great crowd.

He paused at the edge of the circle and looked on the multitude of faces of those who sat there in tiers, one above the other, round the circle, and seemed abashed. He was just turning to run away again when he caught sight of the one who stood in the centre, now glowing with light and glory. Immediately the little lad forgot everybody else, and, running as fast as his little legs would carry him, he went straight to the centre of the circle with outstretched hands and a look of great joy in his face.

The one who stood there then lowered his arms, and, stooping down, took up the little one and laid him on his shoulder, and then, approaching the Prince, he gently laid the little fellow in his lap and began to walk back towards the place where he had stood. But as he went his form grew dim, and, before he had reached the spot he had left, he had become quite invisible, and the whole space was empty. But the little boy lay in the Prince's lap, and looked up into his face — a very beautiful face it was — and smiled.

Then the Prince arose, and, holding the child on his left arm, he reverently laid his right hand on his head, and said, "My brothers, it is written, 'A little child shall lead them', and these words come to my mind but now. What we have seen is a Manifestation of our Lord the Christ, and this little one is of those who are of the Kingdom, as He said. "What message did He give you, child, as you lay in His arms, and He brought you to mine?"

Then for the first time the boy spoke and said, with a child's accent, and still very shy of the large audience, "If you please, Prince, I must be good and do as you instruct me, and then He will show me, from time to time, new things for your City and Realm. But I don't know what it means."

Nor did the Prince, nor the students at first. But he dispersed them and took the little one home to his own house, and thought the matter out. He came to the conclusion it was Eli and Samuel over again, without the more unpleasant details. As a matter of fact, as it turned out, he had read the matter correctly. The child was allowed to play about the laboratories and scientific schools, and watch and listen. He never was in the way, and did not bother them with questions. But now and again, when some extra-difficult piece of work was on hand, he would make some re mark, and when he did so, it was always the key to the solution. Also — and this was considered, as time went on, to be the principal object He had in giving that Manifestation — the students learned simplicity; that is, that the simpler the solution they could find to any problem in particular, the better it fitted into the general scheme with other solutions.

There were many other lessons also which they learned from the Vision itself; for instance, the fact that His Presence was among them always, and that at any time He might become visible, for, when He came that time, He walked out from among the assembly of students. Also, the outstretched arms taught them of self-sacrifice even in those happy realms where glories shone about them, even as it had shone about His form as He stood there.

BOOK I: THE LOWLANDS OF HEAVEN

But the child: he grew as His Divine Sponsor had grown, in wisdom and stature, and when the Prince of that time was taken into a higher sphere, he succeeded him in his high office.

Well, all this is long ago, and still the old hall stands to-day. It is always kept carefully tended and made beautiful without and within with flowers. But it is not used now for lectures and discussions, but for service of worship. One of the artists of the City made a painting of the scene, and that was placed there behind the Altar, like many on earth. And from time to time worship is offered to the Great Father of all, in the sanctifying Presence of His Anointed Son, and, on some of the greater occasions, the Prince who was there when that Vision was given will descend from the higher spheres with the little boy, now a great Angel-Lord, and others who have held the office since their time; and those who assemble there know that some great blessing and Manifestation will be given. But only those who are fitted by their developed state are present at such times, for the Manifestation would not be visible to those who have not reached a certain stage in progress.

God's spheres are wonderful in their beauty of light and glory; but most wonderful of all seems the Presence of His Spirit through all these infinities and eternities, and His tender love to all, both wise and simple; and to you and me, dear, in that He has so ordained the co-operation of the different estates within His Realm that we can talk together thus, you and I, dear, through the thin Veil which hangs between.

Tuesday, October 21, 1913

Of that city I could tell you much more than I have done. But I have other matters to deal with, and will, therefore, give you just one more item of our life there and then pass on to other things.

We were lodging in a cottage within the Palace grounds where the children often came to see us, and my own little one among them. They seemed to be glad to come and see their little friend's mother and her fellow visitors, and were never tired of hearing about the other places we had visited, and especially the children's homes and schools. They would weave garlands of flowers and

103

bring them to us as gifts, with the hope at the back of their minds that we would in return join them in one of their games.

This we often did, and you will easily imagine how I enjoyed those romps with these dear little children in that quiet and peaceful place.

We were once playing with them at a game they had invented among themselves, a kind of jolly Hooper game such as you used to play, and we had won nearly all the others on to our side, when the few who were left facing us suddenly stopped in their song and stood still, looking beyond us. We all turned round, and there, standing in the entrance of a long avenue of trees at the edge of the glade, was no other than Castrel.

He stood there smiling at us, and, although his aspect was so kingly, yet there were so much gentleness and humility blended with his strength and wisdom, that he was very lovely to look upon, and to be near. He came slowly forward and the children ran to him, and he patted one and another on the head as he came. Then he spoke to us. "You see", he said, "I knew where I might find you, and so I needed no guide. And now I am obliged to cut your play short, my sister-visitors, for there is a ceremony on hand at which you ought to be present. So you little ones must continue your games alone while these big children come with me."

Then they ran to us and kissed us happily, and made us promise to come and continue our games as soon as we were at liberty.

So we followed the Prince Castrel along the avenue of trees which formed a leafy tunnel meeting overhead. We walked to the end and emerged into the open country, and here our guide paused and said, "Now I want you to look yonder and tell me what you see".

We, one and all five of us, told him we saw a large undulating plain, with many buildings here and there, and, beyond, what appeared to be a long range of high mountains.

"Nothing else?" he asked.

We replied that we could see nothing else of importance, and he continued, "No, I suppose that is about the limit of your vision at present. But my sight, you see, is more developed than yours, and I can see beyond those mountains yonder. Now listen, and I will tell you what I see. Beyond that range I see other mountains higher still, and beyond them still more lofty peaks. On some of these are buildings, others are bare. I have been in that region also, and I know that among those mountains, which from this point are viewed foreshortened, are plains and tracts of country as wide as this of which this City is the chief.

"I am now looking at the shoulder of a mountain, not on the horizon, as I see it, but far beyond your own range of vision, and I see a large and glorious City, much more extensive and much richer and more magnificent than this. The principal gateway fronts in this direction, and before it is a large flat space. Through this gateway are emerging horses and chariots with drivers, and other horses with riders. They have now assembled and are about to start. Now their leader emerges from the crowd and comes to the front. He gives an order and the crowd of citizens raise their hands and wave a God-speed to them. Now their Prince moves forward to the edge of the cliff on which the City is erected. He leaves the edge and proceeds by aerial flight. His chariot leads the way and the others follow. And they come", he added with a smile, "in this direction. Now we will go to another place, and you shall witness their arrival."

None of us asked the reason of their visit. It was not that we were afraid to do so. I think we could have asked him anything. But we somehow felt that all that it was meet that we should know then had been told us, and so we were content to wait. But he said, "You are curious to know the reason of their coming. That you will shortly be permitted to see." So we went with him to the wall of the City, and stood there looking over the plain towards the hills. We could see no more than we had said.

"Tell me", he said, "which of you first sights them."

We looked long and eagerly, but could not see anything. At last I thought I saw a star begin to twinkle over the mountains far away in the depths of space. Just at that moment one of my companions exclaimed, "I think, my lord, that star was not there when first we came here."

"Yes", he replied, "it was there, but not visible to you. So you are the first to see it?"

THE LIFE BEYOND THE VEIL

I did not like to say I had seen it also. I should have said that before. But he continued, "I think there is some one else who sees that star. Is that not so?" and he turned to me with a quiet smile.

I am afraid I reddened and mumbled something awkwardly. "Well", he said, "watch it. You others will also be able to see it presently. At this moment it is several spheres away, and I did not expect any of you to be able to see quite into that region." Then, turning to us two, he bowed courteously, and said, "Ladies, I congratulate you on your good progress. You are rapidly advancing towards a higher grade, and, if you, continue your sphere of service will soon be enlarged, believe me". We were both made very happy by this speech.

But now the star had considerably brightened, and ever, as we looked, it seemed to enlarge and expand, and this continued a long space of time. Then I noticed that it was no longer a round disc, but was gradually assuming another shape, and, at last, I was able to see what the shape was. It was a harp of light, somewhat in the shape of a lyre, and seemed to be like a jewel set with many diamonds. But as it came nearer and nearer, we were able to see that it was made up of horses and chariots and men, and that in that order they were speeding through space towards us.

Presently we heard shouts of welcome from the people on other parts of the City walls and knew that they had sighted them also.

"Now you see the nature of their business in this City."

"Music", I suggested.

"Yes", he answered, "it has to do with music, That is the main object of this visit, anyway."

As they drew nearer we saw that the company numbered some hundreds. It was a beautiful sight to see. There they came along the path of the heavens, horses and chariots of fire—you know the old familiar phrase; believe me, it is little understood—with riders of light radiating their glory far around them, as they sped along their heavenly way. O, these citizens of those higher realms are all too beautiful for us to describe to you. The lowest in rank of these was just about of Castrel's degree. But his own glory was constrained and hidden, in order that he might be both Prince of this City and also a citizen. Yet, as his companions and peers drew near, we noticed that he also began to change. His face and form glowed with an ever-increasing radiance until, at length, he shone as bright as the least bright of those who came along the sky. I could understand, when I thought of it afterwards, why it was necessary for him to condition himself to the lower sphere in which he served. For, as he stood before us now, even though he had not attained the full intensity of his native brightness, yet none of us dared approach him, but drew a little distance away, and left him to stand alone. We were not afraid, but unaccustomed—that is as well as I can put it.

The members of the flashing jewelled harp at last were speeding over our own country, and when they had come half the way between us and the first range of hills, they slowed down and gradually reformed.

This time the band took the shape of a....[17] Then sweeping down they landed on the space before the principal gate of the City.

Castrel had left us for some time now, and, as they landed, we saw him issue on foot from the City gate, attended by his principal men. He was robed in light—that is nearly all I could see. But the diadem he wore shone more brilliantly than I had ever seen it; and so did the girdle he wore. He approached the leader and knelt before him. This Angel was much brighter even than Castrel. He descended from his chariot and, hastening to our own Prince, lifted him up and embraced him. The action was full of grace and also of love, and, for the few seconds they were together, there was complete silence on the walls. But when the embrace was done, and the words of blessing—in a language we do not understand—were spoken, Castrel bowed his head before the other and then, standing up, looked to the City walls and raised his hand, and there was a burst of music and voices as the citizens broke into a glorious anthem. I have told you of the singing in another region. This was much more sublime, for this was a plane in advance of that. Then they too, followed by the other visitors, entered the City amidst the shouts of the populace and the pealing of bells and strains of instrumental music and the singing of the thousands upon the walls.

---

[17] See p. 162.

So they passed along the street to the Palace, and, as he turned into the avenue which led off the main street, the Angel Prince, our visitor, halted, and, standing in his chariot turned round, and, lifting his hand, blessed the people in their own tongue, and then went on down the avenue and was, with his glittering attendants, lost to view.

Dear, I have tried my very best to give you even a faint description of that incident. I have failed miserably. It was much more glorious than I have been able to describe. I have spent my time also on the description of this arrival scene because that I could understand better than the mission on which they had come. That is far too deep for me, and concerned the teachers of the City and the great men of that land. All I could get to know was that it was chiefly concerned with the studies of the most advanced in that Colony of the connection of music with the creative faculty. I cannot understand more than that. But perhaps others will be able to say more about it than I can.

That word we could not give above was "planet" the second formation, we mean—not "planet",[18] but "planetary systems." I do not know whether it was the solar system, of which the earth is a unit, or other —some other system I rather think; but I do not know.

That is all, dear, to-night. Are you waiting for our blessing? God bless you, dear lad. Lift up your eyes and keep your ideals bright, and believe that the most glorious of glories you can imagine are to the real and actual glories of this life of ours just as candle light to that of a sun.

Wednesday, October 22, 1913

If all the world were one great diamond or pearl reflecting or radiating the light of the sun and distant stars, how bright would be its vicinity. Yet in a measure it does this, but only to a very limited degree because of the lack of lustre on its surface. And as the reflecting capacity of the earth is to that more perfect mirror which

---

[18] See p. 72.

a pearl would furnish, so is the earth life to ours here in these realms of light and beauty, the Summerland of God.

As we gaze out over the wide plains and valleys of the Heavenly Land, we are scarce able to remember the effect of the atmosphere of earth as it had relation to our vision of terrestrial things. But we do remember certain qualities which here are absent. Distance is not obscured, for instance. It fades away. Trees and plants do not appear for a season, and then die. They bloom perpetually, and then, when plucked, they are fresh for a long time, but they do not droop and wither. They, too, fade, or melt, away into the atmosphere. This same atmosphere is not always white. In the neighbourhood of the City of the Prince Castrel there is a sense of golden sunshine all around. It is not a mist, and does not obscure, but bathes all things in its golden radiance without invading the various colours themselves. In other places it is of a faint pink or blue. And every region has its own peculiar tint, or sense, of colour, according to the nature of the people and their employment and bent of mind.

The tint of the atmosphere seems to be governed by this principle; but also it is reflex in its action on the people themselves. Especially is this the case with visitors from other regions. The more highly developed, on coming into a new tract of country, are able to tell by this alone the general character and occupations of the people there. The influence, however, very quickly extends to themselves. It does not change them in character, of course, but it does affect their sensations, and is almost instantaneously seen in the changing hue of their robes.

Thus, as one visits a strange district, one very speedily begins to feel, within and without, that sense of brotherhood and sisterhood which is one of the most delightful of blessings I have found. Everywhere you go you find brothers and sisters. Try to think of it and see what it would mean if it were thus on earth. Then the Angels' greeting of Peace and Goodwill indeed would be realized and earth would be the ante-chamber of the Heavenly Home.

We returned from that City asking ourselves what difference our visit had made in us, and what we had learned. For my own part, it was not difficult to see that the very fact of my own little girl being there was enough. She is a gift I had not expected. But as we returned leisurely across the plain, we found that each had received some special blessing for herself alone.

As we had approached the City by the air, we preferred now to go afoot across the plain until we reached the mountains. And as we went we talked of what we had seen. Now, I could fill many pages with that talk, and I assure you it would not be uninteresting. But time and space are to you, and to publishers, of more account than they are to us, so I will hasten on to what I have to tell.

We reached our own sphere just as our Mother Angel had also returned from a journey to the Bridge of which I have already told you. She brought with her this time one you know.

Name, please.

Mrs. S. She had been through a rather trying experience. When first she came over she was taken to a place where she might have progressed rapidly. Hers was a perplexing case; so many mixed traits that it was very difficult to place her exactly. So she was given the chance and helped in every way. But, you must know, freewill and personality are very important things here, and are never overruled when help is being offered.

She soon grew restless, and it was seen that she would have to be given her way. So she was warned and advised and then taken to the parting of the ways to choose her own road, as she wished to do. A guardian was appointed to keep constant watch in order that if help were sought any time it would be near at hand.

Well, she did not seem to know where to go or what to do, to find what she wanted—peace. So she wandered on and spent a considerable period in the neighbourhood of the Bridge. It was only when she had learned for herself that her own wilful course led again and again into places where the darkness always increased, and people, sights and sounds were of a nature not to radiate happiness, but sometimes terror, that at last she wandered along the borderland, and, by and by, turned a little towards the light and was gradually helped back again to the Home she had left. She is now progressing, slowly, to be sure; but still with an ever softening heart, and more humility and trust, and she will do well in time. That is why I have seen so little of her, and been of so little use. But I may be able to help a little now and again as time goes on. Perhaps that is why she has been brought to the place where I am destined to spend a more or less protracted period of service. I did not know her in the earth life except through you, and your friendship with her children may be the link which will enable her to receive any little help I am able to give.

You see, everything is considered here, even the things which seem so casual and transitory in the earth life. They are all registered and viewed in their relation to one another, all the seemingly casual talks or chance meetings, a book read, a hand shaken in the street for the first time and never again, a few friends meeting, in the same way, at a mutual friend's house and never meeting again—everything and every item is registered, considered, co-ordinated and used when, and if, occasion offers. And so may it be in this case.

Be, therefore, not remiss to weigh well all you do and every word you say; not in anxiety, but rather by cultivating a habit of will to do good; always and everywhere to radiate kindness of heart, for in the Kingdom these are not of small account, but go to make robes bright and bodies radiant.

And so, dear, good night once again—a wish not without its significance to you, if otherwise to us, for here all is good to them who goodness love, and night is absent always where the True Light shines forever, and all is Peace.

CHAPTER V: ANGELIC MINISTRY

Another from the Bridge—Conscience—The Judgment—Self-
delusion—Difficulties and hindrances in communication through the
Veil—"Set a watch, O Lord, before my mouth; keep the door of my
lips"—The method of impression—A meeting in the air— Not
motherless—A mixed character.

Thursday, October 23, 1913

PERCHANCE if we were to tell you of our progress in these
heavenly spheres we should weary you, for much detail has to be
negotiated, and nothing passed over as being too small. But it may
be helpful if we supplement what we wrote in this vein last
evening by giving you now an instance by way of illustration of
this point.

We received a message a short time ago of the arrival of a
sister at the Bridge, who had come over from the further side
where lie the regions of gloom, and I and another were sent to
conduct her to this Home. We went quickly and found our charge
awaiting us. She was quite alone, for her attendants had left her
thus in order that she might profit by a quiet period of meditation
and reflection before beginning her further advance.

She was seated on a slope of grass under a tree whose branches
spread like a canopy over her. Her eyes were closed, and we stood
before her waiting. When she opened them she looked at us for
some time in an inquiring manner. As she did not speak, I at last
addressed her "Sister". At that word she looked at us hesitatingly,
and then her eyes began to fill with tears, and she put her face in
her hands, bowed her head upon her knees, and wept bitterly.

So I went to her and laid my hand upon her head and said,
"You are our sister now, dear, and as we do not weep, so neither
must you".

"How do you know who or what I am?" she replied, as she
raised her face and tried to force back her tears, while there was
just a touch of defiance in her voice.

"We do not know who you are", I answered. "What you were
we do know. We know that you were always a child of our Father,
and so, always our sister. Now you are our sister in a fuller sense.
What else you are lies with you. You are either one whose face is

set toward the Sunshine of His Presence, or one who, fearing the task before you in that direction, will turn back again across the Bridge."

She was silent for a while, and then said, "I dare not. It is all too horrible over there".

"But", I urged, "you must choose; for you cannot remain where you are. And you will come the upward way—will you not?—and we will lend you a sister's hand and give you a sister's love to help you on the way."

"Oh, I wonder how much you know of what lies yonder", she said, and there was agony in her voice. "There they called me sister, too; they called me sister in mockery, while they heaped upon me infamy and torture and—oh, I must not think of it or it will drive me mad again. But I don't know how I shall proceed; I am so stained and vile and weak."

But I saw that this would never do, so I cut her short. I told her that, for the present, she must try to forget these experiences, until we had helped her, and then it would be time enough to begin her task in earnest. I knew that task was going to be a heavy and bitter one; but there is only one way onward, nothing can be glossed over; everything must be viewed and understood for exactly what it is—every act and word up to the present time—God's justice acknowledged, and God's Love through all—and that is the only onward and upward way. But that must rest a while until she was capable of enduring it. And so we comforted her and gradually led her away.

Now, as we went she began to look around and ask about the things she saw, and what kind of country lay ahead, and what the home was like to which she was being led, and so on. We told her all she could understand. We told her of our Angel Mother who had charge of the place, and of our fellow-workers there. In the midst of our conversation she stopped suddenly and said she felt she could go no further. "Why?" we inquired, "are you tired?" and she answered, "No; afraid".

We saw something of what was in her mind, but could not quite understand it as a whole. There was something we could not lay hold of. So we led her on to talk of herself, and at last we unearthed the difficulty.

It seems that when the guardian at the other end of the Bridge had heard her cry for help far away in the gloom, he at once directed a ray of his light in the direction, and sent a messenger to help her. This spirit found her fainting by the side of a dark murky stream whose waters were foul and hot, and bore her to the Bridge Gatehouse. Here she was tended and revived and brought forward across the Bridge to the place where we found her.

Now it chanced that when this spirit worker had found her she had felt a presence but could not see any one near. She therefore called aloud, "May you be cursed if you touch me!" thinking that perhaps it was one of her old tormentors and companions in wickedness. Then she remembered no more until she recovered her senses again in the Gatehouse. As we walked and talked of the workers of these realms the memory of that incident suddenly came back to her mind. She had cursed one of God's ministers, and she was afraid of the light because the words were evil. Truly, she did not know whom she had cursed; but a curse is a curse against whomsoever directed, and it lay upon her heart.

My companions and I consulted together briefly and came to the conclusion that we must return. The other sins of this poor soul might be dealt with presently. This, however, was against one of our fellow workers of the realms of light and love, and we saw that she would find no rest among us, and our services would little avail her until that wrong had been righted. So back to the Bridge we went, and right across it to the Gatehouse at the further end.

There we found the spirit helper who had brought her to that place, and she asked and obtained forgiveness. Indeed, he was awaiting us; for he was stronger and more progressed than we, and so was greater in wisdom, and he knew that she would compel herself to return. So as we drew near he came from the gateway where he had been standing watching us coming along the road, and, when she saw his kind face and forgiving smile, she knew at once it was he whom she sought and, falling on her knees, obtained his blessing.

I fear this is not a very exciting message to-night. I have given it to show you how even the seemingly slight things have to be reckoned with here. As a matter of fact, I believe that some higher intelligence than our own was controlling us all the time; for that little incident proved a very important episode in the progress of that poor sinful woman. It was a long journey back to, and across, the Bridge, and she was very weak and weary.

But when she saw the face of the one against whom she had sinned, and heard his words of love and forgiveness, it showed her, for the first time, that whatever she should have to endure in future it would be sweet in the end, and each task done would earn its own blessing. And that is no mean support to such as she who had so much to face of repentance and agonizing shame of remembrance of the Great Love of God which she had flouted and denied.

What is she doing now?

That was not very long ago, and she has been progressing but slowly. There is so much to keep her back. But she does progress, nevertheless. She is in our Home, but has not yet been given any special work to do for others. She will be so employed eventually, but not for a long time to come.

Sin may be negative in its essential parts, but it is negation of the Love and Fatherhood of God, and that is a far more terrible thing than mere offence against a commandment. It is the contamination of the very nature and spring of our inner spirit life, of the Sanctuary of the Spirit of God. And the cleansing of a polluted Sanctuary is more than the washing of an ordinary dwelling. The very intensity of the Light of the Presence in this spiritual state shows up every speck and mote, and happy are those who keep that Sanctuary clean and bright, for such shall know how sweet it is to live and to love in Him.

Monday, October 27,1913

Once again we take up our tale of the Heavenly Life, and hope to be able to tell you a little more of the love and blessedness which we experience in these bright realms. Our Home is situate on the slope of a thickly-wooded hill in a clearing, and our patients —for they are really such—are tended by us here in peace and quiet after their distressing experiences in one or other part of those lands where the light is dim, and darkness seems to enter into their very souls. They come here more or less exhausted and weak, and are only allowed to go onward when they have become strong enough for the way.

You would perhaps like to know somewhat of our methods here. Chiefly these may be summed up in one word: Love. For that is the guiding principle in all our work. Some are so overjoyed with the realization of the fact that we do not seek to judge and punish, but only to help them, that they are, from that very cause, ill at ease from its unfamiliarity.

One of our poor sisters met our Mother Angel a little while ago in the garden, and was turning down a side-path in order to avoid meeting her, not of fear but of reverence. But our bright Angel went to her and spoke kindly to her, and when she found she could talk quite freely she asked a question. "Where is the judge", she inquired, "and when is the judgment to take place? I am trembling all the while with the thought of it, for I know my punishment will be a very dreadful one; and I would know the worst, and get it over."

To this the Mother replied, "My child, your judgment will take place whenever you desire; and from your own words I can tell you that it has already begun. For you own that your past life is worthy of punishment, and that is the first step in your judgment. As to the judge, well, she is here; for you yourself are judge, and will mete out to yourself your punishment. You will do this of your own free will by reviewing all the life you have lived and, as you bravely own up one sin after another, so you will progress. Much of your punishment you have already inflicted upon yourself in those dark regions from which you have lately come. That punishment, indeed, was dreadful. But that is past and over, and what you have now to endure will be dreadful no longer. All dread should now be past. Painful, deeply painful, I fear it will be. But all through you will feel that He is leading you, and this more and more as you go on in the right way."

"But", persisted the inquirer, "I am perplexed because I do not see the Throne of the Great judge Who will reward some and punish others." "You will, indeed, some day see that Throne, but not yet. The judgment you are thinking of is very different from what you imagine. But you should have no fear and, as you progress, you will learn more, and understand more, of God's great love."

That is what perplexes many who come over here. They expect to find all set ready for their dismissal from the Presence into torture, and cannot understand things as they are.

Others who have cultivated a good opinion of their deserts are much disappointed when they are given a lowly place, sometimes a very lowly one, and not ushered immediately into the Presence of the Enthroned Christ to be hailed with His "Well done". Oh, believe me, dear son, there are many surprises awaiting those who come over here, some of a very joyful kind, and others the reverse.

I have, only lately, seen a very learned writer, who had published several books, talking to a lad who, in the earth life, was a stoker in a gasworks, and being instructed by him. He was glad to learn, too, for he had partly learned humility; and the curious thing was that he did not so much mind sitting at the feet of this young spirit as going to his old friends here and owning up his mistakes and his vanity of intellect in his past life. This, however, he will have to do sooner or later, and the young lad is preparing him for the task. It is also whimsical to us to see him still clinging to his old pride, when we know all about him, and his past and present status, which latter is rather low, and all the time he is trying to think he is hiding his thoughts from us. With such their instructors have to exercise much patience, which is also very good training for them.

And now let us see if we can explain a difficulty which is perplexing many investigators into psychic matters. We mean the difficulty they have in understanding why we do not give them information which they desire about one thing or another which they have in their minds.

You must try to realize that when we come down here we are not in our proper element, but are hampered with limitations which are now strange to us. For instance, we have to work according to the laws which are in vogue in the earth realm, or we could not make you understand what we wish to do or say. Then we often find that when any one has his mind fixed on some particular person whom he wishes to hear or see, or some special matter about which he wishes to inquire, we are limited by the straitened means at our disposal. Other reservoirs of power in that inquirer are closed, and those only are open to us which he himself has willed should be open. And these are frequently not enough for us to work with.

Then again, the activity of his will meets the activity of ours midway, as it were, and there is a clash, and the result is either confusion or nil. It is nearly always better to allow us to work in our own way, trustfully, and afterwards to examine critically what we manage to get through. If information on any particular point is desired, let that point be in your mind at times as you go about your daily occupation. We shall see it and take account of it, and, if it is possible and useful and lawful, we shall find opportunity and means, sooner or later, to answer it. If you ask a question while we are with you manifesting in one way or other, do not demand, but just put your thoughts before us, and then leave it to us to do what we can. Do not insist. You may be sure that, as our desire is to help, we shall do all we can.

And now to a case in point. You have been wanting to know about Ruby and others. You have not insisted, and, therefore, we have been able to use conditions freely and are able to give you some information.

Ruby is happy as ever, and getting quite expert in the work she has in hand. I saw her only lately and she says she will be able to come to speak to you or Rose very soon. Now you are wondering why she cannot come to-night. She has other duties, and also we have to fulfil ours according to plan. One thing she said was this: "Tell dear daddy that his words to the people are brought here, and some of the things he tells them are discussed among us because they happen to be of those things we have not learned of the earth life."

This seems well nigh impossible. Have I got this right?

There you go, you see. Now what do you think these dear angel children are, that you speak so? Do you not understand that the studies of those who came over here very young are mostly of the life and conditions of their new homeland, and that only little by little are they allowed to complete their knowledge of the earth and its life which, nevertheless, has to be learned quite thoroughly as they proceed onward? So it is that every means is used, with discretion, to teach them. And what better or more likely way could you name than by enabling the father to be instructor of his own child? I am not going to say any more about that. It is enough. Think it over in a common sense way and you will perhaps come to a more enlightened frame of mind.

Well, but if what you say is right, one will be almost afraid to instruct one's people at all. And don't be cross.

Dear lad, no, I am not cross. But in you, at least, I have been grateful to find a certain enlightenment as to the conditions of this life and their naturalness, and up crops one of those silly ideas of the nebulous order right in the midst of your mind.

You are quite right, however, to think that you should be careful how you give instruction. But this applies not only to you but to every one; and to all thoughts and words and deeds of every one. They are all known here, one crumb of comfort you can take, however. You may be sure that when anything unworthy or base is thought or spoken, that is never allowed to find its way into such a sphere as that in which Ruby is. So make your mind easy there, my dear, and do not fear to speak out your mind; for silence is sometimes less welcome here than erroneous teaching, when that teaching is sincere.

And now, good night, and best love to you all. God bless you, dead lad, and keep you brave and true.

Tuesday, October 28, 1913

Whatever we have been able to give you in these messages has been transmitted to you by means of impressing your mind with our thoughts and words. In doing this we take, and make use of, as much as we find there, so that we may the more easily get our own thoughts through. Frequently, however, we have been obliged, of necessity, to call your spirit away from the earth surroundings and give you a vision of the places we are describing, and you have written down what you have seen. No, we did not actually take you out of your body, because you have been really conscious all the time.

What we did was to engage and absorb your attention that we might infuse power into your interior sight—the sight of your

119

spiritual body—and at those moments you were scarcely conscious of your surroundings. You forgot them and became oblivious to them, and then we were able to impart to you, in a measure, the power of distant vision; and to this we added the incidents as we had witnessed them ourselves.

For instance, when we described the coming of the Harp of Light to the City of Castrel we showed you the city as it is, but we reconstructed the incidents of the crowds on the walls, and the meeting outside the gates, and all the parts of the ceremony which we wished you to write down. That is what was done. How it was done you will understand some day when you come over here.

We are now going to try to show you another scene. And here we may say that we use the word "try" because, although with a good subject we do not often fail, yet we are not omnipotent, and there are many things which may intervene to hinder our endeavour and modify our success.

Well then, give us your attention a while and we will tell you of a ceremony which we witnessed when a company of people came to visit our colony to learn about our work. You must understand that we go to each other's Homes, and learn of one another in this way, and get to know what we can of the various aspects of work going on in different parts.

We were standing near the top of the hill behind this Home watching their coming. At last we saw them high in the air and far away over the wide-spreading plain. The sky behind them was streaked with horizontal layers of crimson, gold and green; and by that we knew from what region they came, and the nature of their work. They were students in a distant settlement whose principal branch of knowledge was proper use of ceremonial and ritual, and its effects on those who use it.

We watched them coming along the heavenly way, and then a party of our own people, who were waiting on the plain, rose into the air and proceeded to meet the visitors. It was very interesting to see them meet in the air. High up in the heavens they approached each other, and when they were some little distance away our party sounded a welcome on what looked and sounded like post-horns, and then others produced other instruments and, while they played, others sang a welcome.

BOOK I: THE LOWLANDS OF HEAVEN

They had halted now and we saw that behind them was a chariot and two horses. It was very much like the chariots of old times. There is no reason why we should not use carriages of modern build; but shelter is unnecessary, and the old open vehicles have persisted to the present day.

When the visitors came near they halted, and there the two parties faced each other, standing in the air. Try to imagine it. It seems strange to you, but one day you will see that it is quite natural to our present state, and, if progressed enough, we are able not only to stand but to kneel, lie or walk in the midst of space, very much as if it were on solid earth.

Then the leader of our band and the Chief of the visitors approached each other between the two ranks. They took each other by both hands, and kissed each other on the forehead and cheeks. And then our leader took his visitor's left hand in his own right and led him towards the chariot, our party dividing to give them passage, and bowing respectfully as they passed. When the two Chiefs had entered the chariot their followers ran together with outstretched hands and gladly saluted one another as the others had done. And then all turned their faces towards us and came on at a leisurely walking pace until they descended at the foot of the hill.

I cannot make you see the effect of an approach by air. I have tried to do so more than once, but that is outside your imagination. So I can only tell you that it is most beautiful to watch. The movement of these high spirits, such as Castrel and Arnol and others of their rank, when walking on the ground, is not only most graceful, it is fascinating in its beauty of poise and movement. But in the air it is much more so. The soft, graceful, gliding motion, full of quiet and gentle dignity and of strength and power, is princely and angelic. So these two now came to us.

They descended, and then walked by a winding path to the Chief's house. He rules here with our Mother Angel, and I do not think there is much difference in their status or rank. For, except by direct questioning, which we hesitate to use, it is not easy to tell which of two people so nearly, if not quite, equal is the one who by a little degree excels. For so great is the love and harmony between such, that command and obedience seem to blend into

121

one gracious and smiling endeavour of service, and we are at a loss sometimes to distinguish between the estate of two so highly developed as these.

The Chief's residence would very forcibly remind you of a mediaeval castle, set on a rock half-way up a mountain-side and surrounded by waving trees and foliage of many tints—green, red, brown and gold and multitudes of flowers and green patches of grass.

They passed under the gateway, and so within, and we saw them no more. But we noticed that the presence of that radiant company within illuminated the windows of the castle as if suddenly some thousands of electric lamps had been set going. And the coloured lights we saw were most beautiful, for they did not melt into one tint but mingled together, each preserving its own hue, and streaming through the apertures like so many streams of rainbow radiance.

I have often mentioned gateways, but you will have observed that I have not spoken of gates. Now, so far, I have not seen a gate to any of the many gateways I have seen here. You read in the Book of the Revelation of the Holy City and its gates, but I have thought of it, being reminded of it by these gates to what are, evidently, similar cities to that which St. John saw in Presence Form, and I doubt whether that city had gates to the gateways.

And that may be what he means when he says that the gates shall not be shut by day and—remembering that in the cities as he knew them on earth, the gates were not shut by day except in times of war, but were shut by night continually—he adds, by way of explanation, that there is no night here in this land. These are only my thoughts, and may not be correct, but you can look up the passage and refresh your memory and decide for yourself.

I was not present at the festival within the Castle, so will not describe it, as I only heard of it at second hand, and prefer to tell you of things I myself have witnessed, which I can do more vividly. It was a most glorious affair, however, as one can well credit when so many high spirits brought their glory together.

Ah well, dear lad, you will see it all some day soon, when you and your dear ones will all be here in God's good land on which

His love and blessing descend like dew upon sweet meadowlands, with the fragrance all around.

And is it strange if we who learn continually how much more blessed it is to give than to receive, should seek to waft some of this sweetness on our breath through the Veil that those on your side may breathe it too and taste how sweet and gracious the Lord is, and how blessed are they who rest on Him? Whose blessing we invoke on you and yours, now and ever. Amen.

Thursday, October 30, 1913

Place your hand against your head and you will notice that we are then able the more readily to speak to you so that you will be able to understand.

Like this?

Yes. It helps you and us, both.

How?

Because there is a stream of magnetism proceeding from us to you, and by doing as we have suggested it is not so quickly dissipated.

I don't understand a word of all this.

Maybe not. There are many things you have yet to learn, dear, and what we are saying now is one of those things, little in itself but still of account. It is often these small things which help to success.

Now, while we are not over anxious to explain the methods we employ in the transmission of these messages, because we can only make you understand imperfectly, still we may say this: the power we use is best described as magnetism, and by means of this the vibrations of our minds are directed on your own. Your hand being so placed serves as a kind of magnet and reservoir in one, and helps us. But we will not continue this, but get on to something we can better make clear to you.

In our life in the Summerland we endeavour to help both those who come over to us and also their friends still on earth. Indeed, the two phases of service are inseparable, for those who pass over here are often much distressed, and so unable to progress until they know that those they have left behind—are being helped from this side. So we often make excursions to the earth plane for this reason.

Last week we received a woman who had left a husband and three small children, and she begged to be allowed to go and see how they were managing at home. She was so anxious that at last we took her, and arrived at evening time just as they were all sitting

down to supper. The man had just come in from work and he was going to have his meal before putting them to bed. They were two girls, aged about seven and five, and a little boy of two. They all sat round the table in the kitchen, a fairly comfortable room, and the father told the eldest girl to say grace. This is what she said, "God provide for us all, and mother, for Christ's sake. Amen".

The woman went round to the little one, and laid her hand on her hair and spoke to her, but could not make her hear. She was troubled at this, but we bade her wait and watch. By and by the girl spoke, after a long silence, during which she and her father had been thinking of the one who had passed away, and she said, "Dad, do you think mammy knows about us now, and Auntie Lizzie?"

"I don't know", he replied, "but I think she does, because I have felt very miserable the last few days, as if she was worrying about something; and it might be Auntie Lizzie."

"Well", said the child, "then don't let us go. Mrs. — will look after baby, and I can help when I come home from school, and we shan't have to go then".

"Don't you want to go?" he said.

"I don't", answered the child. "Baby and Sissie would go, but I don't want to".

"Well, I'll think about it", he said. "So don't worry. I dare say we shall manage all right."

"And mother will help, and the angels", persisted the little girl, "because she can speak to them now, and they will help if she asks them".

Now, the father said nothing more; but we could see his mind, and read in it the thought that if this little child had such faith, he ought to have as much at least, and by and by he made up his mind to try the thing and see how it would work out. For the parting with his children was not to his mind, and he was very glad to find an excuse to keep them.

I cannot say that the mother obtained much comfort from her visit. But on our way back we told her that the faith of that child, if it was reinforced by that of the father, would form a powerful medium of help, or we were much mistaken.

On our return we reported all to our Mother Angel, and immediately measures were taken to ensure that the family should not be broken up, and the mother was bidden to strive to progress in order that she should be able to help also. Then a change came over her. She set to work in real earnest, and will soon be allowed to join parties on their journeys earthward now and then, and to add her little mite to their stronger service.

But now we must leave that case for a time and tell you of another. A man came to our colony a short time ago who also had lately passed over. He was wandering about seeking somewhere to his mind, and thought this settlement looked something like what he wanted. You must not think he was alone. There accompanied him, but at a distance, a watcher who was ready to help when required. The man was one of those curious mixtures we sometimes get. There was considerable goodness and light in him, but that could not be used for furthering his development on account of its being checked and held in ward by other traits which he could not be brought to rearrange.

He was met on a path some distance away from the hill where our Home is by one of the workers in another Home, and the latter stopped and questioned him, for he noticed a strange and perplexed look in his face. When he stopped he received a signal from, the guardian, who was some distance away, and was informed of the problem, and so, all instantaneously, was equipped to deal with it. He spoke kindly, and the following conversation ensued.

A. You seem to be not very familiar with this region. Can I help you in any way?

B. I don't think so, although it is kind of you to offer to do so.

A. Your difficulty is one which we might deal with here, but not so thoroughly as we would like to do.

B. I am afraid you don't know what that difficulty is.

A. Well, partly, I think. You are perplexed because you have not met any of your friends here, and wonder why.

B. That is so, certainly.

A. But they have met you.

B. I have not seen them; and I have been wondering where I could find them. It seems so strange. I always thought that our friends were the first to meet us when we pass over, and I cannot understand it at all.

A. But they did meet you.

B. I didn't see any one I knew.

A. That is quite correct. They met you and you did not know them—would not know them.

B. I don't understand.

A. What I mean is this. When you came over here you were immediately taken charge of by your friends. But your heart, good in some respects and even enlightened, was hard and blindly obstinate in others. And this is the reason you did not recognize their presence.

The other looked long and doubtfully at his companion, and at last stammered out a question.

B. What is wrong with me, then? Everybody I meet is kind and happy, and yet I don't seem to be able to join any party, or to find my own proper place. What is wrong with me?

A. The first thing you must learn is that your opinions may not be correct. I'll tell you one which is at fault, to begin with. This world is not, as you are trying to imagine it, a place where people are all that is good or all that is evil. They are much as they are on earth. Another thing is this: your wife, who came over here some years ago, is in a higher sphere than the one in which you will be placed when you have at length got the correct perspective of things. She was not mentally your equal in the earth life, and is not so now. But you are on a lower plane than she is, on general lines and all things considered. That is the second thing you have to accept, and accept ex animo. You do not accept it, as I can see by your face. You will have to do so before you can advance. When you have done so, then you will probably be enabled to communicate with her. At present that is not possible.

126

BOOK I: THE LOWLANDS OF HEAVEN

The man's eyes became dimmed with tears, but he smiled rather sweetly and sadly as he quoted, "Sir, I perceive that you are a prophet".

A. Quite right; and that brings me to the third thing you will have to accept; and that is this. There is one watching over you always, always at hand to help you. He is a prophet, or rather a seer, like me; and it was he who put that saying into your mind to repeat to me.

Now the stranger's face became grave and thoughtful. He was trying to get the right and true view of things. He asked, "Is it vanity, then, that is my fault?"

A. Yes; but vanity of a rather difficult kind. In many things you are sweet and humble, and not without love, which is the greatest power of all. But there is a certain hardness in your mind rather than in your heart, which must be softened. You have got into a mental rut, and must get out of it and look farther afield, or you will go about like a blind man who can see—a contradiction and a paradox. There are some things you see clearly enough, and to others you are totally oblivious. Learn that to change your opinions in the face of evidence is not weakness or backsliding, but is the sign of an honest mind. I tell you this, further; had your heart been as hard as your mind you would not be wandering here in the fields of God's sunshine, but in darker regions yonder beyond those hills—far beyond them. Now I have explained, as well as I am able, your rather perplexing case, friend. The rest is for another to do.

B. Who?

A. The one I have already told you of; the one who has you in charge.

B. Where is he?

A. One minute, and he will be here.

The message was sent, and the guardian stood beside his charge, who, however, was unable to see him.

A. Well, he is here. Tell him what you want.

B. Looked full of doubt and anxiety, and then said, "Tell me, my friend, if he is here why I cannot see him".

A. Because in that phase of your mind's activity you are blind. That is the first thing you have to realize. Do you believe me when I say you are, in some directions, blind?

B. I can see very well, and the things I see are fairly plain, and the country quite natural and beautiful. I am not blind in that respect. But I am beginning to think there may be other things just as real which I cannot see, but shall see some day perhaps, but

A. Now, stop there, and leave the "but" alone. And now look, as I take your guide by the hand.

He then took the watching guide's right hand in his own, telling B. to look intently, and tell him if he saw anything. He could not be certain, however. He thought he saw some kind of transparent form which might or might not be real, but was by no means sure.

A. Then take his hand in yours. Take it from me.

The man held out his hand and took that of his guide from the hand of A., and burst into tears.

Had he not progressed so far as to make that action, he would not have seen his guide, nor have been able to feel his touch. The fact that he put out his hand at the command of A. showed that he had progressed during their conversation, and he immediately received his reward. The other held his hand in a firm grasp for some time, and all the while B. saw him and felt him more and more clearly. Then A. left them together. Soon B. would be able to hear, as well as see, his guardian, and no doubt he will go on now from strength to strength.

This will show you what difficult cases we sometimes have to deal with. Light and gross darkness, humility and hard, obstinate pride all mixed up together, and hard to separate or to treat successfully. But such problems are interesting, and, when mastered, give great joy to the workers.

Ruby[19] sends her love and this message to her parents, "Believe me, my darlings, the doing of a good and kind action, and the thinking and speaking of kind words by those we love on earth are immediately telegraphed here, and we use them to adorn our

---

[19] This message from Ruby seems to have reference to boxes of flowers we had been sending to our daughter, who was away at school. G.V.O.

rooms, as Rene adorns her rooms with your flowers". God bless you, dear lad. Good-night.[20]

---

[20] With this message the communication from Mr. Vale   Owen's mother ceased and the messages were continued by a spirit entity named Zabdiel. These are given in a further volume entitled The Highlands of Heaven. H.W.E

CHAPTER VI: ASTRIEL'S MESSAGES [21]

The science of prayer—"Thy prayers are come up"—A present from the spiritual spheres—A lesson on light, vibration and gravitation—The lesson resumed—Orthodoxy and the Truth —Multiform service in the universe—Suns, systems and spheres of power—He giveth to His beloved during sleep—An example—Good-bye.

Tuesday, October 7, 1913

BY the aid of others, who are with us now for the first time, we are going to try to give you a little instruction in the verities of the Faith as they appear to us on this side the Veil.

In regard to those truths which men have embodied in the Creeds we have little to say, for so much has been said already that, until much has been unsaid once again, men are ill-prepared to receive what we should have to say. We, therefore, prefer, for the present time, to leave you to look out for yourselves such truths as you find there, merely observing, as in passing, that all the articles are true if rightly interpreted.

We would pass on, therefore, to speak of things of which men do not consider so much at the present time. These will engage their attention the more when they have finished their wrangling over aspects of the truth which, after all, are aspects merely, and not the fundamental truth itself. If they would endeavour to view things in a right proportion, then many of those matters which absorb so much of their time would stand to them as among the lesser things which matter little, and they would then be the better able to devote their attention to the deeper truths which are established here as well as with you on earth.

One thing it may be well to notice is the efficacy of prayer and meditation. You have already received some instruction on this subject, and we would add to it.

Prayer is not merely the asking for something you wish to attain. It is much more than that, and, because it is so, it should

---

[21] See note on p. 72.

receive more careful consideration than it has yet received. What you have to do in order to make prayer a power is to cast aside the temporal and fix your mind and spirit on the eternal. When you do that you find that many items you would have included in your prayer drop out from the very incongruity of their presence, and the greater and wider issues become to you the focus of your creative powers. For prayer is really creative, as the exercise of the will, as seen in our Lord's miracles, such as the Feeding of the Five Thousand. And when prayer is offered with this conviction then the object is created, and the prayer is answered. That is, the objective answers to the subjective in such a way that an actual creation has taken place.

This does not happen when the prayer is wrongly directed. Then the projection of the will glances off at a tangent, and the effect is only proportionate to the scattered rays by which the objective is touched. Also, when the prayer is mixed with motives unworthy it is proportionately weakened, and also meets with opposing or regulating wills on this side, as the case may require; and so the effect is not attained as desired.

Now, all this may sound rather vague, but it is by no means vague to us. For you must know that there are appointed guardians of prayer here whose duty it is to analyse and sift prayers offered by those on earth, and separate them into divisions and departments, and pass them on to be examined by others, and dealt with according to their merit and power.

In order that this may be done perfectly, it is necessary that we study the vibrations of prayer as your scientists study the vibrations of sound and light. As they are able to analyse and separate and classify the rays of light, so are we able to deal with your prayers. And as there are light-rays with which they are confessedly unable to deal, so many prayers present to us those deeper tones which are beyond the range of our study and knowledge. These we pass on to those of higher grade, to be dealt with in their greater wisdom. And do not think that these latter are always found among the prayers of the wise. They are frequently found in the prayers of children, whose petitions and sighs are as carefully considered here as those of nations.

THE LIFE BEYOND THE VEIL

"Thy prayers and thine alms are come up for a memorial before God." You will remember these words spoken by the Angel to Cornelius. They are often passed over without being understood as the literal description of those prayers and alms as they appeared to that Angel, and were passed on, probably by himself and his fellow workers, into the higher realms. It is as if he had said, "Your prayers and alms came before my own committee, and were duly considered on their merits. We passed them as worthy, and have received notification from those Officers above us that they are of exceptional merit, and required a special treatment. Therefore I have been commissioned to come to you." We are trying to put the case as emphatically as we can in your language of official business in order to help you to understand as much as you may be able of the conditions here obtaining.

If you will examine other instances of prayer in the Bible in the light of the above, you may get some glimpses of the reality as seen by us here in our own land. And what applies to prayer also may be applied to the exercise of the will in directions not so legitimate. Hate and impurity and greed and other sins of the spirit and mind take on here a solidity which is not seen or realized in your sphere; and these also are dealt with according to their merits. And, alas, those who say that Angels cannot grieve, know little of our love for our brethren still battling on earth. Could they see us dealing with some of these misusings of the Father's great gift they would probably love us more and exalt us less.

Now we will leave you to consider this matter further for yourself, if you think it worth while, and, as we see you are willing to continue somewhat, will touch on another matter which may be both of interest and of help to you.

On the top of your church tower there is a weathervane in the form of a cock. You will call to mind that you yourself decided the form that this should take. Is not that so?

I had entirely forgotten it until you called it to mind. You are quite correct, however. The architect asked me about it, and I hesitated between a fish and a cock, and eventually decided on the latter. I am wondering, however, whatever you have to say of it.

No doubt. You see, these things are trifles to you; but there are few things which are trifles to us. Now, the fact that the likeness of a cock stands above your tower is the direct consequence of certain activities which took place in your mind five years ago. That is a case of creation. Many would smile at this, but we do not mind that, for we, too, are able to smile, and some of our smiles would perplex you, I assure you.

The meaning you had in your mind when your apparently not very important decision was made was that all might be reminded that St. Peter denied his Lord. I suppose you meant it as a caution against the repetition of such offence to-day. But you did not realize that that apparently trivial decision was registered here and dealt with quite seriously.

I must tell you that the building of a new church is an event which is the cause of much activity here.

There are officers to be appointed to attend the services and guard the building, and a whole host of ministering spirits to be allotted to the different departments of duty in connection with a new place of worship.

Your clairvoyant friends have been [to] some of these already, but only a very few comparatively. Every detail is considered, not only in respect of the character of the minister and congregation and choir and so on; and the best among us, that is, the most suitable, chosen to help you according to the traits we observe; not only these things but the structure and all structural details are considered minutely, especially where symbolism enters in, for that has an importance not realized among you as it is with us. So it came about that the weather-vane was also considered, and I have chosen that because of its seeming triviality in order to show you that nothing is missed.

It was decided that, as the cock had been chosen in preference to other symbols, we would answer that choice, according to our custom, by giving to the church some appropriate offering in response. And that offering was the church bell, for which a choirboy collected the money. You had no bell when first your church was consecrated. The bird stood aloft, but could not utter his warning as his original had done to St. Peter. And so we gave him voice, and your bell to-day gives tongue—as it did tonight at evensong. And we are glad to see that he who chose the one makes the other speak day by day, for that is surely fitting.

133

Do you think we have our fancies here? Well perhaps that is so; and yet you were thankful for that bell, were you not, good friend?

We were indeed. And I thank you for your kind message. Might I know who you are, if you please?

We are spiritual ministers from a sphere where your own friends and mother have visited from time to time, and she told us of you and said how much she would like us to know you more nearly and, if possible, to give you some message. She and her friends come to us for instruction.

Speaking for my own degree, some members of which are here with me, I would say that we have been glad to come and to know you. But we knew you and your church before your mother told us.

Thank you, sir, for your kindness. Would it be permissible for me to ask your own name?

Permission certainly, but I fear you would not know it, nor understand it.

Nevertheless, sir, tell me, if you will.

Astriel, who leaves you with his blessing. # [22]

Thursday, October 9, 1913

We have come again at the request of your mother, and are glad to have this one more opportunity of speaking to you from this side. Never imagine that we are troubled to come to the earth sphere, for although it does mean an experience of less brightness in environment than is our usual lot, yet the privilege counterbalances that and more.

Perhaps if we endeavour to enlighten you on the chemistry of the heavenly bodies it may be both interesting and helpful to you. We do not mean the physical aspect of the science, as understood by modern astronomical scientists, but the deeper study of their constitution.

---

[22] Astriel always concluded his communications with the sign of the Cross. H.W.E.

BOOK I: THE LOWLANDS OF HEAVEN

Every star, as you know, is itself a centre of a system which comprises in itself not only the planets in revolution round the star, but also the particles of matter which suffuse that system, but are too sublimated to be cognized by any system of chemistry which is possible to those who dwell in physical bodies, and in their research are compelled to use both material instruments and material brains. These particles are between the purely material and spiritual, and indeed may be used both in the physical and the spiritual economics. For the two are merely two of many phases of one progressive economy, and act and react each on the other, like a sun and his planet.

Gravitation is applicable to these particles also on both sides, and it is by means of this force—as we will call it, as being a name you know, and also a very little understand—that we cohere these particles together and are able, from time to time, so to clothe our spiritual bodies as to become visible to the photographic plate, and sometimes to the human eye. But we do more than this, and over a wider range. Were it not for these particles all space would be dark; that is, no light would be able to be transmitted from planet or sun or star to the earth; for it is because of the reflection and refraction of these that the rays are visible. Not that they are transmitted, for their transmission and passage depend on other elements of which we will now say no more than this: It is not the rays of light, nor is it the so-called light-waves which are visible to the human eye, but their action on these minute particles which, on the impact of these rays, become visible as waves.

Your scientists have much to learn yet on this subject, and it is not our business to impart much which men can learn by the powers they possess. If we did so then the benefit derived from your earth schooling would be materially lessened, and that is why we are careful to give you just so much as will help you onward without neutralizing the good effect of individual and collective endeavour. Bear this in mind, and it will then perhaps be seen to have a bearing on whatever we deem it advisable to explain to you in such messages as these.

The stars, then, send forth their light. But in order to send it forth they first must possess it themselves. And as they are not self-constituted personalities, in order that they may have it they must be given it.

Who does this, and how is it done?

Now, of course, it is easy to answer "God, for He is the Source of everything". That is true enough, but, as you know, He employs His ministers, and these are without number, and each unit with an allotted task.

The stars receive their power of transmitting light from the presence of myriads of spiritual beings about them, all ordered and regulated in their spheres, and all working in conjunction. These have the stars in their charge, and it is from them that the energy proceeds which enables the star to do its appointed work.

What we want you to understand is that there is no such thing as blind or unconscious force in all God's Kingdom of Creation. Not a ray of light, not an impulse of heat, not an electrical wave proceeds from your sun, or any other star, but is the effect of a cause, and that cause is a conscious cause; it is the Will of some conscious being energizing in a certain and positive direction. These beings are of many grades and many species. They are not all of the same order, nor all of the same form. But their work is controlled by those above them, and these are controlled by powers of higher grade and sublimity still.

And so these great balls of matter, whether gaseous or liquid or solid, whether star or comet or Planet, are all held together, and their forces energized and given effect not by the operation of some mechanical law, but by conscious, live beings at the back of, and working through, those laws. We use the word "conscious" in preference of "intelligent", because the latter term would not accurately describe all the ministers of the Creator. As you understand the word, indeed, it would describe only a very limited number. And it may surprise you to know that those to whom you would apply the term are those which stand between the lower and the higher. For while the lower workers are not really beings of intelligence, the higher are more sublime than that term would imply.

Between the two there are spheres of beings who would bear describing as intelligent beings. Mark well that I am not speaking now in the terms we should use here, and which you will use when you come over here and have studied the conditions somewhat. I am using earth language, and endeavouring to put the matter from your point of view.

Now you will, from what we have already written, be able to see how intimate is the relationship between spirit and matter, and when the other evening we spoke of your own church building and the allotting of guardians and workers, among other things, for the care of the material edifice, we were only telling you of the same principle at work on a minute scale. Nevertheless it is the same principle exactly. The scheme which provides for the upkeep of all those millions of suns and of their planets took note also of the rearrangement of certain congeries of atoms—some in the form of stone, others wood or brick—which resulted in that new entity which you call a church. These are held together, each atom in its place, by the outflowing power of will. They are not placed there and left solitary. Were this done the building would soon crumble away and fall to pieces.

And now, in the light of what we have written, think of what people call "the difference of feeling" on entering a church, or a theatre, or a dwelling house, or any building. Each has its own suitable emanations, and these are in consequence of this same principle at work which we have tried to describe. It is spirit speaking to spirit—the spirits of the discarnate workers speaking, through the medium of the material particles and their arrangement and purpose, to the spirits of those who enter that place.

You grow tired, and we find it hard to impress you, so, with our blessing, we will leave you now, and, if you will, we shall come again. God be with you and your dear ones and your people, in all things and all days, Astriel. #

Thursday, October 16, 1913

Should we perchance say aught that may seem strange and unreal of this our life in the spiritual spheres you will keep in mind that here are powers and conditions which on earth are hidden from the outer knowledge of men. These powers are not altogether absent from your environment, but they are mostly deeper than the physical brain can bear to penetrate. They may be sensed or felt to a degree by the more spiritually developed—no more than this. For those who spiritually rise above the general level do touch the borders of those spheres which at present are supernormal to the average man.And no amount of mental capacity or knowledge can achieve this exaltation of spirit, for these things are spiritually discerned, and only thus.

We who are present with you this evening have come at the invitation of your mother once again to speak to you of our work and life as it is presented to us, and as we are privileged to know it. This so far as we are able. For the rest, we have told you of our limitations in transmission of such knowledge which, for this reason, must of necessity be incomplete.

Are you Astriel?

Astriel and other friends.

First, my brother, we give you greeting of love and peace in our common Saviour and Lord. He is here to us what He is there to you. But we understand now much which was not clear to us when we walked amidst the shadows on the earth. And this we would say with all solemnity: let those who to-day amongst you are searching into the meaning of His Divinity, and the relation of that to His Humanity, do so fearlessly and reverently. For such are guided more than they know from these realms. And be it always in the mind of those who are sincere that they can do no irreverence to Him Who Himself is Truth in inquiring what the Truth is as He revealed it.

Nevertheless, friend, we tell you, with this same fearlessness, and with great reverence also, that what goes by the name of Orthodoxy among Christians in the Church on earth is not a fair and true presentation, in many ways, of the Truth as we have come to know it here. Also we see among you too much unreadiness to go forward, and lack of courage and faith in the providence of God Who will, if men will follow, lead them more and more into the light, the radiant, glowing light, as it envelops those who are brave, to show them the right and holy way towards His Throne. Let such remember that that Throne shall be shared only by the brave who are strong to overcome, and these are they who are

valiant to do and dare, and pay the price at the hands of those their
fellows who are less courageous and less enlightened.

Now we continue our instruction, and you will accept it so far
as you can. What you do not feel able to receive leave, and
perhaps, as you proceed on your way, you will find it fall into
place little by little until you understand it all. We were telling you
formerly about the heavenly bodies and their correlation to each
other. Now we will tell you somewhat of their creation and of the
aspect they wear to us as viewed on their spiritual side. For you
will understand that every star and planet, and every thing
material, has its spiritual counterpart. You do understand this, we
know, and are going to build what we now have to say on that
knowledge.

The heavenly bodies are the expression in matter, of ideas
originating among those high in the Heavenly Spheres of Creative
Power. They are all and each the effect of thoughts and impulses
proceeding from those spheres. When a world is in process of
creation those High Beings are constantly energizing, and
projecting into the forming matter their spiritual influence and, so
to speak, character. Thus, although the planets of your system are
all conformable to one great scheme of unity, they are diverse in
their individual characteristics. These characteristics answer to the
characters of the Great Lords in Whose charge they severally are.

Astronomers are correct when they say that certain of the
elements which go to form the earth are found in, say Mars and
Jupiter, and in the Sun itself. But they would err if they should say
that they are found in the same proportion, or in similar
combination. Every planet differs in these things from its fellow,
but all conform to the one broader scheme which governs them as
a system. What is here said of the units which go to make up the
Solar system may be applied to the wider range of things.
Considering the Solar realm as a unit, it is not identical, either in
composition of elements or in planetary constitution, with other
systems. Each differs from its fellow also.

Now, we have explained the reason of this. It issues in the
individual mind of the Chief Lord of the particular system. Under
him are other great Lords who work in unison with his one
governing idea. But these also have freedom in those things which

are under their charge, and so on downward to the minute things of creation—the flowers and trees and animals and the formation of the face of the planet. It is on account of this latitude in creation and control that you have such diversity in detail; and because of the limit of restriction to the exercise of that free individuality that you have the unity which you find interpenetrating every department and subdepartment of creation.

Under these supervisors there are also myriads of lesser ministers of different grades downward until some of the lowest orders may scarcely be termed persons, for they merge into the lower species of life which you might term sensory, as distinguishing them from those who, like ourselves, are possessed not only of intelligence, but also of that independence in judgment which we know as freewill.

Are you speaking of fairies, pixies, and elementals generally, of which some writers tell us?

Yes, these are real things, and mostly benevolent; but they are far below the human sphere, and therefore are less known than the higher grades of ministry, such as the spirits of men, and those who have attained to angelic degree.

Now, a little more about the earth itself. Geologists tell how some of the rocks are alluvial and others igneous in formation, and so on. But if you will carefully examine some of these you will find that they give off a certain vapour, or one might almost say magnetic influence. That is the effect of the original inspiration into them by those who formed them originally. And these characteristics are worthy of deeper study than they have hitherto received. The chemical composition has been, more or less, ascertained. But the more subtle influences proceeding from the ever-vibrating particles have been neglected. Yet when it is remembered that no piece of rock or stone is still, but that all its particles are in movement orderly and constant, it is only one step onward then to realize that, in order that this movement be maintained, there must be present some great force and, at the back of that force, a personality of which it is the expression.

This is true, and the baleful influence which some gems do exercise on those whose sentiments towards them are not governed aright, is an evidence of this. On the other hand, you have heard of lucky-stones, which is a phrase which shows some rather vague notion of the underlying truth. Eliminate all idea of chance from these matters, and substitute an orderly system of cause and effect, and remember the consequence of ignorance in traversing all natural law, and you will see that there may be something in what we have been trying to explain.

For the sake of emphasis we have limited our consideration to the mineral creation, but the same truth may be adapted to the vegetable and animal kingdoms also. Of this we will not speak to-night. What we, have said has been said with the object of showing that there is a field for those who have a scientific turn of mind, and who are not afraid to go farther afield than scientists have hitherto allowed themselves to go.

The whole may be summed up in a few words, if which be accepted then the conclusion we have intimated must, of necessity, be accepted too. The whole material creation is nothing in itself and by itself. It is but the expression, on a lower plane, of personalities on higher planes, the effect of which their wills are the causes. As a man leaves the imprint of his character on his work day by day, so these great Creative Lords and their ministers have left the impress of their personality on these material phenomena.

Nothing is still, all moves continuously. This movement is controlled and orderly, and that is a warrant of the constant energizing of personality. As the lower grades of service are dependent on those higher Lords for their existence and continuance, so are these latter to those of grade more sublime, as these are to the One Supreme Energy, the Self- Existent One, Whose Will is our life, and Whose Wisdom is more wonderful than we can express in words or in thoughts. To Whom be reverence done from all who are in Him, and from us who, in the Christ our Lord and Saviour, dwell in Him, and He in us. Amen.

Friday, October 24, 1913

We have come to-night with our friends, your mother and her companions, at their invitation once again, in order to speak to you some message of friendly help and counsel. And in thinking over what would most interest you, we concluded that if we were to say something to you of those powers which watch over the world, we might, perchance, be able to lead you, and those who are willing to follow with you, a little onward towards the great body of knowledge which awaits your searching when you have laid aside those trammels of the earth life, and stand free to progress into the greater glories of the realm of spirit.

Who writes this, please?

We are they who came before, friend; Astriel, as you know me, and my fellow-workers of the Tenth Sphere of progress. Shall we proceed, then?

If you please, and I thank you for your courtesy in coming down here into this dim realm, as it must seem to you.

You say "coming down here", and that fairly well expresses the condition of things from your point of view. Yet not altogether, nor perfectly. For if the planet on which you live your present life is dependent in space, then "up" and "down" are terms which must be very restricted in their meaning. You already have noted this in your writing or, rather, you were impressed to note it.

When we said "the powers which watch over the world", we did not, of course, mean to localize these powers on one side of this planet, but to imply the all-enveloping watch which the heavenly powers keep about the sphere which is called Earth. These powers are resident in zones of which the Earth itself is the centre, and they lie in concentric circles around it.

The inferior zones are those near the planet's surface, and progress in power and glory as the distance is increased. But yet, space must be enlarged in meaning when applied to these spheres, for distance has not the same obstructive sense to us as it has to you.

For instance, when I am in the tenth of these zones, my cognizance is limited, more or less, by that Tenth zone as to its outer or superior boundary. I may, on occasion and by permission, visit the Eleventh zone, or even go higher; but residence in those higher zones is not permitted me.

On the other hand, the zones inferior to the Tenth are not impossible to me; for the zone in which I dwell, being a sphere, includes within itself, even geometrically considered, all the nine inferior spheres. So that we may, for the sake of clarity of understanding, put it thus: The Earth is the centre about which many spheres are; and is enclosed closed in all those spheres. And the residents in the earth life are potentially in touch with all those spheres, and actually so in ratio to their altitude spiritually considered—spiritually, because these spheres are spiritual and not material.

Even the material Sphere of Earth is only so phenomenally, for it is a manifestation in matter of all these zones of spiritual power which envelop it; and of others, too, of other degree which interpenetrate it. Leave these latter aside, for the present at least, and consider the matter as we have limned it.

You will now have some idea of what aspiration and prayer and worship mean. They are the means of communion with the Creator and His High and Holy Ones Who (to put it in a way which you will understand) dwell in the highest, or outermost, of these spheres, and include within Himself and These all the zones within that highest Zone or Sphere.

And so the Earth is enveloped by, and included in and affected by the spiritual powers, of varying degree and kind, entrusted by the Creator— God—to all these ministers of all these spheres which are around it.

But as you progress outward you come into a more complicated state of affairs. For not the Earth only but every planet in this Solar system has its like complement of spiritual zones or spheres. So, as you go farther and farther from the Earth, you come to a realm where the spheres of Earth and the nearest planet interweave with each other. As every planet is served with like attendance, so the complication is multiplied, and you will begin to see that the study of these spheres is not so simple as some good people among you evidently think it to be, who demand from us information as to the meaning of this thing.

Draw a diagram of the Solar system, with the Sun at its centre, and the planets roughly in their respective places around him. Then begin with Earth and encircle him with, say, a hundred circles. Do the same with Jupiter, Mars, Venus and the others, and treat the Sun in like manner; and you will have a faint idea of our

143

work and its absorbing interest, but profound depths of meaning, who include in our studies that of the Spheres of God.

Nor have we yet reached the limit of our problem. For what applies to the Solar system must be applied also to that of every other star and its planets. Then each system having been separately considered, each and all must be studied in their correlation to the others. Think of it a while and you will acknowledge, I think, that there will be no lack of employment for your mental energies when you come over here.

Now, we are sometimes asked how many spheres there be. Well, having explained what we have above, I do not apprehend that we shall be asked that question by you. Did you ask it, we, who are only of the Tenth of these zones, would perforce have to answer, We do not know, and much doubt whether our answer to you would differ were you to put that question a million million of aeons hence, and we having progressed all the while.

And now, friend and fellow spirit, we wish to ask you to consider one other aspect of this matter. We have said that these spheres are spheres of spiritual power. Now, two worlds affect each the other by means of that which your scientists name gravitation. Also, two spheres of spiritual power, coming into contact, cannot fail to act and counteract each on the other. Referring to your mental diagram of the Solar system YOU will see that Earth is, of necessity, acted on by a large number of spheres, and that the greater number of these are they which are those of the Sun and other planets.

Yes, friend, there is, after all, something in the astrological idea, and perhaps your scientists do well to give it a wide berth, for it may not be much understood by, and would probably be fraught with danger to, such as they who do not understand that spiritual power is spiritual power. It is real and tremendous, and every sphere of all these is reinforced or modified by the others. The study of these things should be approached with the utmost reverence and prayer, for these are realms where Angels of high estate go softly, and we of lesser estate look on and wonder after the Sublimity of that Being Who unifies all this in Himself, and Who has no Name that can be transmitted to us who only can reach out after Him a little way and then our arm is shortened;

who only can see a little way and then the light beyond is darkness by reason of its intensity.

But we testify to you, friend, and those who will think reverently of things they cannot understand, that if wonder gives us pause time and again as we proceed, yet never do we lose that sense of a Presence Whose breathing is of Love, and Whose leading is as gentle as a mother's leading of her little child. So we, as you do, take His hand and do not fear; and the music of the Spheres is around us as we go on from glory to the glory beyond. Come this way ever, our brother in Him. Never faint nor weary of the road, for the mists are thinning as you proceed, and the light strengthens into the further light which issues onward into the unknown, but never feared, so we tread gently and humbly, as little children do, amid the glories of the planets and the heavens of suns and spheres, and of the Love of God.

Friend and brother, we say good night to you, and thank you for enabling us in this our service. May it be of some help, however little or much, to few or many seeking after the truth. Good night once more, and be assured of our help in blessing. #

Saturday, October 25, 1913

We will, if it is to your mind, continue our message of yesterday in regard to those spheres of power which affect the earth.

Still concerning the Solar system, we say that, on considering what we have already said, you will see that we have not yet mentioned all the complications which enter into the study of these spheres. For not alone do the concentric circles of zones about all the planets and the sun commingle with all the rest, but also the relative combination is continually changing with the changing positions of these bodies and their consequent proximity to, or distance from, one another. So that it is quite literally correct to say that during no two seconds of time is the influence from them impinging on the surface of the earth the same.

Nor is any combination of their influences identical in its effect or intensity all over the earth at the same time, but differs in different localities. There must further be taken into our

145

calculations the stream of radiation coming to this Solar system from the systems of the other stars.

All these things have to be reckoned in, for bear still in mind that we are speaking of zones and spheres of spiritual beings whose powers are energizing continuously, and whose wakefulness never fails.

This, then, is a rough outline of the conditions which obtain among the planetary systems whose outer manifestation is visible to the eye and telescope of the astronomer. But what is thus observed is but a very little mite when compared with the whole. It is but as a small shower of spray which besprinkles the voyager, as he stands in the prow of the vessel, and scatters itself in globules of mist around him. He sees the miniature globes of water where they float reflecting the light around them, and says they, are innumerable. But if this be so, then what of the ocean itself from whence they came, and of which they are, and to which they will return? As that small cloud of spray-mist is to the ocean, so is the star-bemisted heaven, as seen from the surface of the earth, to the whole. And as the depths of the ocean are to the eye of him who gazes over the vessel's side, so are the depths of space and all that it holds to the human intelligence.

Now let us think a little further afield. Space itself is but a term used to describe the indescribable. It is, therefore, without definite meaning. One of your poets began a poem on space and gave it up in despair. Wisely, for had he intended to do adequate justice to the theme he would have been compelled to continue that poem for ever.

For what is space, and where are the boundaries of it set? Is it illimitable? If so it has no centre. Where, then, is God His Dwelling Place? He is said to be at the Centre of all Creation. But what is Creation? A creation which has relation to space, or a creation which is invisible?

Now it is useless, for all practical purposes, to speculate on things we do not understand. It is well to feel after these things sometimes in order that we may discover our own limitations. This done, let us now speak of such things as we, in a measure, are able to understand.

BOOK I: THE LOWLANDS OF HEAVEN

All these zones of which we have spoken are inhabited by beings according to their degree, who progress from one sphere to a higher as they accumulate knowledge within themselves. You will see from what we already have written that, as we advance from the lowest—to the higher spheres, there comes a region of spheres which are interplanetary, inasmuch as they embrace within their circumference more planets than one. Still advancing, we come to a state where the spheres are of such a diameter that they are interstellar; that is, they embrace within their circumference not only more planets than one, but more stars, or suns, than one. All these are filled with beings, according to their degree of sublimity, of holiness and of power, whose influence extends to all, both spiritual and material, within the sphere to which they have attained. We have but advanced, you see, from planet to star, and from star to stars in their grouping. Beyond are spheres more awful still and more tremendous. But of these we in this Tenth Sphere know but little indeed, and nothing certain.

But you will be able faintly to realize, by a large effort of your imaginative powers, the meaning we had in mind when we wrote last evening of Him Whose Name is to us unknown and unknowable. So, when you worship the Creator, you have, I suppose, no very definite idea of the Order of Creator you intend. It is easy to say you mean the Creator of all. But what do you mean by all?

Now, know this—for this much, at least, we have progressed to know— that you do right to worship the Creator and Father of all, whatever you mean—if you mean anything definite by that very inclusive word. Still, your worship passes first into the lower spheres, and through them to the higher, and some worship goes farther and into higher spheres than other worship does, according to its worth and inherent power. And some goes very far indeed. Far above us is the Christ Sphere of glorious intensity of light and awful beauty. Your worship, then, proceeds to the Father through Him, that is, through the One Who came to earth and manifested the Christ to men.

Now, for all that all we have said is true, yet it is truth expressed quite inadequately by reason of the limitations both of us who are speaking to you, and of your own earth state. For you will understand that when we speak of proceeding through these spheres, we are really using phrasing of a local character, as of a journey from one locality through another to a third. And I fear, friend, that I can do little more at this present time than remind you that these states of which we have been thinking are rather better expressed as spheres than as zones. For, I would repeat, the higher include within themselves the lower, and he who moves in any of them is present in all those inferior to his own. For which reason it is not without some degree of truth that we speak of Him Who is all, and in all, and throughout all; and of the Omnipresence of God.

Now, we feel that we have, laboured this theme over long and should cease further endeavour to put into the little wineglass of earth knowledge and wisdom to understand the vintage of these wide vineyards of the heavens. One thing is enough to know for you and us: The Husbandman and the Vinedresser, both, are sure in their power and in their wisdom to deal with us. Toward them is our journey set, and ours is to do the thing we find to hand, to do it thoroughly and well, and finish it quite, and then to reach out for the task set next in order. When that is finished well, then another will be awaiting us. We shall never find that we have reached the end, I think. For as one progresses one comes to feel the possibility more and more of a truth beneath those words "for evermore", "world without end". But we doubt if you do yet, friend, and we say this with courtesy.

And now we bless you, and leave you in the hope we may come again, for it is well, and there is sweetness in it, to bend to whisper into willing ears of some of the minor glories of our Heavenly Realms. Be sure, friend—and tell others who will hear it—that this life which awaits you is not a mere bodiless dream in a twilight region somewhere beyond the boundary of the real and actual. No; it is strenuous and intense, this life of ours. It is filled with service and endeavours crowned, one after another, with success; of patient pressing onward, and of indomitable wills attuned each to others in comrade service for the Lord of Love, Whose Life we sense and inspire, but Whom we do not see, and Whose Home is too sublime for us to know.

BOOK I: THE LOWLANDS OF HEAVEN

Onward we press, and often take the hand of one a little behind us, and with the other seize the skirt of one a little on before. And so we go, my brother; yes, and so do you, and others working with you. And if we are a little way on before, well, there are many who lag behind. Take their hand in your own, and gently, remembering your own comparative frailty, and if the task be too heavy for you, do not loose that hand you hold, but reach the other out—and here is mine and that of many another with us. You shall not fail, so you keep your own vision and your life both bright and pure. Nay, rather shall that Vision grow more glorious, for is it not written, friend, that such as are pure in heart shall SEE GOD?

Friday, October, 31, 1913

They who say that we come to earth in order to help are correct. But they who hope that we shall help to such a degree that their own endeavours will be unnecessary are in error. It is not permitted to US so to enable you as to lessen the value of earth's schooling. And although this seems so reasonable as to be almost of the nature of a truism, yet many there are who look to us to do what only they themselves can do; and that in no ordinary measure, but almost, as it were, miraculously.

Who is writing, please!

We are with your mother—Astriel and friends.

Thank you. I thought the wording was not quite like that of my mother and her companions.

No, I suppose it is not. Partly, of course, because we are of different character, different sphere, and also different sex, which is not without its peculiar characteristics here as with you. And partly, also, because we are of a different earth period from your mother and her friends.

Do you mean you lived on earth some considerable time ago?

Yes, friend, in England, when George the first was king, and some of us earlier still.

About yourself, Astriel—who, I suppose, are the leader of your band—can you kindly tell me anything?

Certainly. But you do not realize that it is more confusing to give these earth details than it might seem to you. I will say what I

149

can, however. I lived in Warwick, and was a teacher in a school there—head master. I cannot give the exact year when I passed over here with any certainty unless I look it up, and it does not really signify.

Now shall we say what was in our minds? We are permitted to help, but with discretion. When people suppose that we ought to help them in scientific investigation, for instance, they surely forget that God has given them minds of their own to use in His service. And to that end they are left to tread their own natural way, and when they have done what they are able, we, now and again, point the way onward and help them to further knowledge.

Can you give me an instance in point?

I remember that once I was impressing a man who was investigating the laws of psychology in the matter of visions and dreams. He wanted to find out what was the cause of certain dreams being prophetic—the connection between the dream itself and the incident which it foreshadowed. He applied to me, and I told him that he must continue his investigations and use his own mind, and, if it were well, he would be given to understand. That night I met him when he fell asleep and conducted him to one of our observatories where we experiment with the object of portraying, in visible form, the events hovering about the present moment; that is, events which have happened shortly before, and those which will happen shortly in the future. We were not able to go far back or far ahead at that particular establishment. That is done by those in the higher spheres.

We set the instruments in order and cast upon a screen a picture of the neighbourhood in which he lived, and told him to watch intently. One particular item was the entry into the town of some great personage with a large retinue. When the display was over he thanked us and we conducted him back to his earth body again.

He awoke in the morning with a feeling that he had been in the company of certain men who had been experimenting in some branch of science, but could not recall what it had been about. But as he was going about his work that morning the face of the man he had seen in the procession came to his mind vividly, and he then remembered several scraps of his dream experience.

BOOK I: THE LOWLANDS OF HEAVEN

On opening a newspaper a few days afterwards he saw an intimation that a visit was projected to the town and district of this same personage. Then he began to reason things out for himself.

He did not remember the observatory, nor the screen pictures we had shown him, as such. But he did remember the face and the retinue. So he reasoned in this way: when our bodies sleep we ourselves, at least sometimes, go into the sphere of four dimensions, That fourth dimension is such as enables those who dwell there to see into the future. But coming back to this realm of three dimensions, we are not able to carry over with us all we have experienced when we ourselves have been in the realm of four. Yet we do manage to hold such items as are natural to this lower realm, such as the face of an earth dweller and a retinue in procession.

The connection, then, between such a dream as foreseen and the events themselves is the relation of a state of four dimensions to a state of three. And the former, being of greater capacity than the latter, covers at any moment a wider range of view, as to time and sequence of events, than the latter can do.

Now, by such use of his own mental faculties he had arrived at as great an advance in knowledge as I could have given him direct; and by so doing he had also advanced in mental training and power. For although his conclusion was not such as would pass muster here without rectification in several points, yet it was roundly and broadly correct, and serviceable for a practical purpose intellectually. I could not have infused into him more than he had found out for himself.

This, then, is the method of our work, and, when people find fault with us and impatiently demand that this method should be altered to suit their ideas of what is the proper way, well, we have to leave them to themselves, and, when their minds are more humble and receptive, we return and continue.

And now, friend, let us tell you the immediate bearing of this on your own case. You sometimes wonder why we do not make these messages more vivid, as you put it, so that you may have no doubt or difficulty in believing that they come from us to you. Well now, think of it all in the light of the above, and you will see that, from time to time, you are given just so much as will help you to help yourself. Your training, remember, is still proceeding; you have not yet arrived, nor will you while you are in the earth life. But if you go on trustfully and faithfully you will find that things will grow more plain.

Accept what is not self-contradictory. Do not look out too much for proof or disproof; but rather for consistency in these messages. We do not give you too much, but we give you all that will help you. Be critical, certainly, but not unbalanced. There is much more truth than falsehood round about you and your life. Look out more for the truth and you will find it. Beware of the false, but not superstitiously afraid. When you take your way along a mountain-path your mind is alert in two directions—for the right and safe foothold, and against the unsafe places. Yet you give more attention to the positive than the negative; and rightly so, or you would go slow on your journey. So tread that you do not slip; but, go forward also fearlessly, for it is those who fear who lose their balance, and come most often to disaster.

God be with you, friend. His Presence is glorious here, and shines through the mists which envelop the earth, and that radiance may be seen by all—except the blind, and these cannot see.[23]

---

[23] The reader will probably feel that the ending of this present series is somewhat abrupt. I felt so, too, and when at the next sitting Zabdie I took up the tale I stated as much. On which the following conversation ensued:

What of the messages I have received from my mother and her friends? Are they, to cease? They are incomplete—there is no proper conclusion to them.

Yes, they will stand very well as they have been given to you.

Remember, they were not meant to be in the form of a complete history, or novel. Scrappy they are, but not unhelpful to those who read with a right mind.

I confess I am rather disappointed at the ending. It is so abrupt, Lately something was said about publication. Is it your wish that they should go forth as they are?

That we leave to your own discretion. Personally I do not see why they should not. I may tell you, however, that this writing you have been doing lately, as all former writing you have received from us, is preparatory to a further advance—which I now propose to you.

That was all the satisfaction I obtained. So there seemed to be no alternative but to regard this installment as a preliminary to further messages.

G.V.O.

BOOK II: THE HIGHLANDS OF HEAVEN

PREFACE

This volume contains the second of a series of communications from beyond the veil received and written down by the Rev. G. Vale Owen, Vicar of Orford, Lancashire. The messages in this volume are complete in themselves and all are given by one who calls himself Zabdiel and who in the opening line of the messages describes himself as the guide of Mr. Vale Owen.

Following on the communications which Mr. Vale Owen received from his mother, and which terminated on October 30, 1913, in rather an abrupt manner, Mr. Vale Owen again sat in the vestry of the Parish Church, Oxford, on the evening of November 3 and received by automatic writing the words "Zabdiel your guide is here". From that date and until the evening of January 3, 1914, a series of communications amounting to some 60,000 words and occupying some thirty-seven sittings were given by this communicator.

These messages cover a wider range than those the Vicar received from his mother. The inter-relation of this and the after life is more fully explained both in narrative and exposition; and in the last message of all the highest note of spiritual rapture is reached.

To criticise or attempt to elucidate these messages from Zabdiel is not my intention in this preface. The mass of information they contain, the new light they throw on the life beyond the veil, and the knowledge that is unfolded respecting spiritual causes which affect our life here must be left to the understanding of each individual who reads this volume.

That these communications come from a source outside the personality of Mr. Vale Owen will be very apparent to those who follow them closely. On the question of the origin of these scripts I am reminded of a letter which Mr. Vale Owen wrote to me regarding a portion of the messages published in *The Weekly Dispatch* in the latter part of February, 1920, "When I had read the last half-column I put it down with tears in my eyes. I tried it again later—same result. It comes from somebody who knows how to get into my soft places. It all bears out what I said to you:

'You are interpreting to me the script for the first time'."

BOOK II: THE HIGHLANDS OF HEAVEN

THE PERSONALITY OF MR. VALE OWEN

In the London *Evening News* of July 16, 1920, in the course of a review of the first volume of *The Life Beyond the Veil*, Sir William Barrett, F.R.S., referring to Mr. Vale Owen, wrote:

"Here we have a beloved and honoured clergyman, whose saintly and devoted life is known to all his parishioners, retiring to the vestry of his church and in the solemn silence of the place finds his hand guided by soma unseen power, whilst evening after evening there swiftly written down the record of a pilgrim's progress it the spiritual world. And this record is entirely independent of any conscious or voluntary guidance on his part.

"Only on two occasions had the Rev.Vale Owen any idea of what subject was to be treated, and often when he had anticipated

one topic the writing disclosed a wholly different train of thought.

"Reluctant at first to yield to this involuntary guidance, doubtful of its legitimacy and sceptical of the result, he was at last convinced that the messages were wise and helpful; that they did not originate from his own mind; but appeared to be impressed upon him by some extraneous spirit. Believing that these messages would afford hope and consolation to many stricken hearts, the author consented to their publication, but, as

Lord Northcliffe tells us, he refused to touch a penny of the large emolument he might have had. I wonder how many of the Rev. Vale Owen's critics and detractors —with a family to support, as I am informed is the case here—would have acted in this noble and utterly unselfish way!"

Lord Northcliffe has also drawn particular attention to the question of the personality of Mr. Vale Owen as reproduced on page 3. But, although the fierce ray of publicity has penetrated the quietude of the peaceful Vicarage at Orford, Mr. Vale Owen is the last man on earth to whom this would make the slightest material difference.

He has always been most emphatic, both in his letters and to all those with whom he has been brought in contact, in stating that it is the messages that are of paramount importance and not the man.

It is, however, impossible altogether to accede to the wishes of Mr. Vale Owen in this respect. On Tuesday, June 15, 1920 the Vicar of Orford after considerable pressure was prevailed upon by the Hon. and Rev. James Adderley to preach at St. Paul's Church, Covent Garden, London. The scenes that took place in that famous old London church were described in the *Daily Mail* the next morning as follows:

"There were all sorts and conditions of people—clergymen, Army officers, City men, girl typists, Covent Garden porters, women in working garb, women of leisure, widows in their weeds, labourers in corduroys. These and other types of humanity were all there.

"When he left the church Mr. Vale Owen was surrounded by men and women who grasped him by both hands. 'Men bared their heads and a number of women wept. When Mr. Vale Owen freed himself he stood on the steps and to the hushed assemblage addressed a few simple words. As he descended the steps hundreds of people again rushed to greet him. It was with the greatest difficulty that his friends, clerical and lay, were able to escort him to the rectory across the road.

"Thousands of people have written to Mr. Vale Owen congratulating him on his writings. Many people in yesterday's congregation travelled specially from the north of England, Manchester and Leeds in particular, to hear his address."

The advent of Mr. Vale Owen to London on this occasion illustrated at once and in a remarkable manner the value of his personality. The Rev.James Adderley, standing beside the altar of St. Paul's, Covent Garden, before pronouncing the benediction, addressed the vast congregation saying:

"With regard to our preacher to-day, we are perfectly certain there is no fraud and no self-advertisement and no denial of Christianity. That is putting it only in a very negative way. I am not saying anything of the positive things we could say. If we had any doubt about it before we have none now, for if ever a man had an opportunity for self-advertisement and fraud our preacher has had it to-day standing in this church, packed from end to end, hundreds of people outside unable to get in; if he had been out for self-advertisement, was it psychologically possible that he could have preached such a sermon as he has to-day? Anybody knows he could not, and knowing that I asked Mr.Vale Owen to preach here because I thought it would do real good to people of all kinds, convinced believers and those who are sceptical, to have an opportunity of seeing a simple-minded humble Christian parson, who does believe in these experiments, and who has had the most extraordinary psychical experiences, of seeing what manner of man

he is and of hearing what he has to say. If it has done nothing more, it may make people think a little more, make them wonder whether there is not a new spiritual movement going on in the world and whether any religious person can afford to stand altogether outside or is not bound to come inside it, at least to learn something about it, to discuss it, to inquire into it; because if there is any meaning at all in religion, it means that these things are so real that those who believe in God and Jesus Christ cannot possibly neglect them."

MR. VALE OWEN'S WORLDWIDE CORRESPONDENCE

As a natural consequence of the world-wide publicity and interest in these scripts during their publication in *The Weekly Dispatch* and other journals overseas, Mr. Vale Owen has received an enormous number of letters from every part of the globe. Of the great majority expressing gratitude, or making urgent enquiries, many were such as deeply to move him, and also to humble him by bringing realisation of the immense volume of goodwill created. I cannot refrain quoting from a letter written to me by Mr. Vale Owen referring to a certain section of his correspondence, in view of the light it throws on a particular phase of his character. It was in answer to one in which I could not help speaking with indignation on the attitude of certain persons towards the scripts and even towards Mr. Vale Owen himself. Gently rebuking me, he wrote:

"Let us treat our anonymous post-carders and other revilers gently and with patience. They are following, not in a very high-minded way truly, the course they believe to be right and many would be prepared to make sacrifices for their cause—although some are not prepared to do this to the extent of backing up their opinions and convictions by coming out into the open with their names. But viewing the whole matter generally, I cannot but realize what a joy it will be some day, somewhere, to take them by the hand as brothers and sisters and to tell them that we were not too bitter against them * when their rather cruel words of misjudgment and attribution of false motives came from them,

because we realized that they were but treading the road by which we ourselves had come. That is so in my own case, at least. I see my own former self reflected in their present attitude, and I hope it helps to keep me in humility and in love to them. Indeed, I owe them, for this reason, a debt not of resentment, but of gratitude. I refer not to their bitterness, but to their lack of enlightenment."

This letter is typical of the many that I have received from Mr. Vale Owen, and makes it unnecessary for me to insist on what I venture to call the Christ-like nature of G. V. O., as his parishioners, who are also his friends, his comrades and his followers, dearly love to call him. Of his practical energy and foresight in affairs of his parish, his buoyant cheerfulness and untiring labours, I have already spoken in my preface in Vol. I. Manly though his attitude is towards this life and its trials and vicissitudes, and fascinating in every degree as is his personality; I must ask every reader of this volume to respect the wishes of Mr. Vale Owen as far as possible and centre his attention upon the communications of Zabdiel and not on the one who was used as au instrument to give them to the world.

H. W. ENGHOLM, London, *September, 1920.*

BOOK II: THE HIGHLANDS OF HEAVEN

GENERAL NOTES

ABOUT ZABDIEL WHO COMMUNICATED

In the course of these communications Zabdiel has given no indication as to who he may have been during his earth life or of what period of our earth's history he lived here. To Mr. Vale Owen he always addressed himself as his friend and guardian and his spiritual presence is very real to the Vicar of Orford. I am privileged to be able to give for the first time in these notes the full story of an experience that befel a young woman who attended evening service at the parish church of Orford on Palm Sunday, 1917, and it seems to indicate very directly the presence of Zabdiel on this occasion.

I myself have questioned at great length this young girl, Mary A., and her story coupled with the appeal expressed by Mr. Vale Owen to Zabdiel, the same evening, points very clearly to the fact that it was Zabdiel who was seen by the girl and thus came to the help of Mr. Vale Owen in response to his prayer. I give the story from notes made by Mr. Vale Owen himself at the time and I use his own words:

"After Evensong on Palm Sunday, 1917, a girl of about eighteen or nineteen years of age came to me in the vestry. Without any preliminaries she asked, 'Mr. Owen, is there such a thing as seeing angels?' I replied, 'Certainly; why?'

"'Because I have seen one.'

"'When?'

"'To-night, in church.'

"She then in answer to further questions explained that just as I had entered the pulpit she saw an angel near the 'Shield', who passed over the heads of the congregation. As he passed, he turned and smiled—a very beautiful and sweet smile it was—and seemed to go towards me in the pulpit and there disappeared. This was the first experience of the kind she had had, and it gave her so great a shock that she had not recovered from it during the remainder of

159

the service. Indeed, as she spoke to me, she was visibly trembling. I told her that, had she not given way to fright, she would probably have seen him standing with me in the pulpit.

"As to her reference to the 'Shield'; there are six shields on either side of the nave, attached to the corbels. Those on the south are illuminated with ecclesiastical insignia; those on the north with the arms of local families. The third from the chancel arch on the south side is just about half way down the nave, the pulpit stands outside the chancel on the north side.

"The occurrence she related interested me on this particular evening for the following reason:

"On account of extra work owing to the war, I had been feeling very unwell for some weeks past. Palm Sunday is a full day in most parishes, and that evening I was feeling very much spent. As the time for the sermon drew near I began to dread the ordeal and wondered what was going to happen. After saying my usual prayer before going into the

pulpit, therefore, I made an appeal to my guide, Zabdiel. I told him I needed his help very really as I did not feel at all equal to the preaching of a sermon without notes, and was in acute pain. So I asked him to give me his help in a special degree that night.

"What the girl had told me assured me that my request had not been in vain, and it showed me who had brought me the help I already was aware I had received. For on entering the pulpit my pain had suddenly ceased and the preaching was no effort at all. Preoccupation might have explained it had the effect not been so marked and

instantaneous. Before Mary A. had spoken to me I had decided that the effect was too great for such a cause, and had already thanked Zabdiel for acceding to my request."[24]

---

[24]When interviewing Mary A. in reference to the above experience I was very much impressed by the girl's obvious honesty. She is a typical Lancashire lass of the industrial classes, earning her living by working in a metal works. She told me that at the sight of the "angel", as she called the appearance, she was so thoroughly frightened that she bent her head down and clutched at her friend who was seated by her side, and did not dare to leave the pew until the service was over. From her manner in telling of her experience, it was obvious to me that she will never forget it.

A MESSAGE FROM ZABDIEL

On Saturday evening, January 31, 1920, Mr. Vale Owen's wife received a message through the planchette, which instrument had been on various occasions operated by her and through which a considerable number of messages had been given from time to time that proved helpful and instructive to Mr. Vale Owen when he was receiving the different communications now published.

This occasion happened to be on the eve of the publication of the first of the series of the scripts in *The Weekly Dispatch*. The message was spelt out by the pointer of the planchette, running from letter to letter

of the alphabet, written on the board over which the instrument was propelled. I give it here exactly as it was received; it reads as follows:

My son, your Script will be a blessing to the world. Zabdiel gives you his blessing. My son, we lately have done right well, giving you what we can, quietly working with you. When I gave those first writings to you we arranged long ahead what should be done when they came to be published. Long hours of work you gave to me. Do you think I should leave you to fight the great battle alone?'

Any more from Zabdiel?

I have no more to say now except, God bless you all. God's blessings rest upon you in your endeavour to give to the world the truth.

THE REALITY OF ZABDIEL

During the first week of the publication of the Script in *The Weekly Dispatch,* the thoughts of thousands of people were turned towards Orford. This quite insignificant village had become famous in a day and was destined to be known throughout the world. No one realized more than Mr. Vale Owen during that

H.W.E.

momentous week that he had turned his back once and for all on the old order of things and that his outlook on life could never be quite the same again. Controversy about the Scripts was already beginning to rage throughout the country, and the mailbags for the Vicarage were the largest that had ever been seen in that peaceful village of Lancashire. In the midst of this new condition of things I received a letter from the Vicar. A document written straight from the soul of a man who realizes the nature of the high task before him; and its tremendous importance to the world. I publish it because I feel it may be helpful to many who will be reading the messages from Zabdiel for the first time.

Extract from letter addressed to H. W. Engholm, February 11, 1920

"It has taken me some years to think things out. I have done so and made up my mind. I have been down into the Valley of Decision and wrestled it all out. It was rather dark down there at times. But I have now come out of the Valley and I stand to-day upon the hilltop in the fierce light of day. I have given myself at last but wholly to the Great Cause, and any personal feelings count no more at all with me. So never hesitate to tell me what to do and I will do it gladly. When I went into our little church this morning it was quite dark. I knelt in my little corner, but there was so great a surging of spiritual forces all around that I had to get up and walk up and down the church for a time panting. At last I came to a stand in the chancel and this is what I realized. It was quite distinct and real.

"The whole spirit world near the earth was in motion. It was immense, like the ocean beating against the rocks. High above stood Our Lord the Christ. He was stern and immovable, but He looked down our way and with Him there was a great host of fighting men all ready for the battle, and some were already engaged with the enemy. Between Him and me stood Zabdiel. He stood there straight and tall—taller and more majestic than I had ever realized him before. His hands were straight down by his sides, clenched and determined as he poured down upon me a great stream of strength and determination which be in turn seemed to be drawing down from those above him. All this while the forces rushed and surged about him and me, but he was quite calm and like the Christ immovable. And as I stood there still, but still panting—for the power was really overwhelming—he gradually came down and stood on my right-hand side. But he towered above me as we stood together there comrades both."

To Mr. Vale Owen, I know, the life to come is a living reality. He feels that he is now carrying out his humble duty to those fair angel friends, whose continual presence strengthens and sustains him night and day, and he will continue to do so until he is called to the presence of the Christ whom he daily strives to serve as a faithful and loving servant.

H. W. E.

ANGELIC LOVE

I

Open your world to me,
Fair angel friends,
Your world of peace and beauty and delight,
Of people robed in radiance and bedight,
On brow and breast and shoulder, with the gem
Of Order and Degree of Ministry
In those broad acres of Eternity
Or here below, as is allotted them.
Open your world to me:
Yet not too broad make the Shekinah beam
To fall upon my poor dull vision yet,
Lest I lose heart by contrast; lest I fret
To leave my duty now, before the theme
Of this my present course be here complete
But just enough to keep and guide my feet
Till this life blends
Into the Life Supreme,
Fair angel friends.

II

Open your hearts to me,
Fair angel friends;
Open to me your large, untiring love,
And let me see how placidly you move
Amid the wonders of the Universe,
Where wish is act accomplished; where each breast
Heaves glowing and responsive to the quest
Of kindred spirit seeking to converse.
Open your loves to me —
Yet you will know, your clearer eyes will see
How much 'tis well to give and to withhold —
Lest I to claim for earth be over bold
The license of your larger liberty;
But just a gleam vouchsafe, nor seek to hide
How blest are loves where love is purified;
How our love tends
Toward the love to be,
Fair angel friends.[25]

---

[25] Subsequent to the reception of the portion of the script in this volume, I received the verses printed above. It was intimated to me that it should be regarded as the keynote to this series of messages. G. V. O.

CHAPTER I : INTRODUCTORY

Divine Love —Human blindness —Evil and good — Evolution —Unity in diversity.

Monday, November 3, 1913

ZABDIEL, your guide, is here and would speak with you.
I shall be glad if he will be good enough to do so.

I am able now for the first time, friend, to join in these messages which your mother and her friends are giving through you to your fellows. Now the time has come when I may continue to develop, with your help, the instructions given you, if it be your wish so to continue.

I am much indebted to you, sir. Please tell me what is your wish now.

That you sit and write down my messages, here and at this time, as you have done for the past few weeks for your mother and her friends.

Will my mother, then, cease and give place to you?

Yes, that is her wish. From time to time, however, you shall hear of her, and from her and others of your circle of friends.

And what is the nature of your projected course of instruction?

That of the development of evil and good, and of God's present and future purpose with the Church of the Christ and, throughout, of mankind generally. It is for you, my friend and charge, to say whether you will proceed, or cease here and go no further. I warn you that, although I shall observe the rule here held advisable of leading onward rather than revealing by cataclysm, yet much that I shall have to say will be of a nature disturbing to you for a time until you have assimilated it and have come to understand the logical sequence of the teaching I shall have to impart.

What of those messages I have received from my mother and her friends? Are they to cease? They are incomplete—there is no proper conclusion to them.

Yes, they will stand very well as they have been given to you.

Remember, they were not meant to be in the form of a complete history or a novel. Scrappy they may be, but not unhelpful to those who read with a right mind.

I confess I am rather disappointed at the ending, it is so abrupt. Lately something was said about publication. Is it your wish that they should go forth as they are?

That we leave to your own discretion. Personally I do not see why they should not. I may tell you, however, that this writing you have been doing lately, as all former writing you have received from us, is preparatory to a further advance—which I now propose to you.

When do you wish to begin?

Now; and you may proceed as you are able from day to day, as you already have done. I know your work and your engagements and shall order my own accordingly, so far as my work with you is concerned.

Yes, I will do my best. But I confess, quite candidly, I fear the task. What I mean is, I do not feel developed enough, for, from what you say, sir, there is some pretty stiff mental work afoot in what you propose.

My grace shall be sufficient in the strength of our Lord the Christ, as heretofore.

Well, then, will you begin by telling me something more than I know about yourself?

It is not on myself that I would fix your mind, friend, but on the messages proceeding through me to you, and through you to our fellow-Christians fighting their way through the mists of controversy and doubt and misdirected zeal. I want to help them and you, my charge; and to such as have shall be given, and these shall hand it on to others. It is for you still to choose.

I have already chosen. I said so. If you are good enough, Zabdiel, to use a poor instrument like me, that is your business, not mine. I will do my best. I can only promise so much as that. Now, what of yourself?

My mission is of more importance than my own personality which will best be delineated through the thoughts I am able to give you. The world is suspicious of one who claims more than they can understand. They believe when they read, "I am Gabriel who stand in the Presence", because that was said long ago. But if I should say to you, "I am Zabdiel who comes to you from High Places with a message from those who are accounted in the Heavenly Realms as Holy Ones and Princes of Love and Light"—well, you know, my friend and charge, what shape their lips would take. And so I pray you let me speak, and judge me and us by what message I am charged with—whether it be true and high or no—and it will suffice for you and for me. One day, dear friend, you shall look on me as I am, and know me better in that day, and be glad.

Very well, sir, I leave it to you. You know my limitations. I am neither clairvoyant nor clairaudient nor a psychic in any real way, I take it. But what has already been written, I admit, has convinced me that it is external to myself, I think I am convinced that far. So, if you will, I will. I cannot say more, and I know I am not offering you much.

It is enough, and what you lack I must endeavour to supply of my own strength. Now, I will say no more at this time, for I know you have to go; you have work to do. God be with you, my charge, in the Lord Christ Amen. #[26]

Tuesday, November 4, 1913

May grace and peace be yours, friend, and quietness of mind.

In order that what I have to say be not misunderstood, I would begin by telling you that in these realms we do not dwell so much on those things which are not of immediate importance but search out such matters as most concern our present onward way, master them, and so proceed from step to step on firm and sure ground. Truly, the things of infinity are not altogether absent from our minds—the nature and presence of the Absolute and Ultimate One, and those conditions which are about Him, these are not altogether thrust aside. Yet we are content to let them rest not understood, knowing, as we judge from our own experience in these lower realms, that those beyond us must hold for us blessing

---

[26] Zabdiel always concluded his communications with the sign of the Cross. H.W.E.

even greater than our present state. And so we go onward in perfect trust and confidence, happy to advance, and yet not impatient of the future towards which we surely move.

So when I tell you of evil and good I shall deal more of those things which we are able to make plain to you, and these will be but as one dewdrop is to a rainbow, and less than this indeed.

There are those who say there is no evil. These are in error. If evil is the negative of positive good, it is real as the good is real. For it were as rational to say there were no such condition as night, but that this is but the negative aspect of light and day, as to say that evil is not and yet good is. For both are conditions of attitude which individual beings assume toward the One Who Is, and, as each attitude is a qualifying medium of an appropriate effect, so a condition of rebellion is the secondary cause of trouble and disaster to the rebel.

The very intensity of the Love of God becomes terrible when it meets with an opposing obstacle. The swifter the torrent the greater the surf about the opposing rocks. The greater the heat of a fire the more complete the dissolution of the fuel which is cast into it, and on which it feeds. And although to some such words may seem horrible in the saying of them, yet it is the very intensity of the Love which energizes and flows through the creation of the Father which, meeting opposing and, disharmonious obstruction, causes the greater pain.

Even in the earth life you may test and prove this true. For the most bitter of all remorse and repentance is that which follows on the realization of the love borne to us by the one we have wronged.

This is the fire of hell, and none else. And if this do not make hell a reality, then what thing could? We who have seen know that only on repentance and the realization that all God's actions are acts of love do the pangs of hell descend upon the sinner, and not until then in their full intensity.

But if this be so, if evil be real, then also are evil beings real. Blindness is inability to see. But not only is there such a condition as blindness; there are also people who are blind. Blindness is also a negative condition, or less. It is the condition of one who has four senses instead of five. But real it is, nevertheless. Yet it is only when one who is born blind is told of the sense of sight that be begins to feet his lack of it, and the more he understands the lack of it the more his lack is felt. So it is with sin.

It is usual here to call those who are in the darkness the "undeveloped". This is not a negative term, which would be "retrogressed". So of both I say not "loss" but "lack". The one born blind has not lost a faculty but lacks it. The sinner also rather lacks than loses his faculty to apprehend the good. His is rather the condition of the blind from birth than the blind from misadventure.

And herein is the explanation of the words of St. John that they who have been brought into the knowledge of the truth cannot sin—not as theoretically considered, but as practically considered. For it is difficult to see how they who have enjoyed the light and all the beauty it reveals should put out their eyes and so become blind.

Those, therefore, who sin do so from lack of knowledge, and inability to appreciate the good and beautiful, and as the blind come to disaster unless they be warded by those who can see—guides either incarnate or discarnate—so with those who are spiritually blind.

Yet you may say that people do go back and fall from grace. Those who do so are such as those who are partly blind or of imperfect sight—colourblind as to one or more colours. These have never seen perfectly, and their lack is only unknown to them until opportunity offers, and then their imperfection is manifest. For a colour-blind person is one whose sight is, in little or more measure, undeveloped. It is only by using his vision that he maintains what vision he has, and if he neglects to do this then he retrogresses. So with the sinner.

But it may perplex you to be told that many who live apparently good and upright lives on earth are found here among the undeveloped. Yet so it is. They have gone through life with many of their higher spiritual faculties undeveloped, and when they step into the world where all is spiritual, their lack is seen, and only gradually do they come to understand what they have lacked unknowing so long,—just as many colour-blind people live their lives and pass hence and never know their imperfect state of vision; which also is hidden from their fellows.

Suppose you give me a case by way of illustration.

One who teaches the truth in part only must learn here to teach it whole. Quite a large number of people accept the fact of inspiration, but deny that it is an ordinary and perpetual means of God's grace for men. When they come over here they, in turn, become inspirers, if so qualified, and then learn by how much they were indebted in their earthly course to those who used this method with them unknown. They must first develop this lacking knowledge and then they may progress, and not till then.

Now, evil is the antithesis of good, but both may be present, as you know, in one person. It is only by freewill that that person is held responsible for both good and evil in his heart. Of this freewill, and the nature and use of it, I must further speak at another time.

God be with you, friend, and keep you in His Grace. Amen. #

Saturday, November 8, 1913

If you will give me your mind now for a little while I will endeavour to continue my words in reference to the problem of evil and its relation to that which is good. These are indeed relative terms and neither of them absolute as considered from the point of view of a man on earth. For it is not possible that one in whom both have a part be able to define either perfectly, but only, or chiefly, as the effect of each is seen in its working.

Also, let it be remembered that what seems to be good or evil to one man does not of necessity so appear in the eyes of another. Especially is this true of those of different creed and habit of thought and manner of life in community. What, therefore, is possible in the matter of distinction between these two is that the broad and fundamental principles which underlie each should be grasped clearly, and the minor shades of these qualities be entrusted to the future when they will be gradually made more plain.

Now, evil is rebellion against those laws of God which are manifest in His working. It is the endeavour of a wise man that he should walk in the same direction as that towards which these laws flow. He who from willfulness or ignorance opposes this current

170

finds at once that an obstacle is presented to him, and if he persists in his opposition, then disaster will ensue.

For the Life of the Supreme, which operates and energizes through creation, is a force to oppose which is destruction. And if a man were powerful enough in himself to bring such opposition to stand in the way of that tremendous force as would check, even for a moment, its flow, annihilation would be his lot when the pent-up energy once again burst forth upon him. But no man is able thus, and to this degree, to oppose God; and it is therefore that our weakness itself is our surety against annihilation such as this.

For a longer or shorter period sometimes, and often indeed for some thousands of years, as you reckon time on earth, a man may maintain his obduracy. But no man is created who is able to continue so everlastingly. And that is a merciful limit which our Father Creator has placed around and in us lest He lose us, or any one of His children, away from Him, and without return for ever.

Let us therefore, having looked on this phase of aberration from man's natural walking with God, now look the other way in the direction in which all things are tending. For truly, evil is but a transitory phase and, whether it pass away from His economy in whole or no, from every individual most surely it will pass away when its opposing force is spent, and he be left free to follow on in the glorious train of those who brighten as they go from glory to further and greater glory.

For this reason also will the Kingdom of the Christ one day be altogether purged of evil, because individuals make up that Church and, when the last has been ingathered, then will it be complete in its radiating glory to minister perhaps, and as many here believe, to other worlds in need of such help and succour as your world is to-day.

As we stand on the earth plane, where I stand now, and look through the Veil of difference of condition which is between us and you in the earth life, we often see many people at one time, and sometimes but few. These people differ in brightness according to the degree of holiness in each; that is, according to the degree in which each individual in himself is able to reflect the divine light of spirit which streams past and through us to you.

Some appear very dim, and these, when they come over here, will go to regions dim or less dim according to their own dimness.

So that every one will both appear to others and others will appear to him, as natural to the particular environment and atmosphere in which their lot is cast. This is "their own place". Let me illustrate this in order to make it more plain to you. If an electric spark be projected into thick darkness the contrast is too great to appear congruous. We should say that that spark was out of its proper element, and created a disturbance amid the darkness which brought, just for a minute, things to a standstill. Men groping their way along the dark country lane stand still and rub their eyes until they can see to pursue their way once more. The night animals also for a moment are startled and cease to move.

But if that flash be projected into the atmosphere in the daylight of noon, the disturbance is less, and if it could be projected into the sun it would there lose contrast and blend with his brightness.

So those whose radiance is great go into those spheres whose brightness agrees with their own; and every one into the sphere which agrees with his—be it less or more. But those whose bodies—spiritual bodies I mean—are of gross texture, and do not radiate much light, but are dim, go into those dim spheres where only they may be so much at ease that they may work out their own salvation. They are not at ease indeed in any sense of the word; but only they would be less at ease in a brighter sphere than in those dim regions until they have grown in brightness themselves.

All who pass over here from the earth have some of the darkness which envelops it like a thick pall of mist. But many of these have already in their wills endeavoured to rise through that mist into the clearer realms: and these do quickly here what they fain would have done below. And now we are looking upward, and there indeed lies the Royal Road, the King's Highway to His Holy City and the Dwelling Place of His present Majesty. Along that way we follow step by step; and every step we go we see that far away the light increases ever, and our comrades and ourselves grow in brightness, as in beauty, the further we go. And it is a matter of no small joy that we are permitted, for periods differing according to the needs of you on earth, to come back on our steps and help you on the road we know to be so radiant and so full of the Beauty of His Presence.

And this, my friend and ward, we will endeavour, if you still keep of the mind you are at this present time. I think you will so persevere. But know you that many do set out and then, distrusting the brightness because it dazzles their unaccustomed eyes, turn back to paths more dim where their sight is less distrained. And so we look upon them as they go, and sigh, and turn to seek another, if perchance he should prove strong to bear more of our brightness than the one for whose return hither in our ways we must await, till the due time shall come to us and Him.

God keep your feet that they do not slip, and your eyes that they be not dimmed, and, although in words of earth you will not be able to write down what you may know, yet so much of it will we endeavour that you write that others may be led so to ask that they may have, so to seek that they shall find, and (if they be very courageous—these two cities being taken) so to dare as to knock, and so to knock that that Gate be opened and the brightness and glory within revealed. #

Monday, November 10, 1913

As I stand on the plane of earth, above and beyond lie the spheres, into some of which I have penetrated, and of the Tenth of which I am a member. These spheres are not so much what would correspond to localities on earth, but rather estates of life and power, according to the development of the individual. You have already received some instruction as to the multiplicity of these spheres of power, and I do not purpose to pursue my own on those lines. I would rather lift your mind into the realms of light and activity by another channel, and this I now proceed to do.

All that is good is potent to accomplish things in two directions. By the power within, a good man, be, he incarnate or discarnate, can and does both lift up that which is below him, and also draw down that which is above; not alone as by prayer, but also, of his own right, by power.

Now, this is by reason of his attunement to the Divine Will; for by so much as he is able to correspond with his Divine environment, by so much is he able to work through that environment; that is, to energize and to accomplish things. The things he may so accomplish are manifold even to one who has risen only into a small number of spheres, and these things, when projected through the Veil into your earth life, are accounted wonderful.

For instance. There are here such as have charge of the elements which condition the earth and those things which grow upon the earth. Let us take one example which will serve to illustrate the others: Those who have charge of vegetation. These are under one Mighty Prince; and are divided and subdivided into departments, all in perfect order. Under these again are others of lower estate who carry out their work under direction, and in conformity to certain unalterable laws laid down in the higher spheres. These are what you know as elemental spirits, and are multiple in number and in form.

The laws of which I speak are very complex the further we proceed from the sphere of their origin; but if we could trace them up-stream and arrive at their origin we should find, I think, that they were few and simple, and at last, in the source and spring of their origin, unity. Of this I, who have been only a little way, can but reason on what I have observed in my upward progress; and this would lead me to hazard that the one law, or principle, from which all the lesser laws and principles are radiated might best be described by the word Love.

For, understood as we understand things, Love and Unity are not much diverse, if not actually identical. We have discovered this much at least, that everything which divides in all the regions and estates on this our own level, and in those spheres below us down to the earth sphere, is in one way or another an abnegation of Love in its most intense and truest meaning.

But this is a most difficult problem to discuss with you here and now; for it would be very difficult to explain to you how all the diversity you see around you is due, as it seems to us, to this same disintegrating action, and yet is all so wonderfully wise and so beautiful. Still, if you substitute for the word negation the idea of Unity less one part, and then Unity less two parts, and so on, you may perchance get some glimmer of what philosophy is held among us on this subject of Unity radiating into diversity of operativeness. Although the activity of these lower orders is all regulated by law, yet a great amount of freedom is found within its bounds. And this is to us a matter of much charm because, as you will agree, there is much beauty in diversity, and in the ingenuity displayed by those who energize among plant life.

Some of these laws which govern the elementals and those above them I am unable to understand yet. Some I do understand but am unable to transmit to you. But a few I may tell you, and you will, in your own proper time, learn more as you progress in these heavenly mansions.

It would seem, then, that one rule they must observe in their work is that, having planned out any scheme of development for a family of plants, that scheme must be pursued, in its main elements and essentials, to its natural consummation. All their armies of subordinates are kept within the limits of that unalterable law of evolution. If an oak family is planned, then an oak family that must remain. It may evolve into subdivisions, but these must be subdivisions of the oak. It must not be allowed to branch off into the fern family, or seaweed. These also will be developed along their own line.

Another law is that no department of spiritual workers shall be able to negative the operations of another. They may not, and often do not, work in conformity; but their operations must be along lines of modification, rather than absolute negation, which would mean destruction. Thus we find that if the seed of two plants of the same family be mixed the result will be a mule plant, or a blend, or a modification. But the seed of one family being mixed with that of another family is without effect. And in neither case is the effect annihilation.

A parasite may entwine itself around a tree. But then ensues a fight. In the end the tree is usually worsted and pays the penalty of defeat. But it is not suddenly laid low. The fight proceeds, and indeed sometimes the tree wins. But it is recognized here that those who invented and carried out the parasitic idea have in the main won the battle of forces. Thus the war goes on, and when

175

you view it from this side you will see how very interesting it all is.

And now I must tell you something which I have hinted already, and which you may find difficult of acceptance. All these main principles, even when diverse in action, are planned in spheres higher than my own by high and powerful Princes who hold their commission secure under others higher still, who hold theirs from others above them.

I use the word "diverse" in preference to "antagonistic", for among those High Ones antagonism does not find a place, but diversity of quality in wisdom does, and is the cause of the wonderful diversity in nature as it works out in its procession from those Higher Heavens outward through the lower spheres into that of matter which is visible to you on earth. Where antagonism enters is in those spheres where the radiating wisdom has become more attenuated by reason of its journey outward in every direction through spheres of innumerable myriads of freewilled beings, and diluted and refracted in its passage.

And yet, when you consider the stars of different size and complement, and the waters of the sea, naturally still but by the motion of the earth and the gravitation of bodies at a distance is allowed to have no rest; and then the more rarefied atmosphere which, also responding to the pulls and pushes of the forces which impinge upon the earth, whips into motion the heavier liquid; and all the diversity of form and colour of grass and plant and tree and flower and insect life and life more evolved, the birds and animals, and of the continuous movement among them all; and the way in which they are permitted one to prey upon another, and yet not to annihilate wholly, but every species must run its race before it pass away—all this and more; then will you not, my ward and friend, confess that God is indeed most wonderful in the manner of His working, and that the wonder justifies most fully the measures He has permitted His higher servants to adopt and use, and the manner also of their using?

In His Holy Name I bless you, friend—and that is peace. #

CHAPTER II: MEN AND ANGELS

Degrees of light in the spheres — Geometrical astronomy — The orbit of human life — Angel visitants to earth — The wrestling of Jacob — The power of a name — Courage in thinking — The Divinity of the Christ — Love and its opposite — " Now we see through a glass darkly" — Zabdiel's Heavenly Home

Wednesday, November 12, 1913

IF it were possible, friend, that we should be so united as to be enabled to, look out on things from one point of view and vantage, these matters in hand would be so much the easier to explain. But you look hence from one side the Veil which hangs between things and the region of their causation, and I from the other side. So that our outlook is normally in opposition, and when I would make things appear simple to you I must perforce turn me about and look the other way and, so far as I am able, with your eyes rather than my own.

This doing so far as in me: lies, therefore, I call you to gaze with me into the upward reaches of creation, inversely to their natural course and flow from the High Ones outward towards the spheres where what is material begins to assume and claim a place. As we go we find that what things we have known as belonging to our environment in the lower spheres begin to assume other aspects: they are transformed to the vision, and transubstantiated to the sense of inward perception, and yet are related to those things which obtain in the sphere of matter, or those next above as the sun is related to the twilight of earth.

Taking first this same matter of light. Light is known on earth by reason of its contrast with darkness, which is merely a state of absence of light, and intrinsically of no content or value. So that when we speak of darkness we mean a lack of certain vibrations which enable the retina of the eye to register the presence of external things.

Now in the regions of spiritual darkness on this side of the Veil a like condition of affairs also obtains. For those who are in darkness are those whose sense of sight lacks the vibrations from without which enable others to have knowledge of those things which to them are external but present withal. Their state is a state of inability to receive these vibrations. When their spiritual faculties do undergo change then they are able to see more or less clearly.

But also these vibrations which convey the knowledge of things to their sense of sight are, in those regions, of a more gross quality than in the regions of spiritual health. So that even to those good spirits who penetrate into those regions, and whose sense of sight is more perfect, yet the darkness is quite apparent, and the light by which they see is dim. So that, as you will understand, there is response between the spirit and the spirit's environment, and that response is so accurate and perpetual and sustained as to constitute a permanent state of life.

As we go higher in the spheres this responsive action between the spirits and their environment is also maintained and that which we may call the external light becomes more and more perfect and intense the higher we go. So it is that those who dwell in, as we will say, the Fourth Sphere may not penetrate into the fifth, to remain there, until they have become so developed as to sustain with ease the degree of intensity of light there obtaining. Having attained to that Fifth Sphere they soon become used to its light. And if they return to the Fourth, as they do from time to time, that Fourth Sphere seems dimmer to them, while still they are able to see with comparative ease. But if they should descend straight to the Second or First Sphere, they would only with difficulty be able to use those denser vibrations of light and, in order to do so, are obliged to train themselves to see in that same sphere which once was but their normal abode.

When we come down to your earth sphere we see by reason of the spiritual light which men have in themselves. And those who are of higher spiritual grade than others we see so much the more clearly.

Were it not for faculties we possess other than that of sight, we should, as I suppose, have difficulty in finding our way about, and to those to whom we wish to come. But we have these other faculties, and by their use are able to do our work in ministering to you.

BOOK II: THE HIGHLANDS OF HEAVEN

You will now be able to understand that there is a quite literal truth in the words, "Who dwells in light which no man can approach". For few in the earth life are able to rise many spheres beyond; and the light which streams from above is blinding even to those who are much progressed.

Now think what of beauty this evermore perfect light implies. You have colours on earth which to mortal eyes are entrancing. Just over the border on this side are colours which are much more beautiful and more varied. What then must be the beauty in this one thing alone as we advance into the greater light! Even what I myself have seen, who have only come this little way, is more than I can even hint at in this language in which I am trying to speak to you now, and which to-day is as a foreign tongue to me, who am also limited to the use of what store of words you yourself possess.

But those who love beauty will find a never-failing supply to their great joy and, as light and holiness go hand in hand, so, as they progress in the one, will they in the larger enjoyment of the other. This is the Beauty of Holiness, and it is past all imagination of mortal men. But it is worthy of meditation, and if you will keep it in mind then what things are beautiful on earth will speak to you more really of the greater beauties of the Heavenly Realms where the joy of life is all one can desire. Which one day shall be yours, good friend, if you keep in the right and onward way. #

Saturday, November 15, 1913

And now, my friend and ward, I would that I might enable you to see one other matter from this standpoint where I stand, and that is the real relation of spirit power and energy to the phenomena of development among the heavenly bodies as men of science have observed them and tabulated them and, reckoning up their joint message, have made their deductions, and from these have, with some penetration and wisdom, formulated the laws according to which these things come about.

The term "heavenly bodies" has a dual significance and will be interpreted according to the measure and quality of the individual mind. To some these orbs are creatures of the heavens material, and to others they are none else but manifestations and

179

results of the energizing of spirit life. The mode of operation of this spirit life, also, is not understood by all alike; and by some the term is used most vaguely. To say that God made all things is to say a big thing in few words. But the significance of the truth herein embodied is somewhat tremendous; and for all but those who are able to rise into clearer light than that which hovers about the dim places of the earth plane, it would be nearer the truth to say that herein is a truth not so much embodied as entombed. Out of the simplest wisdom are made the greatest things; and out of the most elementary of geometrical figures arise the most wonderful combinations of perpetual movement.

For it is only the purest and simplest things that are competent to be used most freely and without entanglement. And this state of affairs alone gives warrant of perpetuity, whether on earth, or in the vast reaches of space through which go these worlds and systems, eternally because perfectly ordered in their course.

Now, it is not too much to say that the appointed paths of all these bodies of the heavenly systems are shaped of two principles: that of the right line, and that of the curve. It is even more true and exact to say that their orbits may be said to be shaped out of one form only, and that the right line itself. All go onward impelled in a right and straight course and yet not one that is known to us but travels in a curve. Astronomers will explain why this is, but I will note one instance by way of example here.

The earth, we will suppose, is set forth on its journey. It travels in a straight line from one point. That is its potential movement. But directly it leaves that point it begins to fall towards the sun, and we find after a while that it is moving in an ellipse. There is no straight line here, but a series of curves worked together in one figure, which is the orbit of the earth. And yet the pull of the sun was not in the fashion of a curve, but in a right line, direct. It was the combination of these two straight lines of energy—the impetus of the earth and the gravitation of the sun—which, being perpetually exerted, bent the orbit of the earth from a straight into an elliptical shape, and one in which many elements of curve entered to build it up complete. I leave out other influences which modify this one again in order to concentrate your mind on this one great principle.

BOOK II: THE HIGHLANDS OF HEAVEN

I put it in formula, thus: Two straight lines of energy operating on one another produce a closed curve. Both, you will note, are quite orderly in their working; and both are beautiful and of wonderful power. For, that any body of matter move at all should seem Wonderful, and is so in truth. Yet each modifying the other, and the greater dominating the lesser without depriving it of its essential power and freedom of movement, these by their joint action—exerted and directed apparently in opposition—produce a figure of greater beauty than the two straight lines, which are as the parents to the child.

Now, you would not, I take it, say because these forces are seen to be exerted against one another that this is a bad scheme and plan whose origin is of evil. For you see these two bodies still continuing their journey through space year after year, and century after century, and you come to think it rather a matter for awe and reverence than for contumely. It displays a Wisdom which is beautiful in its working and mighty in operation; and you praise God Whose mind conceived all this, for He must be very wise and very great indeed. And you do well.

Yet when other His works you contemplate, but understand them not so well as this, sometimes you men are too ready to doubt Him and His ways of working. You see a like opposition of forces in human life, and you say His plan is here imperfect. You think He might have made a better way; and many doubt His wisdom and His love because, seeing but a minute section of the curve of the great orbit of existence, they cannot but conclude that all is falling, falling to destruction; or at least that a straight and right line would be the better course, and not these combinations which curve the impetus of human life from its direct onward way of evolution: without disaster and without pain.

My dear friend and ward, these things might be otherwise than as they are, but they would not be near so lovely in their completed orbit then as they will be in the path on which He Who made all and sees the end of things sent them forth. These forces which in opposition produce straining and travail and pain are as those which make the orbit of the earth what it is; and He Who sees the perfect form has seen it well to work thus, and in patience looks on towards the consummation of this His perfect scheme.

THE LIFE BEYOND THE VEIL

We here do see not all nor much of the road ahead; yet more than you we see, and so much as enables us to content ourselves and press onward, helping others on the road, content and trusting that all will be well ahead however far we go. For now we do not seek with much labour to reckon on the course we are travelling wrapped round with earth mist which hinders us to see, but we view the way from the clear sunlight atmosphere of these heavenly realms; and I tell you the orbit of human life, as it works out towards completion, is beautiful too: so beautiful and so lovely withal that we are full often brought to arrest in wondering awe at His Majesty of Love and blended Wisdom, to Whom we bow in lowly adoration not to be expressed in any words of mine, but only in the, yearning of my heart.

Amen, and my blessing upon you, friend. Look up and be fearless for, believe me, all is fair ahead and all is well. #

Monday, November 17, 1913

"What thou seest write in a book." These words were spoken by an Angel to John in Patmos, and he carried out the command as he was able. He wrote his account and handed it to his brethren; and from a time till now men have striven to wrest from that account its meaning. They have tried one method and another, and confess themselves perplexed. Yet their perplexity is of their own making, friend, for had they read as little children read they would have been able to turn the door with the right key, and to enter into the Kingdom to see what beauties there await such as are able to take a simple man's simple words simply, and believe.

But men have loved perplexity ever, and seek in it to find profundity and depth of wisdom. And they fail, for, looking on the surface of the glass, they are dazzled and blinded at the reflected light, which they should have looked through and beyond at the glories there revealed.

So do men add perplexity to perplexity and call it knowledge. But knowledge is in no wise perplexing, but the lack of it is. So when I seek to explain aught to you, and through you to others, do you not, look so much on the surface of things, at the precise method by which this comes to pass; and do not start in doubt at words and phrases familiar to you as your own, for these are my material by which I build up my house; and only such as I find stored in your mind can I use.

Moreover, all these years past you have been watched and prepared, partly to this very end, that we should use you thus, and that where we lack, for further contact with your material sphere, there you yourself should come to our aid. We can show you things—you must write them down. Thus what thou seest write in a book, and send it forth to be dealt with by men, each according to the measure of his own capacity, and each as his faculties are quickened to the perception of spiritual things. Let that suffice, then. Come with us and we will tell you what we are able.

You say "we." Are there others besides?

We work all together, friend. Some are here present with me bodily, others still in their several spheres are able to send forth their help from those realms without their leaving them. Also there is a certain help which only may be given thus, For you will know that, as the diver at the bottom of the sea must be tended with air by those above continually for his support, so it is likewise helpful that we be ministered to the while we also minister. By this we are enabled the more clearly to speak to your mind of the higher verities while we stand on this dim and grosser lower plane as on the bed of the ocean where our natural air is scanty and our light looms far above. Think of it and us in this wise and you will be able to understand a part of our task.

Some there are who ask why angels do not come in plenty nowadays as in the olden times. Here are many errors in few words, and two preeminent. For first, angels of high estate did never come in plenty to the earth plane, but one here and another there amid the ages; and those were accounted worthy of a forward place in the annals of great events. Angels do not in this wise come to earth and visibly appear, except it be on some very rare and special commission. This were an extension of our difficult task: first must the diver get to the dark and very deep waters, and then must he so condition himself that he become visible to those nearly blind creatures whose habitat is on the ocean floor.

No; we work for men, and are present with them, but in other ways than this, according to rule and varying method as each task requires. And that is the second error made; for we are present and do come to earth continually. But in that word "come" more lies hidden than I may reveal.

For even those on this side, in the spheres between us and you, do not understand yet our powers and the ways of their using, but only in part as they learn in the course of their progress. And so let it rest thus. And now I will explain to you another matter of interest.

The audience which Jacob had of the Angel at Jabbok when he wrestled with him and prevailed: What, think you, was that wrestling; and what the reason of the withholding of the Angel's name?

I think that the wrestling was a bodily wrestling; and that Jacob was allowed to prevail in order to show him that his wrestling with his own nature during his residence in Padan Aram had not been in vain—that he had prevailed. I think the Angel withheld his name because it was not lawful to give it to a man still in the flesh.

Well, the first answer is better than the second, which, my charge, is not saying a very great deal. For, see you, if he did not give it because it was not lawful to give, why was it not lawful?

Now, the wrestling was real and actual, but not form to form as men do usually wrestle. The Angel might not be touched of mortal hands with impunity. He had manifested in visible form, and that form was even tangible, but not rudely to be treated. For the power of that Angel was such that the mere touching of the thigh of Jacob produced dislocation. What, then, had Jacob taken that form within his arms?

But the Angel was held there by the will of Jacob: not because Jacob's was the stronger will, but because of the Angel's condescension and courtesy.

While Jacob wished he stayed, but courteously asked to be permitted to go. Do you wonder at this great indulgence? Think of the Christ of God and His humiliation among men and you will wonder no longer. Courtesy is one of the outward manifestations of love, and may not be disregarded in that long course of training which makes us what we are and do become. So was the Angel held because he gave that much. But Jacob is not so winning. In him his newly realized strength of will and character overbears his finer sentiments for the time, and demands a blessing. This he obtains, but not the Angel's name.

It were not quite accurate to say it was not lawful that it should be given. Sometimes the names are given. But in this case not; and for this reason: There is much power in the use of a name. Know this, and remember it; for much disaster continually ensues by reason of the misuse of holy names, disaster wondered at and often felt to be unmerited. Jacob for his own sake was denied that name. He had shown his willingness to demand a blessing, but must not be given to be enabled to demand too much. He had come into contact very nearly with great power, and must be restrained in the drawing on that power, or the fight he had still to fight would not be then his own.

Now, I see in your mind a question as to the possibility of demanding unwisely from us and thus obtaining. Things are so ordered that not alone is this possible but continually is it done. Strange as it may seem to you, help is often demanded from these spheres in such a way that it must be given, and yet it were, time and again, better that the asker's own resources should have been employed, and he thereby have risen to greater strength than by this the other way. If a name be called with vehemence by those on earth the owner of that name cannot but be notified of it. He attends and acts as possible and best.

I cannot but think that Jacob made a better advance in his contest with Esau, and with his sons and with the famine, and with the many trials he had to meet, by bringing to bear on them his own strength of personality than had he been able continually to call to his aid his Angel-guide to do what he could do himself. This help would be often refused and he, unable to understand, would probably have been hindered in his faith and perplexed. Sometimes the help would have been given, and in so patent a way as to require little aspiration to understand, and so, little advancement.

But I will not pursue this to greater length. My object in citing Jacob's case was to show you that you are not farther from us, nor we from you, because you do not see us nor hear our voices. We speak and you hear, but more deeply in yourself than with the outward ear. You do see, but the vision is more inward than that of the outward faculty of sight. And so do you be content; for we are so, and will continue to use you, so you continue in quietness of spirit and in prayer to the Highest through His Son, Whose ministers we are, and in Whose NAME: we come.

Tuesday, November 18, 1913

When all things visible were created one thing was left not quite complete because the last and greatest of all, and that was man. He was left to develop and, being given to possess great power, he was shown the onward way that he should tread, and left to tread it. But not alone. For all the hierarchy of the heavenly realms were his beholders to see how he would do with those gifts which had been given him.

I do not speak at this time of evolution expressly, as understood by scientists, nor of fall and uprising again, as taught by those who profess theological knowledge, but rather of the broader aspect, as we contemplate man's aspirations and what has come of them. And looking forward, also, it is permitted us to weigh his future, and to see a little way ahead into those long reaches and realms of wide expanse which lie before us all.

Nor in doing this am I able to constrain myself within the limits of doctrinal theology as understood by you. For it is indeed constrained and straitened so greatly that one who has lived so long in wider room would fear to stretch himself lest he foul his elbows against the confining walls of that narrow channel; and hesitates to go at any pace ahead, fain as he is to travel, lest worse than this be his lot.

No, my friend, shocking and startling as it be to those whose orthodoxy is as the breath of their body to them, more saddening is it to us to see them so much afraid to use what freedom of will and reason they have lest they go astray, mistaking rigid obedience to code and table for loyalty to Him Whose Truth is free.

Think you for a moment. What manner of Master-Friend is He to them who tremble so at His displeasure? Is it that He is waiting and watching, with sinister smile, to catch them in His net who dare to think and think in error sincerely? Or is this He Who said, "Because you are lukewarm, and neither cold nor hot, I will reject you"? Move and live and use what powers are given prayerfully and reverently and then, if you do chance to err, it will not be of obduracy and willfulness but of good intent. Shoot with strong arm and feet well and firmly set, and if you miss the mark by once or by twice, your feet shall still be firm and the word "Well done!" for you shot amiss, yet in His good service, and as you were able to do, so you did. Be not afraid. It is not those who strike and shoot and sometimes miss the mark whom He rejects, but the craven who fear to fight for Him at all.

This I say boldly for I know it is true, having seen the outcome of both manner of lives when those who have lived them issue forth among us here, and seek their proper place and the gate by which they may pass onward this way.

And now, my ward and fellow-servant in the Army of the Lord, listen well awhile, for I have that to say which may be not very familiar to your way of thinking, and I would that you record it aright.

Many there are among you who do not find it in them to accept the Christ as God. Now, there is much light talk of this matter on both sides of the Veil. For not with you on earth alone but also here we have to seek in order to know, and miracles of revelation are not thrust upon us; nor is our own freedom of reasoning constrained by any higher power than our own.

Guided we are, as you are, too, but not forced to believe this or that in any of the many ways in which this might be done. So there are here, also, many who say that Christ is not God, and so saying think they have made an end of the matter.

It is not my present purpose to prove to you the contrary and positive truth, nor even to state that truth affirmatively. It is rather that I would endeavour to show you and them what manner of question this is, and how it is not conducive to an understanding of it, by even the little we may, to speak in terms without first defining them.

First, then, what is meant by God? Do they mean a localized personality when they think of the Father —a person such as a man is? If so it is obvious that the Christ is not He, or this would create a double person, or two personalities in one in such a way that distinction of each would be impossible. It is not that way the Oneness of which He spoke is to be sought. Two equal Persons united is an unthinkable condition, and one which reason rejects at once.

Or is it meant that He is the Father in manifestation as Man? So, then, are you and so am I His servants. For the Father is in all of us. Or is it that in Him was the fullness of the Father, undivided? So in you and in me also dwells the Father, for Him it is not possible to divide.

Yet if it be said that the Whole of the Father dwells in Him but not in us, I say that is an opinion and no more, and also an illogical one; for if the Father as a Whole dwells in the Christ, then either the Christ is the Father without distinction, and none else, or the Whole Father dwelling in the Christ must cease to dwell in Himself of necessity. This also is not reason.

So it is first necessary that we understand that the Father is the Name we give to the highest aspect of God we are able to think of. And even this we do not understand, for it is frankly confessed that He is beyond our understanding. I cannot define Him to you, for I have not seen Him Who to all less than Himself is not visible entirely. What I have seen is a Manifestation of Him in Presence Form, and that is the highest I have attained hereto.

Then the Christ in His Unity with the Father must be also above us as to our understanding, as He is above us in Himself. He tells us so much as we are able to think of, but not to understand very much. He manifested the Father, and such qualities of the Holy Supreme as were capable of manifestation in the body to us. Little more we know, but grow in knowledge as we grow in humility and reverential love. As He is One with the Father, so we are One with Him. And we dwell in the Father by our dwelling in Him Who is the blending of what we call the Human and the Divine. The Father is greater than He, as He Himself once said. By how much greater He did not say, and we could not have understood had He told us.

It may be said by those who read this that I have cut away the scaffolding and left no building within. My purpose, friend, I stated at the first. It was not now to rear a building, but rather to point out that the first thing to build is a sure foundation; and that any structure raised on one not sure must, now or later, fall, and much labour be in vain. And this indeed have men been doing more than they realize; and that is why so much is misty when it might be plain to view. Not all, of course, but enough to make the road much brighter than it is.

I speak not so much to instruct, in this present message, but rather to give men pause. For ratiocination may be fascinating to certain minds, but is not meat for the soldier. It flatters with its perfect logic and well balanced argument, but is not durable to withstand the wear and tear of the wide elements of the spheres. It is not always so wise to affirm, as to say, "I do not know this—yet". Pride often blinds one to the beauty of a humble mind; and it is not true that he who answers a deep problem off-hand is a fountain of wisdom; for assurance is sometimes nearly akin to arrogance, and arrogance is nowise true or lovely.

You and I, my friend and ward, are One in Him Whose Life is our assurance of Life continued. In Him we meet and bless each other, as I bless you now, and thank you for your kindly thoughts towards me. #

Wednesday, November 19, 1913

And so, dear friend and ward, my words to you are such as many will not receive; yet know this, that many shall come from east and west and sit down at the Feast of the Christ who without knowing Him as to His Natural Divinity, yet love Him for His human kindness and love; for that, at least, they all can understand. And none can comprehend the other His aspect in the fullness of its meaning. And so let us think of other things, and first the relation men incarnate should foster towards Him if they would progress in the way He showed them.

Foremost must they love. That is the first commandment of all, and the greatest. And hard have men found it to keep. They all agree that to love one another is good; and when they come to translate the sentiment into action, how sadly do they fail. And yet, without love no thing in all the universe would stand, but fall into

189

decay and dissolution. It is the love of God which energizes through all that is; and we can see that love, if we look for it, everywhere. The best way to understand many things is to contrast them with their opposites. The opposite of love is dissolution; because that comes of refraining from the exertion to love. Hatred is also of the opposite, and yet not the essence of it; because hatred of one person is often a mistaken method of expressing love to another.

And what is said of persons is also true of doctrines and aims. Many express their devotion to one cause by their hatred of another. It is foolish and faulty, but not altogether of evil. When a man hates another man, however, he is likely to cease to love more and more until it becomes an effort to love anything at all.

This is one of those things which make for difficulty in this life of the spheres. For not until a man has learned to love all without hating any is he able to progress in this land where love means light, and those who do not love move in dim places where they lose their way, and often become so dull in mind and heart that their perception of the truth is as vague as that of outward things.

There are, on the other part, mansions here which sparkle with light in every stone, and send forth radiance over the country round to a great distance by reason of the high purity in love of those who dwell in them.

Will you describe such a, residence as this, and those who live in it? It would help more than this general description, I think.

It is not easy, as you will know one day. And if I accede to your request, you will understand the result will not be true to fact, inasmuch as it will be inadequate. Nevertheless, I will do as you desire. What residence particularly would you wish me to describe?

Tell me of your own, please.

In the Tenth Sphere are conditions which do not obtain in those of lower degree, least of all in your own sphere of earth. If it were possible that I should take you now into that sphere you would not see anything at all, because your condition is not yet fitted to it. What you would see would be a mist of light, more or less intense according to what region of that sphere you were in. In the lower spheres you would see more, but not all, and what you were able to see you would not understand in every part.

Suppose you take a fish out of the water and put him in a globe and take him through a town, how, much, think you, would he firstly see, and secondly understand? I think he would see some few inches beyond the circumference of his habitat—the water, which is his natural environment. Put your face where he can see you, and then your hand instead. What would he know of these things?

So would you be in these spheres; and only by training would you be able to energize and use your faculties therein with ease and profit. Now further, how would you, in the language of the fishes, describe to them the Abbey of Westminster, or even your own village church? If that fish were to make known to you how unreasonable you were when you told him you were hindered by his own limitations; or if he told you that he did not believe there was such a place as the church or Abbey, which you named but could not describe to him, how would you convince him that the unreason was of his own, and not of your making?

Still, since you wish it, I will tell you what I can of my own house and home; and you will probably think I might have done better when I finish, and best of all had I refrained altogether.

The country in which we built our house touches many spheres, and among them those whose natures radiate many colours according to their virtues, and which coincide most nearly with those of the people with whom I dwell. These colours are mostly other than those you know, but all those you know are here, and in almost infinite combination and hue. According to the occupation in which we are mentally engaged at any time the blend of colours varies, and the atmosphere takes on that tint. Then the house also vibrates and responds to the thoughts and aspirations, whether of prayer sent onwards, or help willed backward through the spheres behind us, in which direction lies the earth plane.

Music also proceeds from us, not necessarily by mouth, but more often directly from the heart; and this is taken up also in response by the buildings around us, which are part of our energizing; and also the trees and flowers and all plant life is affected and responds. Thus colour and music are not merely inanimate here, but fraught with our life, and vibrate to our will.

The house is four-square, and yet the walls are not four alone, nor at angles each to the others. They, too, are blended, and the outer and inner atmosphere mingles through them. These walls are not for our protection, but for other uses, and one is to concentric our vibrations, to focus them in their transmission to distant regions where our help is needed and desired. Thus we reach the earth also and sense your doings there, and send you words of instruction, or help in other forms, in answer to the prayers which come to us for us to deal with.

Here also descend those of higher spheres and, by means of these houses and other influences prepared, become tangible to us that we may commune with them on matters which perplex us. From this house also we send such strength to those who from time to time are commissioned to us from the lower spheres as enables them, for the period of their sojourn among us, to endure the conditions of this sphere with no great discomfort; and also to converse with and to see and hear us, which otherwise they might not do.

As to the aspect of this house from without, I will give you the description of one of those of a lower sphere which is nearer your own. He told me that when he came in sight of it he was reminded of the words, "a city which is set on a hill whose light cannot be hid". He was a long distance away, but paused and descended to the ground to rest (for he came so far by aerial travel). He shaded his eyes, and gradually was able to look again at the mansion on the hill, far away, in its brightness.

He said he saw the great towers; but they shone so brightly with their blue light that he could not tell where they actually ended, because the light shot up into the heavens above and seemed to continue them there indefinitely. Then the domes—some were red and some gold, and the light from these was likewise too dazzling to see where they ended, or what was their size. The gates and walls likewise shone silver and blue and red and violet, and blazed with dazzling light which bathed the hill below, and the foliage of the trees around, and he wondered how he would enter and not be consumed.

BOOK II: THE HIGHLANDS OF HEAVEN

But we saw him, and sent messengers to deal with that his difficulty; and when at last he turned to bless us and depart, his mission being ended, he said to us, "A thought strikes upon me at this time of parting. My fellow-workers will ask me what manner of place is that to which I have been; and how shall I tell them of this glory when once again I am altogether of my own sphere, and resume its more straitened powers?" And we replied, "Son, you will never quite be as you were, hereafter. For in you will remain somewhat of this sphere's light and perception. But what you in your heart are able to remember will be of larger measure than you can give to them. For they would not understand if you could tell them; and to tell them you would perforce have to use the language which is current here.

"Therefore tell them to bend their wills to further development, and one day they shall come and see for themselves what you have seen but are unable to relate."

And so he went away in great joy uplifted. This be your own also, friend, and the words we gave him now I give to you. #

CHAPTER III: THE EARTHLY AND THE HEAVENLY

Recurring science—Tales of faerie and magic—The passing of materialism—The interrelation of spheres—Purified by suffering—Origin of species—Man's place in the universe.

Friday, November 21, 1913

NOT every one who runs reads aright, for they who run are sometimes of too impatient a mind in regard to those things which are not of apparent importance, and only the apparent is of importance to such as these. And so it comes to pass that much that is written very plainly is no word to them, and its message of significance is left unheeded. This is so in the various signs which are written in what men term nature; that is, the surface phenomena of spirit power energizing in and through matter. Thus it is also in the movement of peoples and nations, as they work out their destiny according to their own proper and peculiar characters.

And thus it is, in perhaps a less degree, in the discoveries of science, as popularly understood. Let us for a short while consider this last and see if there is any message to those who would search more deeply than most, who have time to run only and not to read.

Science, as history, repeats itself, but never in exact duplicate. Broad principles govern, from time to time, the search for knowledge, and are succeeded by others in their turn which, having served, then also fall behind into a secondary place in order that other principles may receive the more concentrated and undivided attention of the race. But from time to time, as the ages go by, these principles return again—not in the same order of sequence—to receive the attention of a new race. And so the march of human progress goes on. Items of discovery also are lost and found anew, often in other than their original guise, and with some strange features added, and other old features lacking.

In order to make what is here set down more plain, I will come to details by way of example. There was a time when science did not mean what it means to men today: when there was a soul in science, and the outer manifestation in matter was of secondary interest. Thus it was with alchemy, astrology, and even engineering. It was known in those days that the world was ruled from many spheres, and ministered to by countless hosts of servants, acting freely of their own will but within certain strait limits laid down by those of greater power and higher authority. And men in those days studied to find out the different grades and degrees of those spiritual workers, and the manner of their service in the different departments of nature and of human life, and the amount of power exercised by each several class. And they found out a considerable number of facts, and classified them.

But inasmuch as these facts, laws and regulations and conditions were not of the earth sphere but of the spiritual, they were fain to express them in a language apart from that of common use. When another generation grew up whose energies, were directed in other ways, these, not considering well what manner of knowledge was contained in the lore of their ancestors, said the language was allegorical, or symbolic; and thus doing they also made the facts themselves assume a shadowy form, until at last there was little of reality left.

Thus it happened with regard to the study of the spiritual powers of varying degree and race, and this issued in the fairy tales of Europe and the magic stories of the East. These are really the surviving lineal and legitimate descendants of the science of the past, added to, subtracted from, and distorted in many ways. And yet if you study to read these tales in the light of what I have said, you will see that, when you have separated the essentials from the more modern embroidering, there are to be found there embedded, like the cities of Egypt under the sands of the ages, solid facts of science or knowledge as spiritually considered.

Would you, please, give a specific instance, by way of illustration?

There is the story of Jack and the Beanstalk. In the first place, look at the name. Jack is colloquial for John, and the original John was he who wrote the Book of the Revelation. The Beanstalk is an adaptation of Jacob's Ladder, by which the upper, or spiritual, spheres were reached.

Those spheres once attained, are found to be real countries and regions, with natural scenery, houses and treasures. But these are sometimes held by guardians not altogether in amity with the human race who, nevertheless, by boldness and skill of mind are able to wrest those treasures away and return to earth with them. And also they are able, by natural quickness of character, to prevent those guardians from regaining possession of these treasures of wisdom and depriving the human race of the right won by the conquest of the bolder sort.

Now, this is picturesque, and is made to assume a quaint and even ludicrous guise by reason of its being handed down from age to age by those who did not understand its deeper import. Had they done so most certainly they had not nicknamed the original as Jack. But, as his customary attire of dress will show you, this came about in an age when things holy and spiritual were had in light esteem by reason of the inability of men to realize the actual presence of spiritual beings among them. So, also, they garbed a demon, and gave him spiked ears and a tail, and for a similar reason—that his actuality to them was mythical. The personality they made of him was mythical indeed.

The story I have named is one of many. Punch and Judy might represent the transactions in which the two who stood out most reprobate were Pilate and Iscariot. And from the manner in which these solemn, and indeed awful, incidents are related, the levity of the age in such matters is apparent. Well, so it is, and has been ever. But now, to-day, the spiritual is returning among men to claim a place, if not adequate to its importance, at least of greater consideration than of these last centuries.

Thus, in other guise outwardly, but inwardly more akin, the broad principle which governed the Egyptian astrologers, and the wisdom which Moses learned and used to such effect, is returning to-day to lift men up a little higher and to put a meaning into that dead materialism of the past which, handling things produced of the energizing of life-shells, bones and fossil stones—denied the Author of Life His place in life's grand arena. It spoke of the orderly working of natural law—and denied the One Source of all order and all working. It spoke of beauty—and forgot that beauty is not unless the spirit of man perceives it, and that spirit is because He Who is Spirit is for ever.

We are watching, and we are guiding as we may and opportunity is given us. If men respond to our prompting there is

196

an age to come more full of light and the beauty of love and life than that just passing away. And I think they will respond, for the new is better than the old, and from behind us we feel the pressing of those of higher wisdom and power as we look earthward. And so we do what we are impressed is their intention and desire.

We are not given to be able to see very far ahead. That is a special study, and it is not of the duties of the band of workers to which I am attached. But we are glad to find our endeavours in many hearts meet with ready response, and we hope for greater opportunity, as years go by, to show men how near we are to them, and how great they are potentially if they but be humble in spirit, and quiet, and strive after holiness and purity in thought and desire, looking to Him, the Example of man at his greatest, and seeking to reproduce in themselves that beauty of holiness they may read, even as they run; for a glance at that One His Life should entrance one who has in himself to see what beauty is. For Him we love, and to Him we do reverence, Whose peace be to you in all things, all your days, dear friend. Amen. #

Monday, November 24, 1913

Moreover, friend, it is a good thing and a helpful to bear in mind our presence at all times; for we are near, and that in ways both many and various. When we are personally near at hand we are able to impress you with helpful thoughts and intuitions, and so to order events that your work may be facilitated and your way more clear than otherwise it would appear to you. When in person we are in our own spheres, we still have means whereby we are informed not alone of what has happened in and around you, but also what is about to happen, if the composition of circumstances pursue its normal course.

Thus preserving contact with you, we maintain and ensure our guardianship that it be continuous and unceasing, and our watchfulness that it shall in nowise fail on your behalf. For here, and through the spheres between us and you, are contrivances by which intelligence is sent on from one sphere to those beyond and, when necessity require it, we enjoin others to carry out some mission to you, or, if the occasion so requires, we come to earth ourselves, as I have done at this time.

But further still, and in addition to this, we are able each to come into contact with his own charge direct in certain ways, and to influence events from our own place. Thus you will understand that the whole economy of the Creator, through its manifold spheres of light, is unified in action and correlated. So that no part is but is influenced by all those other parts, and what you do on earth not only is registered in the heavens, but has effect on our minds and thoughts, and so on our lives.

Be, therefore, of very careful mind and will; for your doings in thought and your doings in word and your doings in act are all of great import, not alone to those you see and touch around you, but also to those around you unseen and untouched by you, but who see and touch you constantly and often. Not these alone, but those who go about their business in their own spheres are so affected. It is so in my own, I know, and how much higher I do not hazard to say.

But, were you to ask me, I would reply that your doings are multiplied by transmission through the spheres of light by seventy times seven; and that no end is found to their journey within the ken of man or angel. For I little doubt, if that at all, they find out at last the very Heart of God. Be ye, therefore, perfect, because your Father Who is in the Heaven of the Heavens is perfect; and no imperfect thing can find acceptance and approval to enter where He is in His awful Beauty.

And what, then, of those spheres where they who do not love good and beauty dwell? Well, we are also in touch with those, and the help sent there is as readily sent as to the earth sphere; for those realms of darkness are but further removed, and not disconnected, from us. Those who are there are learning their lesson as are you in your earth sphere, but theirs is more dim than yours—no more than this. For still are they sons and daughters of the One All Father, and so our brothers and sisters too. And these we help when they cry, as we help you at your petition. It has been given you already to know somewhat of the conditions of life there obtaining. But what your mother wrote I may here supplement a little.

BOOK II: THE HIGHLANDS OF HEAVEN

Light and darkness are states of the spirit, as you know. When those dwelling 'in the darkness' cry for light, that means that they are become out of touch with their environment. So we send them what help is needed; and that is usually direction by which they find their way—not into regions of light, where they would be in torture, and utterly blinded, but, into a region less dark, and tinctured by just so much of light as they may bear until they outgrow that state and cry in their longing for more.

When a spirit leaves a dark region for one less dark he experiences an immediate sense of relief and comfort by comparison with his former state. For now his environment is in harmony with his own inner state of development. But as he continues to develop in aspiration after good, he gradually becomes out of harmony with his surroundings, and then, in ratio to his progress, so his discomfort increases until it becomes not less than agony. Then in his helplessness, and approaching near to despair, having come to that pass when his own endeavours can go no further, he cries for help to those who are able to give it in God's Name, and they enable him one stage onward nearer to the region where dimness, rather than darkness, reigns. And so he at last comes to the place where light is seen to be light, and his onward way is henceforth not through pain and anguish, but from joy to greater joy, and hence to glory and glory greater still.

But oh, the long, long ages some do take until they come into that light, ages of anguish and bitterness; and know all the time that they may not come to their friends who wait them until their own unfitness is done away; and that those great regions of darkness and lovelessness must first be trod. But do not mistake my words of their meaning. This is no vengeance of an angry God, my ward and friend. GOD IS OUR FATHER; AND HE IS LOVE.

All this sorrow is of necessity, and is ordered by those laws which govern the sowing, and the reaping of that which is sown. Even here, in my own place, where many things both wonderful and lovely we have learned, yet not yet have we attained to plumb and sound this mystery to its lowest depth. We do understand, as we were unable when in the earth life, that it is of love that these things are ordained. I say we are able to understand where formerly we were able but to say we trusted and believed. Yet

199

little more of this awful mystery do we know; and are content to wait until it is made more plain to us. For we know enough to be able to believe that all is wise and good; as those in those dark hells will know one day. And this is our comfort that they will and must be drawn onward and upward into this great and beautiful universe of light, and that then they will confess, not only that what is is just, but that it is of love and wisdom too, and be content.

Such have I known, and do know, and am of their number in the service of the Father. And it seems to me their praise and blessing of Him are nowise lacking in love in comparison of ours who have not journeyed

through those awful depths. Nay, friend, for I will confess to you this one thing else: that sometimes, as we have paid our united worship together prostrate before the Light of the Throne of the Heavens, I have felt that there is something in their worship lacking in mine; and have almost half wished that I might have that in me too. Yet this would not be right; and doubtless the Father takes, in His Love, that is in us to give Him. Nevertheless, it is very sweet, that saying of the Master, and rings true here where love is seen in the beauty of its nakedness: Because she is forgiven much, therefore she loves the more.

God keep you in His Love, my friend and ward, and nought else matters so you do respond to His sweet caress, and rest in Him. Amen. #

Tuesday, November 25, 1913

If it were but a little of faith a man should have in him he would be able to understand what I have written by your mind and hand. But not to many is it given to see into the truth of things, and to know them as true indeed. So has it been down the ages, friend, and so will it be yet for ages many. So far it is given to see, but yet we look forward and onward still, and ahead we think we see a world of men moving and doing in a greater light than that which is about them to-day; and in that day they will see and understand how near are we to them, not in books alone, but in the daily lives they lead. Meanwhile we do our part, ever watchful, ever hopeful

200

and, if our joy is sometimes mingled with a sadness we cannot altogether put away while men and we do not go hand in hand, as is our wish, still, again, we know that we are coming nearer together; and all is well.

And now to our present task, my ward; for while it is day I would that we work together; for when the night descends then you will find another day, but not as now; and other opportunities of service, but not such as these. So let us do what we can while we have command of these present conditions, and we shall do better work when wider spheres are opened to us, both to you and me.

Science, as you know it, is not coterminous with what you know, for we look deeper into those fundamentals which are of spiritual origin; and worldly science is but now beginning to admit this truth into her councils. Thus we are already drawing nearer each to other; or rather it would be more true to say that those among you who are searching into the meaning of the phenomena of your sphere are coming nearer to us as we draw them upward to higher and deeper searching. For this we are thankful, and it emboldens us to continue in the same path; and this we do in sure faith that men will continue to follow where we lead, so we be careful to lead them wisely and well.

I now would tell you somewhat of the inner meaning of what men call the origin of species in animal life. But now, and at once, I would say the term is all too large; for the origin of the different creations in animal life is not found in the realm of matter, but has its genesis in these realms. We have learned here that, when the Universe of systems was moving towards its present form and constitution, those who had charge to watch and work took their counsels from those of higher degree, and on those counsels shaped their own wisdom.

At that time it was seen that in the heavenly spheres there were many diversities both of the forms of life as bodily manifest, and of mind in its working. And it was resolved that the universe was meant to reflect the personalities and types of those who were commissioned to carry out the work of its development. To this conclusion they were divinely guided, for when their plan was completed it was given them by revelation to know that the Divine

201

approval was upon it in general kind; but that it was not of absolute perfection. Nevertheless, it received the imprimatur of the All Father Who vouchsafed them freedom to work out His will according to their own capacities and powers.

Thus arose the different orders and species of animal and vegetable and mineral life, and also of human type and racial character. And these things being initiated, again the Divine Mind pronounced His general approval or, as our Bible has it, He found it to be "very good".

But high as were those who were chief in this matter of creation, yet they were less than the Only Omnipotent and, as the work of ordering the universe was very great, and wide in extent, the imperfections of their work became magnified as they worked out; so that, to a single mind, and one of low degree, as is that of a man, those imperfections loomed vast and great. For it is not competent to one who is so small and undeveloped to be able to see both good and evil equally, but the evil is the easier seen to him, and the good too high and wonderful for him to grasp its meaning and power.

But if men would keep in mind one thing, they would find the existence of this imperfection, mingled with so much more that is wonderful and wise, the easier to understand. That one thing is this: that the Universe was not created for him alone, any more than the sea was created alone for the use of the sea-animals that dwell therein, or the air for the birds. Man invades both sea and air and calls them of his kingdom to conquer and to use. And he is right. They do not belong to the fish and the birds. The dominion is to the greater being, and that being is man. He is lord by permission, and rules the earth in which, and over which, his Maker has placed him.

But there are greater than he and, as he rules the lesser and uses them for the development of his faculties and personality, so these rule him and use him likewise. And this is just and wise, for these Angels and Archangels and Princes and Powers of God are His servants also, and their development and training are necessary as that of men. But by how much these are greater than he, respectively, so must the means and material of their training be of higher nature and sublimity than those which are given him to use.

BOOK II: THE HIGHLANDS OF HEAVEN

According to the innate power of any being, man or angel, so is his environment proportioned and constituted.

Let men remember this and keep it in mind, and then they will the better appreciate the dower of freewill given to them, a gift which no one of all the heavenly hierarchy may take from him. And they would not if they might; for in so doing their material would be deteriorated in quality, and the less capable of enabling them in their own advancement.

Now, I fear that some who read what I have written will say that hereby man becomes merely the tool of those of higher grade, to do with him what they will for their own advantage. Not so; and for the reason I have just stated—that he is, and ever must remain, a freewill being.

But more, the one great power which animates those, who serve the Father here is Love. These are no mere despots of oppression. Power and oppression are correlatives of earth creation. Here power means an issuing forth of love, and the greater the power the greater the love which is sent forth. And this, moreover. Let those whose fight with evil is fierce and dire remember and realize well the privilege and high destiny which is theirs to attain. For in this is a warrant and sure token that man has been permitted into the Council and work of those of very high degree, to join with them in this great task of working out salvation for the whole universe on the lines laid down so long ago. And this task is one which a man with courage will grapple with full eagerly, for it is he who will understand so much as this: that what angels and Princes of high estate are doing he is doing with them in his own sphere and degree and, knowing this, he will rejoice and be strong.

Seeing also that his work is one with our own, and ours is his, and with only one object set before us both, which is the betterment of all life and all things, he will know that our strength is at his call, so he call wisely and with due humility and simple trust. For so we delight to help men, who are our comrades in this fight, and our fellow-workers in the one great field of the Universe of God.

We see more than you do of the awful travail of those who err from this service, and yet we do not despair, because we see also the more clearly the meaning and purpose of it all. And thus seeing, we know that men will one day rejoice as we do when they too shall, each in his own time, ascend to the higher spheres of service and, from this point of vantage, continue his development. In that day he too will use for his training the material we are using, and of which he is a part and portion, when others have taken his place, and he the place of those who now are lifting him upward. "To him that overcometh", said the Christ, "will I give to sit with Me in My Throne, even as I overcame, and am set down with My Father in His Throne". To the strong is the Kingdom, my dear charge and ward, and to the one who has shall be given. This much now, and I must cease for this time. But the matter is much greater than I have been able to tell in this short message. If God permit I will tell you more anon.

And now, do well and you shall fare well: and if you be strong, then out of your strength shall sweetness come. For so it is in these realms that they are most sweet and lovely whose strength is greatest. This remember, and it shall solve many problems which perplex men much. God's light be with and around you always, and you shall not stumble then. #

CHAPTER IV: EARTH THE VESTIBULE OF HEAVEN

Inspiration—Like attracts like—The squire and his wife—Our spiritual status—The man who thought he knew—The penalty of spiritual blindness.

Wednesday, November 26, 1913

MANY things there are of which I might speak to you, matters of organization, and of the exercise of power as its influence and effect are seen by us as it passes on its way through our spheres to that of earth.

Some of these things you would not be able to understand, and others, perhaps, but few among you would believe if they understood them. So I confine myself to the simpler principles and the mode of their working; and one of these is the modus operandi of the connection obtaining between us and you in the matter of inspiration.

Now, this is a word very expressive if understood aright; and very misleading if not so understood. For, that we inbreathe into the hearts of men knowledge of the truth of God is true. But it is only a very little of the truth. For more than this we do give to them and, with other things, strength to progress and to work God's will, love to work that will from high motive, and wisdom (which is knowledge blended with love) to work God's will aright. And if a man be said to be inspired, this is not a singular case, nor one exceptional.

For all who try to live well, and few do not in some degree, are by us inspired, and so helped. But the act of inbreathing is not a very close way of describing the method of our work. It would the better apply as used subjectively of the one so-called inspired. He breathes in our waves of vibrating energy as we direct those waves to him. So a man breathes in and fills his lungs of the fresh breeze on the hill-side, and is refreshed. Even so he breathes in the refreshing streams of power we waft towards him.

But we would not limit the meaning of the word to those alone who in elegant words tell out to the world some new truth of God, or some old truth refurbished and made as new. The mother tending her child in sickness, the driver of the engine along the railway, the navigator guiding the ship, all, and others, do their work of their peculiar powers self contained, but, as occasion and circumstances require, modified and supplemented by our own. This is so even when the receiver of our help is unaware of our presence; and this more often than not. We give gladly while we are able; and we are able so long as no barrier is opposed to us by him we would help.

This barrier may be raised in many ways. If he be of obstinate mind, then we may not impose on him our counsel; for he is free to will and to do. And some times when we see great need of our help being given, the barrier of sin is interposed and we cannot get through it. Then those who counsel wrongly do their work, and grievous is the plight of those to whom they minister. Each man, and every woman too, chooses his own companions wittingly or unwittingly. If he flout the idea that we are present in the earth sphere, or that any influence may proceed from what to him is the unseen and unknown, that matters not so he be of good intent and right motive. He opposes to us no barrier of absolute negation. We help him gladly, for he is honest, and will some day in his honesty own his error—some day soon.

Only this, that he is not then so sensitive to catch our meaning; and he will often mistake us, not knowing what we would impress upon his mind. If the water-wheel be well oiled on its axle, then the water turns it easily; but if it be rusty, then the force must be increased in volume, and the wear, both of the wheel and its axle, is greater, and it moves more heavily. Also, the sailors may be accurate in obeying the instructions of the captain, even if he were totally strange to them. But if he be known to them well, then they are the better able in the storm, of a dark night, to catch his meaning in the orders he gives, for they know his mind and need little words and few to tell them of his wishes. So they who know us more naturally and more intimately than others are in better fettle to receive our words.

Inspiration, therefore, is of wide meaning and extent in practice. The prophets of old time—and those of to-day—received our instruction according to the quickening of their faculties. Some were able to hear our words, some to see us—both as to their spiritual bodies—others were impressed mentally. These and other ways we employ, and all to one end, namely: to impart through them to their fellow-men instruction as to the way they should go, and in what way they should order their lives to please God, as we are able to understand His will from this higher plane. Our counsel is not of perfection, nor infallible. But it never leads astray those who seek worthily and with much prayer, and with great love. These are God's own, and they are a great joy to us their fellow servants.

Nor need we go far afield to find them, for there is more good in the world than evil, and, as in each good and evil is proportioned, so are we able to help, and so is our ability limited.

So do every one these two things—see that your light is kept burning as they who wait for their Lord, for it is His will we do in this matter, and it is His strength we bring. Prayers are allotted us to answer and His answer is sent by us His servants. So be watchful and wakeful for our coming, who are of those who came to Him in the Wilderness, and in Gethsemane (albeit I think they would be of much higher degree than I). And the other to bear in your mind is this: See you keep your motive high and noble, and seek not selfishly, but for others' welfare. We minister best to the progress of those who seek our help for the benefit of their brethren rather than their own. In giving we ourselves receive, and so do you. But the larger part of motive must be to give, as He said, and that way the greater blessing lies, and that for all.

Remember His word, "I have power to lay down My life—but I lay it down for My sheep". This He did in very truth, and with no dissembling of motive. Nevertheless, in laying down that life He took life up again more glorious, and that only because His gift was empty of self, and full of love. So do you, and you will find your sweetness in the giving and receiving, both. It is a task most difficult of perfect fulfillment. But it is the right and good way, and must needs be trod. And He has shown us how. The vessels of the flower empty themselves of their scent to the enjoyment of man, but only to be filled again with more and, so doing, come to more perfect maturity day by day. The word of kindness is returned, and two people made happy by the initial act of one. Kind words later beget kind deeds. And so is love multiplied, and with love, joy and peace. And they who love to give, and give for love's own sake are shooting golden darts which fall into the streets of the Heavenly City, and are gathered up and carefully stored away till they who sent them come and receive their treasure once again with increase. #

Thursday, November 27, 1913

Following on what I have given you, I may add that very few there are who realize in any great degree the magnitude of the forces which are ambient around men as they go about their business day by day. These forces are real, nevertheless, and close at hand. Nay, they mingle with your own endeavours, whether you will or no. And these powers are not all good, but some are malicious, and some are betweenwise, and neither definitely good nor bad.

When I say "powers" and "forces", it is of necessary consequence that personalities be present with them to use them. For know this, not as of formal assent, but consenting thereto *ex animo*, that you are not alone, and cannot be or act alone, but must act and will and contrive in partnership, and your partners you do elect, whether you do so willingly or no.

So it behooves that all be curious in their selection, and this may be assured by prayer and a right life. Think of God with reverence and awe, and of your fellow-men with reverence and love; and do all things as knowing we watch you and mark down your inner mind with exact precision, and that, as you are and become now, so you will be when you are awakened here; and what things now to you are material and positive and seem very real will then be of another sphere, and your eyes will open on other scenes, and earth be spoken of as that other sphere, and the life of earth as a journey made and finished, and the money and furniture, and the trees in your garden, and all you now seem to own as your peculiar property will not be any more at hand.

Then you will be shown what place and treasures and friends you have earned in the school of endeavour just ended and left behind for ever. And you will be either full of sorrow and regret, or compassed with joy unspeakable and light and beauty and love, all at your service, and those your friends who have come on before, now eager to show you some of the scenes and beauties of their present home. Now what, think you, will that man do whose life on earth has been a close compartment, with no window for outlook into these spiritual realms? He will do as I have seen many do. He will do according as his heart is fashioned. Most such are unready to own their error, for such are usually positive that the opinions builded up during a lifetime, and which have served them so well, cannot be so grievously in error. These have much to pass through before the light will serve their atrophied spiritual sight.

But those who have schooled themselves to sit loose to what are counted for riches and pleasures on earth shall find their laps not large enough for the treasures brought by loving hands, nor their eyes so quick as they may catch all the many smiles of welcome and delight at the surprise they show that, after all, the real reality is just begun, and the new is much better than the old. And now, my ward and friend, let me show you a scene which will point what I have written.

On a hill-side green and golden, and with the perfume of many flowers hovering about like music kissed by colour, there is an old gabled house with many turrets and windows like those which first in England were filled with glass. Trees and lawns and, down in the hollow, a large lake where birds of many colours, and very beautiful, sport themselves. This is not a scene of your sphere, but one on this side of the Veil. It were of little profit that I argue to show the reasonableness of such things being here. It is so, and that men should doubt that all that is good and beautiful on earth is here with beauty enhanced, and loveliness made more lovely is, on our part, a matter of wonder quite as great.

On one of the towers there stands a woman. She is clad in the colour of her order, and that colour is not one you know on earth; so I cannot give it a name. But I would describe it as golden-purple; and that will, I fear, convey little to you. She looks out towards the horizon far away across the lake, where low-lying hills are touched by the light beyond. She is fair to look upon. Her figure is more perfect and beautiful than that of any woman on earth, and her face more lovely. Her eyes shine out a radiance of lovely violet hue, and on her brow a silver star shines and sparkles as it answers to her thoughts within. This is the jewel of her order. And if beauty were wanted to make her beauty more complete, it is there in just a tinge of wistfulness, which but adds to the peace and joy of her countenance. This is the Lady of the House where live a large number of maidens who are in her charge to do her will and go forth on what mission she desires from time to time. For the House is very spacious.

Now, if you study her face you will see at once that she is there expectant; and presently a light springs up and flashes from her eyes those beautiful violet rays; and from her lips a message goes; and you know that by reason of the flash of light of blue and pink and crimson which darts from beneath her lips and seems to take wing far too quickly for you to follow it across the lake.

Then a boat is seen coming quickly from the right between the trees which grow on its borders, and the oars flash and sparkle, and the spray around the gilded prow is like small spheres of golden glass mingled with emeralds and rubies as it falls behind. The boat comes to the landing-place, and a brilliantly robed throng leap on to the marble steps which lead them up to the green lawn above. One is not so quick, however. His face is suffused with joy, but he seems also full of wonder, and his eyes are not quite used to the quality of the light which bathes all things in a soft shimmering radiance.

Then from the great entrance, and down towards the party, comes the Lady of the House, and pauses a short distance from the party. The newcomer looks on her as she stands there, and utter perplexity is in his gaze, rapt and intent. Then, at last, she addresses him, and in homely words this shining saint of God welcomes her husband, "Well, James, now you have come to me—at last, dear, at last". But he hesitates. The voice is hers, but different. Moreover, she died an old woman with grey hair, and an invalid. And now she stands before him a lovely woman, not young nor old, but of perfect grace and beauty of eternal youth.

"And I have watched you, dear, and been so near you a the time. And that is past and over now, and your loneliness is gone for ever, dear. For now we are together once again, and this is God's Summerland where you and I will never grow old again, and where our boys and Nellie will come when they have finished what is theirs to do in the earth life." Thus she talked, that he might get his bearings; and this he did at last, and suddenly. He burst into tears of joy, for it came to him that this indeed was his wife and sweetheart; and love overcame his awe. He came forward with his left hand over his eyes, just glancing up now and then, and when he was near she came quickly and took him into her arms and kissed him, and then throwing one arm about his neck, she took his hand in hers and led him up the steps, with slow and gentle dignity, into the House she had prepared for him.

Yes, that House was the heavenly counterpart of their home in Dorset, where they had lived all their married life until she passed hence, and where he had remained to mourn her absence. This, my ward, I have set down by way of pointing, with homely incident, the fact that the treasures of heaven are not mere words of sentiment, but solid and real and, if you will not press the word, material. Houses and friends and pastures and all things dear and beautiful you have on earth are here. Only here they are of more sublime beauty, even as the people of these realms are of a beauty not of earth. Those two had lived a good life as country squire and wife, both simple and God fearing, and kindly to the poor and the rich alike. These have their reward here; and that reward is often unexpected in its nature as it was to him.

This meeting I myself witnessed, for I was one of those who brought him on his way to the House, being then of that sphere where this took place.

What sphere was it, please?

The Sixth. And now, friend, I will close, and would I might show you now some of these beauties which are in store for the simple-hearted who do what they can of love, and seek the righteousness of God to please Him rather than the high places among men. These shall shine as the stars and as the sun, and all around them shall take on more loveliness by reason of their presence near. It is written so, and it is true. #

Friday, November 28, 1913

We will now try to think of that passage where the Christ of God and Saviour of man speaks to His own as being chosen out of the world. Not alone chosen of the world, but taken out of it. If, then, out of the world, in what abode do they dwell?

First it is necessary to understand in what sense our Saviour speaks of the world. The world in this case is the realm where matter is of dominant importance to the mind, and those who count it so are dwelling, as to their spiritual state and spiritual bodies, in another sphere than those who hold the inverse idea, namely, that matter is but the mode of manifestation adopted and used by spiritual beings, and subservient to those who use it, as a workman uses clay or iron.

Those who are held to be in the world, therefore, are spiritually in the sphere which is near the earth, and these are sometimes called earthbound spirits. It matters not whether they be clothed with material bodies, or have shed them and stand discarnate; these are bound and chained to the world, and cannot rise into the spheres of light, but have their conversation among those who move in the dim regions about the planet's surface. These, then, are holden of the earth, and are actually within the circumference of the earth sphere.

But He had lifted His chosen out of this sphere into the spheres of light and, although still incarnate, yet as to their spiritual bodies, they were in those higher spheres. And this explains their manner of life and conduct subsequently. It was from these spheres that they drew all that indomitable courage and great joy and fearlessness which enabled them to count the world as being not of their necessity, but merely as the field where they must fight their battle, and then go home to their friends awaiting. What is true of them is true to-day.

It is from the spheres of gloom that fear and uncertainty come to so many, for these are the lot of those who dwell therein discarnate, and not quickened so that they may be able to realize their spiritual environment nevertheless; move and energize in it, and receive in themselves those qualities for which they have fitted themselves by their manner of thinking and of life.

So it is scientifically exact to say that a man may be in the world as to his material body, but not of the world as to his spiritual body.

BOOK II: THE HIGHLANDS OF HEAVEN

When these two sorts of men come over here they go each to his own proper sphere and, for lack of clarity of reasoning and judgment, many are very much surprised to find themselves allotted to a place of which they had heard with their outer ears, but had not further inquired as to its reality.

Now, in order to make this more clear, which is of the very elements of knowledge to us on this side, I will tell you of an incident of my own knowledge and experience.

I was once sent to receive a man who required some careful dealing with, for he was one who had many rather decided opinions as to these realms, and whose mind had been filled with ideas of what was right and proper as to the life continued here. I met him as his spirit attendants brought him from the earth region, and led him to the grove of trees where I awaited him. 'He walked between them and seemed dazed somewhat, as if he sought what he could not find.

I motioned the two to set him to stand alone before me, and they retired some little distance behind him.

He could not see me plainly at first; but I concentrated my will upon him, and at last he looked at me searchingly.

Then I said to him, "Sir, you seek what you cannot find, and I may help you. First tell me, how long have you been in this country of ours?"

"That," he answered, "I find difficult to say. I had certainly arranged to go abroad, and thought it was into Africa I was going. But I do not find this place in any way what I expected."

"No, for this is not Africa; and from that country you are a long distance away."

"What is the name of this country, then? And what tribe of people are these? They are white, and very handsome, but I never came on any quite like them, even in my reading."

"Well, there you are not quite exact for a scientist such as you are. You have read of these people without realizing that they were anything more than puppets without life and natural qualities. These are those you have read of as saints and angels. And such am UP

"But," he began, and then paused. He did not believe me, and feared to offend, not knowing what consequences should ensue;

for he was in a strange country, among strange folk, and without escort.

"Now," I told him, "you have the biggest task before you you have ever encountered. In all your journeys you have come to no barrier so high and thick as this. For I will be quite plain to you and tell you the truth. You will not believe it. But, believe me, until you do believe it and understand, you will not have peace of mind, nor will you be able to make any progress. What you have before you to do is to take the opinions of a lifetime, turn them upside down and inside out, and own yourself no longer a scholar and great scientist, but the veriest babe in knowledge; and that nearly all you thought worthy of any consideration at all as to this country was either unworthy a thinking being, or absolutely wrong. These are hard words because they are such of necessity. But look well on me, and tell me, if you can read me, whether I be honest and friendly or no."

He looked on me long and very seriously, and said at last, "Though I am altogether at sea as to what you mean, and your words seem to me like those of some misguided enthusiast, yet your face is honest enough, and I think you wish me well. Now, what is it you want me to believe?"

"You have heard of death?"

"Faced it many a time!"

"As you are now facing me. And yet you know neither one nor the other. What kind of knowledge call you that which looks on a thing without knowing what it is?"

"If you will be plain, and tell me something I can understand, I may be able to get the hang of things a little better."

"So. Then first of all you are what you would call dead." At this he laughed outright and said, "Who, are you, and what are you trying to do with me? If you are bent on trying to make a fool of me, say so and be done with it, and let me get on my way. Is there any village near at hand where I can get food and shelter while I think over my future course?"

"You do not require food, for you are not hungry. Nor do you require shelter, for you are not bodily tired. Nor do you observe any sign of night at all."

BOOK II: THE HIGHLANDS OF HEAVEN

At this he paused once again, and then replied, "You are quite right; I am not hungry. It is strange, but it is quite true; I am not hungry. And this day, certainly, has been the longest on record. I don't understand it all."

And he fell into a reverie again. Then I said, "You are what you would call dead, and this is the spirit land. You have left the earth, and this is the life beyond, which you must now live, and come to understand. Until you grasp this initial truth further help I cannot give you. I leave you to think it over; and when you wish for me, if you so should wish, I will come to you. These two gentlemen who led you here are spirits attendant. You may question them and they will answer. Only, this remember. You shall not be suffered to ridicule what they say, and laugh at them, as you did but now at my words. Only if you be humble and courteous will I allow you their company. You have in you much that is of worth; and you have also, as many more I have met, much vanity and foolishness of mind. This I will not suffer you to flaunt in the faces of my friends. So be wise in time and remember. For you are now on the borderland between the spheres of light and those of shade, and it lies in you to be led into the one, or to go, of your own freewill, into the other. May God help you, and that He will if you will."

Then I motioned to the two attendant spirits, and they came and sat down by him; and I left them sitting there together.

What happened? Did he go up or down?

He did not call for me again, and I did not go to him for a long time. He was very inquisitive, and the two, his companions, helped him in every possible way. But he gradually found the light and atmosphere of the place uncomfortable, and was forced to withdraw to a region more dim. Here he made a strenuous effort, and the good at length prevailed in him. But it was a fierce and protracted fight, and one of much galling and bitter humiliation.

Still, he was a brave soul and won. Then they were called by those to whom he had been committed by them, and led him once again to the brighter country.

There I went to meet him, in that same spot in the grove of trees. He was a much more thoughtful man, and gentler, and less ready to scoff. So I looked on him silently, and he looked on me and knew me, and then bent his head in shame and contrition. He was very sorry that he had laughed at my words.

Then he came forward slowly and knelt before me, and I saw his shoulders shake with sobbing as he hid his face in his hands.

So I blessed him, with my hand upon his head, and spoke words of comfort and left him.

It is often thus. #

Monday, December 1, 1913.

Not to many is it given to see the light amid the darkness, nor to know the darkness for what it is. But that is a state of their own making; for to every one who would know the truth there is sent out from these spheres such help and enablement as is needed according to his nature and capacity.

This has ever been, and thus it is to-day. For God is One, not alone as to His Nature, but also as to His manifestation in the outer spheres of His Kingdom.

When He sent forth this present universe of matter He endowed His servants with qualities which made them competent to carry out His purpose, giving them liberty within certain bounds, as I have formerly explained. And one of the laws which governed them was that, among all minor and temporal variations and seeming diversity in the operation of the powers which were put into their hands, unity should be the guiding principle of all, and to that end all should tend eventually.

This principle of unity and consistency has ever been before those high Princes and Dominions, and has never been departed from. Neither is it unregarded today. This men forget, and themselves disregard who marvel that we should interest ourselves in you, our brethren less developed, insomuch as to touch you, and to speak to you and guide you personally and by personal contact of our presence.

Also, it is on our part a marvel that men should be found who hesitate on the way, and fear that to speak to us is a wrong, and displeasing to Him Who Himself came into the world for this same reason; that He might show how both spiritual and material were but two phases of one great Kingdom, and the unity of both together.

Throughout His teaching this is the one great motive, and for this it was that His enemies put Him to death. Had His Kingdom been of this world alone He had not discounted their temporal aspirations, nor their manner of life as to its ease and grandeur. But He showed that the Kingdom was of those higher realms, and that the Church on Earth was but the vestibule to the Presence Chamber. This being so, then the virtues by which nobility should be measured were those which governed rank in these brighter regions, and not the mixed conditions of the lower portion of that Kingdom, as interpreted by the world.

For that they killed Him; and to-day there is remaining too much, as we see it, of their sentiment, both in the Church and in the world outside. And until men do realize us our presence, and our right of consideration as fellow-members of this same Kingdom of the Father, and not until this come to pass, shall men make much advance in the discerning between the light and the darkness. Blind guides there are too many, friend; and they displease us much by their arrogant sniffing at our work and commission.

"Had they known they would not have killed Him—the Lord of Glory."

No, surely; but they did kill Him withal.

Did these present know that we who come to earth on our loving enterprise were angels, they would not have reviled our work of communion and those who rise above the ruck that we may make our whispers heard. No, but they do revile us and those our friends and brethren. And they shall plead their unknowing and their blindness with like effect as those who killed the Master Christ.

Zabdiel, this is no doubt all quite true and just. But I think you are, perhaps, speaking with some heat. Also, it was St. Peter who pleaded for the Jews, was it not, and not the Jews themselves?

Aye, friend, I do speak with heat somewhat, in indignation. But there is another heat more generous, and that is the heat of love. It is not true to think of us as always placid and unmoved. We sometimes are angry; and our anger is always just, or it would

217

soon be corrected from those who are over us and see with eyes more clear than our own. But we do never avenge ourselves—remember you that, and remember it well. Nevertheless, in justice, and in love of our friends and co-workers on the earth plane, we do mete out punishment, and that of duty, to those who deal with them unkindly. But I see you do not favour me in this. I will defer to your inclination, therefore, and leave this matter for this time. But what I have said is true every whit, and worthy to ponder well of those whom it shall be seen to touch.

As to that matter of St. Peter's pleading. Yes, so did he. But keep in mind one more thing also. I speak from this hither side the Veil, and you hear me through it on the earth side. Now, we have here, as you have there, records of history—the history of these realms—which are carefully kept. And from these records we know that in their judgment here those His accusers did plead this blindness, and to little avail. Light was as darkness to them, and darkness to them was as light, because they were themselves of the darkness. They did not know the Light when He came to them, for this same reason. Very well, they were blind and did not know. Now, blindness here in these spheres is not the effect of the shutting off of the outer light, but proceeds from deeper cause. It is not outward but inward, of the essence of a man's nature. Because, therefore, they were blind, to the place of the blind were they sent; that is, to the regions of gloom and anguish.

This age is one of great activity in these regions of light. Much energy is being directed on the earth in all its parts. There is scarcely a church or creed unstirred. It is the light being directed into the darkness, and it is a matter of very great responsibility to those who are still in training in the earth sphere. Let them be curious and very brave to see and own this light.

This is my warning, and I give it with solemn thoughts. For I speak after much experience in this school where we learn much, and more quickly than by the use of a material brain. Let men search humbly and find out the truth of these matters.

For the rest, we do not sue on bended knee. That let them also keep in mind. We do not proffer gifts as slaves to princes. But we do come and stand by you with gifts which gold of earth cannot buy; and to those who are humble and good and of a pure mind we give these gifts of ability to understand the Truth as it is in Jesus of certain conviction of life beyond and of the joy of it, of fearlessness of disaster here or hereafter, and of companionship and comradeship with angels.

Friend, I leave you now, and beg you bear with me if I have said what you have less willingly recorded than at other times. I have not unwittingly thus impressed you. And at another time I will endeavor your compensation in messages of brighter hue. Peace and joy be in your heart, my ward. Amen.

CHAPTER V

THE SCIENCE OF THE HEAVENS

Transmission of spiritual power—The relation of Spirit to
matter—Consider the Heavens—The web of light—Spiritual
reality—The reality of Heaven—The city by the lake—Old comrades
meet—The Temple and its Sanctuary.

Tuesday, December 2, 1913.

DEAR friend and ward, I will to-night speak to you of certain
matters which connect with the question of transmutation of
energy. Energy, as I now employ the word, is to be understood as
that intermediary which couples up the motion of will with the
effect as displayed to the minds of men. We here are trained to this
end that we may, by the motion of our wills, transmit, by what we
may call vibration, our thoughts through the intervening spheres,
or states, into the earth plane. It is this movement in vibration
which I call energy.

Now, you must understand that in using earth-phrasing I am
employing a medium which is not adequate to express, either
exactly or fully, the science of these spheres and realms. It is
necessary, therefore, that I qualify my terms, and when I use the
term vibration I do not speak merely of oscillation to and fro
alone, but of movements which are sometimes elliptical,
sometimes spiral, and sometimes a combination of these and other
qualities.

TRANSMISSION OF SPIRITUAL POWER.

From this point of view the atomic system of vibration, which
has but of late been revealed to men of science, is to us one with
the movements of the planets of this solar sphere, and of other
systems far away in space.

The motion of earth round the sun, and the motion of the
molecules of the atom are vibrations. It matters not by what degree

you measure them, or what the diameter of their orbit, they are one in kind, and in degree only do they differ each from other.

But transmutation brings into any such system a change of movement, and the quality of movement being changed, there is also, and of necessity, a change of result. Thus we, acting always in perfect obedience to laws laid down by those higher and wiser than ourselves, concentrate our wills on the movement of certain vibrations, which become deflected and transmuted into other qualities of vibrations, and thus change is wrought.

Usually we do this work slowly and gradually, in order to obtain the exact quantity of divergence from the original quality of vibration intended, and not less or more.

It is by this method that we deal with the actions of men, and the course of nature in all its parts. There are manifold classes and companies who have in charge the various departments of creation—mineral, vegetable, animal, human, terrestrial, solar, and stellar. Beyond this, also, the stars are grouped together and dealt with by hierarchies qualified for that great task. It is by this same method, then, of the transmutation of energy that systems are gradually developed into worlds, and these worlds furnished with form, and then enabled to produce vegetation and animal life. But, this being so, you will note that all life, and all development, is consequent on the operation of spiritual energy obeying the dictates of the will of spiritual beings. This once grasped, blind force disappears, and intention takes its place intention of intelligent and powerful spiritual workers of various grades operating according to certain fixed laws but, within the bounds of those laws, free and mighty.

THE RELATION OF SPIRIT TO MATTER.

Moreover, matter itself is the result of the transmutation of spiritual vibrations into those of grosser sort, and these latter are now being analysed by scientists who have come to the knowledge that matter is indeed the result of vibrations, and that no particle of matter is still, but in ceaseless movement. That is correct, but not conclusive. For it does not pursue the matter to the end of it. It were truer to say, not that matter is in vibration, but that matter is vibration, the result of vibration of a quality more refined, which is found, not in the phenomenon of material things, but in those spheres proper to its quality.

Thus you will see how little it matters that, when the time comes for you to cast off the body of earth, you stand discarnate. Your earth body was a body of vibrations and no more. Very well, you now have a body of vibrations more substantial and enduring, because of a higher quality, and nearer to the energizing Will which brought it into existence, and so sustains it That body will serve you while you sojourn in the lower spheres and, when you have progressed, that body will be transmuted into one still more permanent, and of quality more sublime. This process will be repeated as the ages go by and you proceed from glory to higher glory in the infinite reaches of progress before you.

It follows also that, as those in the lower spheres in this spiritual realm are not normally visible in the earth sphere, so those of the higher spheres are not normally visible in those lower spheres, and so on in like order as we rise from sphere to sphere and pursue our way along this glorious road of light and high endeavour.

So it is then, friend and ward, and when you come hither one day you will be the better able to understand. For although you do now employ this same method, of which I have spoken in your own daily life, and so does every man, yet you little understand the manner of its working. Did you so it were well that all men be of one mind with us who try to use our powers for the glory and worship of God; for the weapon, to be used for good or evil, which man would then find to his hand would pass in might and strength all his present knowledge; as that exceeds the mental endowment of the fly or little ant.

It is well that we are able to co-ordinate the progress in knowledge and in holiness that they journey together.

For this is so—not perfectly, but within certain boundary lines, wide but sure. Were it otherwise the world would not be what it is to-day; nor order rule comparatively.

This, however, is one aspect of our care for the human race; and what the future holds I cannot say. For I cannot see so far as to conjecture how far men will go in this new knowledge, the threshold of which they now have crossed. But things will be well ordered by those who watch with jealous care, and wisdom very great; and all will be well while this is so. #

Wednesday, December 3, 1913.

It may be well to pursue our subject in hand a little further in order that my meaning may be made more explicit. Know then, my friend and ward, that what I have said already in respect of the transmutation of energy is by way of defining, rather than explaining in detail, the use of my terms.

CONSIDER THE HEAVENS.

If you will look out into the display around you of God's life manifest in the elements of your sphere you will observe several points of interest.

First you would not be able to use the sense of sight to help you to understand His working were it not that light, which is external to you, were poured upon your planet. But light also is merely vibration, and also is not consistent in its vibrating quality from first to last.

For you observe the sun to be visible, and the source of those vibrations.

But outside the atmospheric envelope of the solar sphere those vibrations are transmuted by the variant medium into which they have entered. Thus the stream of light passes through regions of darkness, and so continues until it approach another atmospheric zone, such as that which is about the earth, when once again that energy is transmuted as to its quality, and becomes once again what men call light. Yet one entity alone is that stream from sun to earth, a stream of light energizing from its source, passing through a vast region of darkness, and emerging once again in its native quality wherever it strikes upon a planet in its course.

You will remember the words, "The light shineth in the darkness, and the darkness does not comprehend it." This, then, is more than an analogy merely. It is the mode of working which

God adopts in His universe both of matter and spirit. And He is One; and His Kingdom is one.

It is obvious, therefore, that certain conditions are necessary in order that light may become operative to reveal things to men. Those conditions are the environment upon which light acts, and by which it is also affected by reflex action.

So is it in respect of spiritual environment. It is only when a genial environment is found that we spiritual ministers are able to become operative. And that is why to some we are able to reveal things in measure greater, and with greater ease, than to others whose environment is not so congenial. Whatsoever makes manifest is light, whether the thing manifest be material or spiritual.

And I tell you of another similitude. This is that as over the intervening region of darkness the light is directed from the sun to the planet far away, so from higher spheres is the light sent over the spheres intervening, and is received in the earth plane as direct, in a manner, as the earth itself receives the sun's light.

Now, look on another field. Far away beyond the farthest star you see from earth is a zone of wondrous beauty where suns have evolved to a much more conclusive system than those you observe. It is seen here that light is measured in proportion as heat is decreased; which would point to the fact that heat is by evolution of ages transmuted into those vibrations which constitute light. The moon is colder than the earth and reflects a greater light in proportion to its bulk. The older a system becomes the colder it grows, and more brilliant withal. This is as we believe in my sphere; and I may tell you that no observed fact has to this present time been found to oppose our conclusion.

THE WEB OF LIGHT.

I once observed a very beautiful instance of the transmutation of energy here in my own land.

There was a company of visitors from another sphere, and they were about to return to their own, their mission having been finished. A party of our own, of whom I was one, went with them to the large lake over which they had come to us. Here they embarked barked in boats, and were giving us their parting words of thanks and goodwill, when one of our Princes was seen approaching with a company of attendants, from behind us. They came through the air and hovered about us and the boats while we, knowing their habits, but not their present intention, waited to see what manner of thing they—or rather, he, had in his mind to do. For it is a delight in these realms to give pleasure, each to other, by exercising such powers as we possess, and that in varying combinations by which effects are differently produced.

Far up in the heavens we saw them, as they moved slowly, circling about the Prince from whom to those in circle went threads of vibrations of different quality, and so of different colour. These he of his will sent forth, and those his subordinates wove them into a network of curious design and very beautiful; and where two threads crossed there the intensified light shone like a stone of brilliant hue. And the knots were of many colours owing to the varying combination of threads entering into their construction.

When this was complete the circle widened out and drew away and left their Prince alone in the midst. And be held the net by its middle in his hand, and it floated out around him like a many-coloured spiderweb. It was very beautiful.

Now, that net was really a system of many qualities of vibrations woven together. He loosed it of his hand and it began slowly to sink as he rose through it, until it was level with his feet. Then he raised his hands and descended with it. And as he came he looked through the net at the boats below; and he made slow movements with his hands in their direction.

Then they began to move on the water as of themselves, and so continued until they floated in a circle. Then the net descended and settled over them, and we saw that they were all within its circumference, and also that, as it lighted on them, they passed through it and it sank and rested upon the water. Then the Prince, standing on the net and on the water, in the midst of the boats, waved his hand in greeting to them. And the net slowly arose from the water, lifting the boats with it, and floated upward into the air.

So away over the lake they went together, and the company of our sphere closed in around them, and sent up a song of Godspeed as they floated away towards the horizon over the lake.

It was merely one of those little tokens of love which we here delight to show our brethren of other spheres of labour—nothing more. My reason for relating this—which was, in display, much more beautiful than I am able to show you thus writing—was to illustrate the effect of the will of a powerful Angel Lord concentrated on the forces to hand and transmuting them in quality.

Beauty is not alone the minister of pleasure to the sight. It is rather a characteristic of these realms. For beauty and utility go together here. And the more useful a man becomes the more beautiful is he in person, The beauty of holiness is literal and real, friend; and it were well if all men could accept that truth. #

Thursday, December 4, 1913.

Having now explained, somewhat briefly, some of those principles, which are found in operation in your own sphere of earth, as also of these of more rarefied substance, I will continue in slightly different vein. For although it is not of your ability, nor helpful, to speak of those things which exist in these higher spheres alone more properly, yet a man must look ahead as he journeys; and the more he is able to understand of that land for which he is set out upon the road, the more sure will be his stepping onward, and less strange will appear that land on his arrival.

Beginning, then, at this point, it is one of the first tasks we have to learn here—having passed through the veil of flesh into the clearer realms of spiritual life, and having first to make familiar to ourselves the conditions here found existent, and that accomplished —to hand on to those who come on after us that same knowledge.

SPIRITUAL REALITY.

BOOK II: THE HIGHLANDS OF HEAVEN

One matter which causes much distress and distrust to many souls is the fact that all they see here is real . You have already been shown this; but so strange it is and contrary to all rational expectation, that I would fain add to what you already have received a little more. For it is of primary import to every one that he realize that the existence before him is no dream, as a man would say—but not we—but that it is indeed the fuller life developed, and the life for which the earth life is both a preparation and beginning. Why do men imagine that the sapling is of larger strength than the full-grown oak, or that the spring is of more reality and power than the river? The sapling and the spring are of your present earth life; the oak and the river are here.

The body you now wear, and the trees and rivers and other of material substance, which you call real, are not so enduring, nor so real, as their counterparts in these spheres. For here is found the energy which comes to your systems, and is as the electric dynamo to the single lamp as to its power and intensity.

When, therefore, men think of us as whiffs of smoke, and of our environment as drifting shadows, let them pause and ask if there is any sound reason to bottom their view. Nay, there is no reason in it whatsoever, but, on the contrary part, it is foolishness, and unworthy thinking beings of spirit estate.

THE REALITY OF HEAVEN.

Let me describe you a scene in one of these spheres, or regions, as I will say to make it more natural seeming to you, a scene and an incident, by way of showing you what kind and manner of life you will take your part in one day soon. For when you step over into the sunlight, and think backward of your earth life, it will surely stand out very vivid and plain, and the reason of things you now discern but in part will be seen to be both ordered and wisely beneficent. Nevertheless, how short a day will your present life then seem to you when around you unfolds ever one infinitude after another, and eternity begins to be of your life, which now you reckon day by day.

Far away a light is rising in the sky which overlaps the horizon like a violet-tinted veil, and seems to drop behind it, curtaining the further distance from my sight. Between that horizon and the high rock on which I stand to view is a wide-stretching plain. Here at my feet, far down below, I see a temple which, in its turn, is still high above the City which stretches round the base of the mountain.

Domes and halls and mansions surrounded by lawns of emerald, and flowers flashing and sparkling like gems of many colours I see, and squares and statues and fountains and many people, whose robes outshine the flower-beds and out-number their colours, move about in groups. One colour is seen to be dominant over the rest, however, and that is gold, for that colour is the principal of this City.

THE CITY BY THE LAKE.

High walls stretch, crescent-wise, along the outer part and embrace the City as the horns bend in towards the mountain on either side. On these walls are watchers,—not against foe, but to give tidings of what is forward out on the vast plain from time to time, and to welcome friends who journey hither from regions far away.

The walls are lapped by the waters of a lake which is in extent as a sea or ocean on earth would be measured. But yet it is possible for those who are trained to watch to see, beyond it, the land on the farther shore where the light is growing, and is seen kissing the sails and flashing oars of the ships as they go, some in one direction and some in another, upon the bosom of the gently swelling sea.

And now I descend and stand on the walls to watch what is enacting.

Presently I hear a rumbling as of thunder coming from the direction of that violet cloud of light. This grows in volume and rhythm, and gains in pleasurable tone, until it has become one sustained chord of music.

Then from the temple above me I see emerge a great throng who wear white glistering robes, with golden bands about their middles, and each a fillet of gold upon his head. These take hands upon the platform of rock before the Temple and, looking upward, seem to be lost in adoration. They are really gathering power to answer the salutation of the party who are travelling towards us beyond the horizon yonder.

Then another man comes forth and stands before .them, looking towards the violet cloud of light. He is of larger build than the rest, clothed like them of white and gold, but more beautiful and bright of face, and whose eyes are like a flame of quivering light.

Presently, as they stand thus, a cloud begins to gather around them and, as it thickens, we see it in movement revolving, until it takes the shape of a sphere, and is in colour golden, but full of many-coloured lights. It enlarges until at length it hides the Temple from view. And then a very notable thing ensues.

The sphere, revolving and sending out flash after flash of light—gold, crimson, purple, blue, green and other, slowly rises into the air, and higher still it goes until it is level with the topmost peak of the mountain behind and above the Temple. Higher still it rises, and its light radiates far afield.

And I notice that the platform where stood the party of Temple-dwellers is bare of them. They have ascended in that globe of living light and flame. This is not possible but for those who have developed in training to endure that intensity of spiritual power which generates such phenomena as this. Higher still rises the sphere until it rests suspended, and the brilliancy of its flashing is increased.

Then I notice a shadow stealing from out its midst, and settling and spreading over that half of it which opposes itself to the region behind; but the front which is toward the violet light in the horizon is naked, and its brightness is increased by so much that I may not look at it, but only at the rays as they travel high over the plain in answer to that message coming from afar.

Then, too, we hear a humming noise, like that of bees, which comes from the sphere of light; and this increases like the other, like a chord of great orchestras, as it swells out, high in the heavens now, and floods the plain and the sea both with light and music, — for here these are often made to go hand in hand, blended in condition and effect.

THE LIFE BEYOND THE VEIL

Our friends are seen and heard by those who come towards us from far away, and the two streams of light gradually approach, and so do the two strains of harmony, and all blend together in wonderful beauty. But they are not near together. That which in these realms answers to distance in yours is immense. These two in opposition are as if one of the stars you see from earth should salute a sister star billions of billions of miles away, and send her music to her in greeting, receiving answer in like responsive light and sound together blended. Then, could these two stars leave their moorings in the ends of space, and begin to come nearer each to other along the heavenly road, century after century, approaching at awful speed and, for greeting sending out from time to time floods of radiance and music, as throwing kisses by the way, ahead of their meeting—so imagine this approachment of those two spheres of the spiritual universe, and you do not over-estimate either their beauties or powers of movement thus displayed.

I leave them thus, and go about my business, and all the time the light increases, and the people of the City tell the news, and hazard who it is who comes for this time, and remember one to another he meets, who came last, and what it was transpired then of glories new and not before seen in that city while they had been citizens.

So each goes about his work in happy expectation, for all visitors here bring joy, and joy receive in themselves of their hosts, and take it back to their own people when they again depart.

Now, I would that I might describe for you the meeting. That I am unable, for it is of those things that are not possible to utter in words of earth. Even thus far I have been much hampered, and have only found it possible to picture the scene hereto by lopping and chopping off all the more beautiful parts and giving you just a skeleton frame to hang your imagination upon. If the glory of it all in separation be tenfold more glorious than I have been able to indite, what shall serve me of language to tell you of the blending of those two glories when they were come together? The heaven was transformed into a blaze of light, and thousands of beings flashing hither and thither, with many species of transport animals, and wagons of different construction, and banners and devices, and flashing, radiating, shimmering lights and colours, and voices which were like instruments of music falling upon us below, as they wheeled and circled in the heavens above, like showers of golden rain mingled with violet flowers and diamonds.

Rhapsody? Yes, friend, to those who would measure heaven by earth's drab pageants, tawdry and tinsel in their trappings, and enacted in an atmosphere which to this of our own land is as fog to sunlight. Yet in the midst of all the dull dampness of earth and earth life, you yourselves are not of earth but of those heavenly Spheres potentially and by reason of your destiny. Be you, therefore, not so sordid to grovel about with nose to earth smelling for gold which discomposes composes itself, and is not of lasting and persisting quality. Use what things you have, and be glad that your world is so wisely ordered and so wonderful as it is, but do not rate this land by what you find normal in that lower sphere.

Look onward, friend and ward, for this is yours; and all those beauties and delights we hold in trust for you. Stretch forth your hand in faith, and I drop into it just one small gem of all these heavenly treasures. Open your heart to us and we will breathe into your being some of the music and love of your own future home.

And so, be you content awhile, and do what you find at hand to do. We keep your inheritance sure and safe for your coming, and, so you do your work as faithfully and as well as you are able, you and all such shall come to us as Kings and Princes of the Blood—of the Blood—which is His Life for all who love holiness as He loved it and, because He loved its beauty, did not flinch to do His Father's Will—at Whom men scoffed, and for which they crucified Him.

Tread in His way, for that way led Him to the Throne, and shall lead you thither, you and all who do their parts nobly and with love.

Of such He is their King. #

Monday, December 8, 1913.

And now, my friend and ward, I am of a mind to-night to continue that of which I made a beginning when last I impressed you.

231

That violet cloud of glory and the one of my own sphere were commingled and, as I looked up at the sight, I saw, as I told you, the movement of those who were within. Then the glory settled down upon our City, and all the buildings and trees and people and all things therein were bathed in that violet-golden shower, and took on a more lovely aspect by reason of the baptism.

For you will understand that it was from a sphere more advanced than my own from which these our visitors were come; and none come so but they bring a blessing in gift to leave behind. Thus when they had departed we had received that which enabled us nearer to our next step onward, and the whole city glowed with somewhat more of sublimity than heretofore.

Now, it chanced that I had business in the Temple at that time, and thither I made my way along the mountain path. It was a long ascent, but usually I went afoot by way of meditation and preparing of myself for whatever I had in hand on such occasions as this.

OLD COMRADES MEET.

Here and there along the path ascending are shrines, set a little off the way, like those in many lands of earth. And as I stood before one of these, a little removed, I covered my eyes with my hands, and stood thus awhile to commune with Him Who of His Life gives strength to us to follow after Him in the Heavenly road. Thus it was that I did not hear when some drew nigh me until their steps were present with me on the path behind. Then they ceased and I, having finished my offering, turned and saw those whose light showed me of their degree that it was not as mine, but higher in the spheres. So I bowed myself to them, and stood with eyes to look upon the ground, and waited for them to tell out their will and purpose with me.

But I stood for long and they did not speak to me. So, making bold from the silence of them, I raised my eyes and looked upon them, first at the girdle of their robes to understand of what order they might be. Thus I understood that they were of those messengers who attended their Chief on his journeyings, both.

Such they were as you shall call them aides-decamp to their Leader.

Then, they still continuing in silence, I looked on their faces. They were aglow with smiling; and amusement was not lacking in their smile. So I steadfastly gazed upon them, and at first I could discern little, for it was no easy matter that I should penetrate through that radiance shimmering around them then, to see their features whether I knew them or no. But, catching some of their power, as is the manner at such times, I did at length come to a knowledge of their countenances. Then I understood. They were two old comrades who, when we did service nearer to the earth plane, had fought for souls and won them out of the darker regions into the light of the Presence. And I had been their minister then, and their companion.

They came to me, when they saw the dawning recognition in my eyes, and, taking each a hand in his, we went together tip the hill ascending, and on towards the Temple plateau, they kissing me first on either cheek, and so imparting to me further of their strength, to be and to converse with them.

Oh, the bliss and the great pleasure of that walk, when they who had been advanced beyond my present estate spoke first of old times and service together and, gradually leading, came to present times in this my own sphere, and then spoke, in sequence, of their own more bright and glorious, to which soon, perhaps, I should be called.

THE TEMPLE AND ITS SANCTUARY.

So we came to the Temple, and the way seemed not so long by much as at other times for the beauty of their presence and the entrancement of the talk they gave me of the added glory of their Home.

They bore a message to the Temple-keeper that their Chief and Lord would sometime soon come, with our own Ruler, to bless the Temple and to offer worship there, both for his own retinue and himself, and for the City at which, for the time being, he was guest.

Will you describe the Temple to me, Zabdiel?

THE LIFE BEYOND THE VEIL

What I am able in your words at my disposal I will give you.

There is no wall between the facade and the edge of the precipice, so that the Temple is seen most clearly from the plain a little out from the City walls. It rises sheer from the platform of rock, one arch topping another, and mounting upward in perfect harmony, and in colour growing lighter as the higher arches are reached. The dominating colour I cannot tell you, for you have no such on earth. If I name it a combination of pink and grey that is all I can do; and it does not give you a very exact idea of its aspect. But let that suffice, and indeed I come little nearer in my description of the architecture itself.

There is not one great porch alone, as in most of your cathedrals, but there are five. They are of different build and hue, and are so constructed for the accommodation of those who come hither to worship. For were all to be admitted through one gate, those of lesser power would experience an enervation which would take from their ability to worship when within. So these five door-ways are made to lead them into that nave where they may recover to be strengthened. Here they pay their first vows and devotions.

Then they pass on into the great central hall of the Sanctuary, where they all mingle together without discomfort.

There is a square tower over this central space, open to the top and to the sky above. And over the tower bangs a moving, luminous cloud, which is like the Shekinah of old, the Dwelling Place from which, at certain times, descends into the Temple, and upon the worshippers, an access of His Life and blessing.

On the farther side of this space there is another nave; and here are angels who come to meet with those who are called. These minister to us by teaching of those Mysteries which are of the Higher Realms, and only those who have progressed much may receive their teaching, for it is both very high in wisdom of Divine things and powers, and also it is given sparingly, for, as a moth is destroyed of the flame it seeks too eagerly, so it is not with impunity that the higher Wisdom may be either had or given. Into that inner Sanctuary I never yet have looked, for my time is not yet at hand to do so. And when it comes I shall be ready. I shall not be bidden thither before I am fully prepared. Yet before I am advanced to my next sphere onward I must pass through the learning to be had there, and there alone. Towards this I am at present endeavouring.

I have told you somewhat of that mighty Shrine, but falteringly, for it is too glorious to put into your words. Of such a theme St. John of the Revelation strove to tell to those his brethren who had been less favoured than he. But he could but tell them of precious stones and pearls and light and crystal and no more. Well, that is my present case, my brother, and I am at pause. So let me leave it there with some sorrow that I can do no more than this which falls so short of the glory which crowns and suffuses all that Temple which stands on that Heavenly Mountain in the Tenth Sphere of these long reaches of progress in knowledge and wisdom and power and strength and blessing towards Him Who is the Source and Spring of them all. #

Zabdiel, I feel it rather a strain to come on succeeding days. Would you rather that I came on every other day; or on every day I can, as at present?

As you will, friend. Only remember this: that the power is here now, and it may not continue. I will sustain you for so long as I am able, and when that fails by reason of your limitations—then I can no more. I will make my journal so completed as I can, however, while you are in this state of receptivity. But do as you think well. If you decide to continue daily, then do not task your mind with other writing more than is necessary for your dutiful fulfilment of your obligation to your people and friends. Take exercise and recuperation without-doors, as you feel it helpful. And I will give you what I can of my strength and sustenance. But my ability to give is greater than is yours to receive. So, if you feel able, come daily, or as nearly so as your duties permit. We have not once failed hitherto on any day, and may be able so to continue.

CHAPTER VI

THE SUMMERLAND OF GOD

"Teach me Thy way"—The glade of the statue—Flora of the
Tenth Sphere—The Sanctuary of Festivals—A Heavenly vista—The
meeting at the Valley of the Peaks—Themeeting with Harolen—To
the Gate of the Sea Lau Deo—The altar on the raft—" One Lord,
One Faith"—A Heavenly Transfiguration—The Son of Man.

Tuesday, December 9, 1913.

So you come to me, my ward, as I desired you. I think you will
find my endeavours none too feeble but that I shall be able to say
some little thing which will be of help to you, and to others, to-
night. For there are forces on hand which will enable you when
you do not know it, and I use them to put my thoughts in order
before you. So do not falter in your distrust of your own faculty to
reproduce them. When you are no longer fortified to do so I will
inform you, and we will close up our book for the time being and
give our minds to other matters.

Now give me your mind that I may continue on my way, for I
will that to-night you should be given to know a little further of
our doings here in this Tenth Sphere. Only remember always that I
am constrained, and that of necessity, in my narration, to model
my description, in some measure, on the conditions as they are
found in the spheres lower than this of mine, even as, once again,
these pictures are further reduced within the compass of the
language and imagery of earth. This of necessity, I say, for it is not
competent to put a bushel of wheat into a pint measure, nor to
confine light within the darkness of a leaden casket.

"TEACH ME THY WAY."

The Temple-shrine of which I spoke is of use not for worship
alone, but for instruction of those competent to receive it. This is
the High School of the sphere, and only those who have passed
through the lower forms may come here for their final learning. At

various points in that region are other schools or colleges, each for some special class of instruction in wisdom, and some few for the co-ordination of some of these branches together.

The City itself has three of these colleges, where those who have passed through what I will call the provincial schools come to learn the relative value of the various teachings they have received, and to combine them together. In many spheres this line is followed. But each sphere is both continuous, and also in advance of, the sphere inferior to itself. So that from the lower to the higher spheres there is a graded system of progress, and every step onward implies an added capacity, not alone of power, but in enjoyment in the using of it.

Instructors are mostly of those who have qualified for the next sphere in advance, but who elect to stay in order to teach those who, in their turn, shall succeed them when at length they go on into their own proper place of abode.

From time to time these preceptors do make their journey into the sphere above, and then return to continue their task. For they are enabled to bear its enhanced glory, while those who are of less degree are not able to do, so.

And also there come once and again those of the higher spheres into the lower for friendly intercourse and conversation with their fellows who teach there; and then they nearly always are willing to condition themselves according to the environment of that same lower sphere, in order that they may impart some loving words of encouragement to the pupils.

When a spirit from one of these spheres descends to your earth, it is necessary, in order that he may make contact with you who dwell there, to condition himself in like manner, and this in more or less degree. So it is here between the higher and lower conditions obtaining in the spheres of various quality and elevation.

But it is easier for us to commune with some of you than with others, and that according to your degree of advancement spiritually. So again, is it here in the spirit land. There are those in the Third Sphere who know of the presence of those of the Fourth or Fifth or even higher spheres, by reason of their advancement spiritually beyond their fellows. If to these latter such visitors wish to become visible and audible they must the more completely condition themselves to the environment of that sphere, and this they do.

This description is in outline, and you will see that what seems at first to complicate life here really serves to its orderly arrangement. The leading principles which govern the communion of saints on earth with those passed higher are produced hither, and continued on into the higher places upward in orderly sequence. And if you wish to know what regulates our own communion with those above us, then reason it out by analogy, and you will have as fair a knowledge of it as is possible to you while still on earth incarnate.

Thank you. Would you describe a little more in detail the City and the country of the Tenth Sphere?

Yes. But first as to the name "Tenth Sphere." That is what we name it by way of brevity. But in every sphere other spheres are found to touch it. What we will call the Tenth is the dominant note: but the harmony of the spheres is one and blended. For this reason a man may aspire to that above him, and is lifted up by reason of the contact of that higher zone interpenetrating his own.

But also, having progressed to, let us say, the Seventh, he is initiate into all those spheres below, through which he has passed. Thus, as others come down to him, so he can go down to others, so he condition himself always according to that sphere into which he goes. And he may from his own sphere reach forth his power to those in the spheres below. This we continually do, even from our own projecting our cognisance, and power to aid, into the earth for those with whom we have established contact. We do not always leave our own home when we help you; but on occasion we do so, as necessity compels.

Where are you now—in your own, or here in the earth sphere?

I am now calling to you from near by. For, although I count little of bricks and mortar, yet, on account of your incarnate condition, and your inability to rise far hitherward of yourself, needs must I meet you on the way. So I come to you and stand within call of you, or you would produce my thoughts, but not in the order and manner I wish.

BOOK II: THE HIGHLANDS OF HEAVEN

And now to answer your inquiry of this land which is my own. Bear in mind the words with which I began to-night, and I will tell you.

The City stretches round the base of the mountain. Between the walls of it and the Lake are mansions and their grounds which extend left and right, and most of them approach the Lake itself. We embark on the water and take a straight course ahead and, landing on the opposite shore, we find it is wooded with trees, many of a kind only found in this Sphere. Here also we find paths set out and, taking the one before us, we go a long journey inland, and at length emerge into a glade.

In this clearing there is a statue. It is that of a woman who stands looking upward into the heavens above. Her arms hang down against her sides, and her dress is a plain robe without ornament. The statue was placed there long ago, and has stood gazing upward for many ages.

But you are spent, my brother, to-night. So I must leave this theme and renew it, if I may, at another time.

Look up, as the face of that statue does, and you shall receive a baptism of light upon your eyes that you may see some of the glories which are there. #

Thursday, December 11, 1913.

To continue:

The glade in which the statue stands is one where we often meet to receive direction from those above us who, from time to time, find it convenient to call us away from the throng of our brethren in order that they may commend to us some line of special study, to be done. Here we meet and they come to us and in that beautiful glade are more beautiful than the setting in which they shine.

Out of the open space lead several paths. We take one to the right of the further side, and pursue it. On either hand as we go we see flowers blooming, some of the daisy family, and the pansy, and others standing aloft as if rejoicing in their beauty of foliage and colouring, like the dahlia and the peony and the rose, All these, and more too; for we in this sphere know no flowers in their seasons, but all bloom together in the perpetual, but never-wearying summertime.

Then, here and there are other kinds, and some are of great diameter, a veritable galaxy of beauty, like great shields of flashing light, and hues all beautiful, and all giving forth delight to the beholder. The flora of this sphere is beyond description to you, for, as I have already explained, there are colours here which earth knows not, by reason of its grosser vibrations, and also because the senses of the human body are not enough refined for their perception.

Thus, to digress a little, there are colours and sounds about you ever which are not cognisable of your senses. And here we have these, and more added, to help the gorgeous display of loveliness, and to show us some little of what the Beauty of Holiness must be like nearer to the Central Bliss where the Holiest dwell in the Heart of the One Alone.

Presently we come to a river which bisects our path, and here we turn to the left, for we must visit a colony which will be of interest to you. And what, think you, do we find here at the edge of the forest which bends away from the river and leaves an open plain to view? Naught else but a Sanctuary of Seasons or—shall I say?—Festivals.

Now, you in the earth plane have small wit of the nearness of us who seem to you so far away. Why, not a sparrow falls but your Heavenly Father knows and marks it. So all you do is open to us, and scanned with interest and much care, if perchance we may be able to throw into your worship, from time to time, some sprinkling of heavenly dew which shall tincture it and you with thoughts of Heaven.

Here, then, in this colony are curious[27] ministers who seek to weigh your Festivals on earth as they come round year by year; and these add their own offering to that of those who attend your worship[28] to strengthen them in their helping of you as to that particular bent of mind which directs your thoughts and aspiration at the greater Festivals of your cycle.

---

[27] Meaning "zealously careful" (old use).
[28] I.e. spirit attendants.

BOOK II: THE HIGHLANDS OF HEAVEN

This is not of my own special work, so that I do not speak expertly. But I know that all those ideas which with you do cluster about such as Christmas and Epiphany and Easter and Whit and the like are reinforced from such colonies as these.

I have heard, moreover, and believe it true, that those who worship the Father God by other rules than the Christian are likewise tended at their great Festivals by their own special guiding, watching angels.

Thus it is that you will note at such times an added fervour in the worshippers at their Shrines of grace, and much of it, I believe, is the result of streams of spiritual power directed from these schools, and flowing into the hearts of the congregations on earth, united in praise and worshipping of God.

You would like something to be told of the buildings of the settlement. There are many, and most of them are lofty. And they assemble around a Dominant structure which rises on many arches and is storied far and high into the space above. The top of this is spread out and hangs, with lip-like festoons, over the houses below it, as it were a lily opening ever but never quite fully in bloom. It is of blue and green, but shaded in its folds with rich brown, like gold intensified. It is lovely to look up to, and speaks of worship unfolding heavenward, like a flower whose perfume ascends while the very heart is expanding itself to the gaze of those above, and to the Heavenly Creator and Lover, Who is over all, and yet sees and knows and finds pleasure in the breathing of the heart's life back to Him Who gave it and sustains it unceasingly and for ever.

We leave this beauteous flower to hover like a bird with mother-wings above her brood of clustering dwellings which fondle one another below and seem safe in the protection, as it were, of their mother Sanctuary and Shrine. We leave these and continue.

After a long journey up-river we begin to ascend, and continue. Thus we come to the Mountainland; and here we look far away into the distance. This is on the borderland between our Sphere and the one next in ascent.

Some of us are able to see farther and in more detail than are those who have not attained to develop themselves so far, What I see I tell you now.

241

We are on the summit of a mountain, which is one of many. Before us is but a little valley and then

rises range after range of higher peaks and summits; and the farther you move to focus your gaze the brighter is the light which bathes them. But that light is in nowise still. It moves and shimmers and dazzles and darts among those far mountains as if they lay within an ocean of heaving crystal or of electricity. That is the aspect, and I can no more than that for you.

Streams and buildings there are, but these are far away. I know that among those mountains there is grass, and there are flowering plants and trees and meadows and gardens and mansions of those who dwell in that

Sphere. But these are not to view for me, who can only see the outstanding landmarks.

And over all, and throughout all, I see the Love of God and His most exceeding and excellent comeliness and beauty: and my heart leaps forward to rejoice me on my way. For thither I am going, and, when I have fulfilled my task here as it is given me to do, and not until then, I know that some fair denizen of that enchanting land will come and call me, and I shall leap in joy to hasten thither.

Ah but, my brother, is it not thus with you also? What that farther sphere is to my own heart, the next of your advancement should be to you, and as lovely by comparison.

I have told you but only a very little of this sphere, but enough to give you zest and appetite to urge forward on your march.

I would now recur to the glade and bid you keep your eyes full steady gazing upward. Nay, your foot shall in nowise stumble because your eyes are not groundward bent. For those who look aloft look in the way they are going; and we look downward to keep your stepping sure.

So all is well, my ward; yea, all is well for such an one, for, because he trusts us who serve our Lord, on Him his heart is stayed; and none shall make him stumble.

So be it, then. The world is dull and wearying, times and oft, yet there is beauty, too, and love and holy aspiration. Take of these and enjoy them.

BOOK II: THE HIGHLANDS OF HEAVEN

Give of them freely to others, and the gloom will seem less gloomy, and the light beyond will dawn more clearly and brightly, and the sons of the morning will lead you on into their own more lovely Summerland. #

Friday, December 12, 1913.

Standing on that high peak radiant with the light which strikes it from the realms behind me, and bathed in the greater light of those before, I commune with those of both spheres and, through them, with the spheres beyond. Such moments are of bliss too great for utterance, and open the eyes of spiritual understanding to see things glorious and mighty, and infinitudes vast, and all-embracing love.

Once I stood thus, with face turned towards my future home, and closed my eyes, for the intensity of light as it moved before me was more than I could bear continuously. It was there I first was permitted to see and speak to my guide and guardian.

He stood upon the summit over against me opposite; and the; valley was between. When I opened my eyes I saw him there, as if he had suddenly taken on a visible form for me, that I might see him the more plainly. And so it was indeed, and he smiled on me, and stood there watching me in my perplexity.

He was clad of glittering silk—like tunic to the knees, and round his middle was a belt of silver. His arms and legs below were bare of covering, and seemed to glow and give forth light of his holiness and purity of heart; and his face was the brightest of all. He wore a cap of blue upon his hair which was like silver just turning into gold; and in the cap shone the jewel of his order. I had not seen one of this kind before. It was a brown stone and emitted a brown light, very beautiful and glowing with the life which was all about us.

At last, "Come over to me," he said; and I was thereupon afraid, but not with any terror, but rather abashed of awe. In that way I feared, not else.

So I said, "I know you for my guide, sir, for my heart tells me this much.

And I delight to look upon you thus; for it is very lovely and sweet to me.

In presence you have been with me often on my heavenly road, but always just before, that I have not been able to overtake you. And now that I am given to see you thus in visible form I am glad to thank you for all your love and tending. But, my lord and guardian, I fear to come to you. For, while I descend into the valley, the brightness of your sphere will dazzle me and make my feet unsure. And when I should ascend to you I think I should faint by reason of the greater glory which is about you. Even here I, from this distance, feel it scarce to be borne for long."

"Yes, for this time," he replied, "I will be your strength, as many times before I have been, not always of your knowledge; and at times again when you have known me near but only in part. We have been so much together that I am able now to give you more than hitherto. Only be strong, and with all your courage to the fore; for no harm shall fall upon you. It is to this same end that I have impressed you to come to this place, as often I have come to you."

Then I saw him for awhile stand very still indeed, as he might have been a statue very well. But presently his form took on another aspect. He seemed to be in tension as to the muscles of his arms and legs; and I could see, beneath the thin gossamer—like garment, that his body there was in like manner exerting its every power. His hands were hanging at his side, and turned outward a little, and his eyes were closed. Then a strange thing happened.

From beneath his feet there came a cloud of blue and pink mingled; and it moved across from him to me until it was a bridge between the two summits, and spanned the valley below. It was in height little more than that of a man, and in breadth a little broader. This gradually came upon me and enveloped me, and when I looked I could see him through the mist, and he seemed very near.

Then he said, "Now come to me, my friend. Tread firmly forward to me, and you shall have no hurt."

So I began to walk to him through that shaft of luminous cloud which was all about me, and, although as I went it was elastic beneath my feet, like very thick velvet, yet I did not sink through the floor of it into the valley, but continued my way uplifted with great joy. For he looked on me and smiled as I went to him.

But although he seemed so near, yet I did not reach him, and yet again, he stood still and did not retreat from me.

But at last he held out his hand and, in a few steps more, I had it in mine, and he drew me on to firmer footing.

Then the shaft of light faded and I found I stood on the further side of the valley, and looked across on my own sphere. For I had crossed over by that bridge of heavenly light and power.

Then we sat down and communed together of many things. He called to my mind past endeavours, and showed me where I might have done my task in better ways; and sometimes he commended me, and sometimes did not commend, but never blamed, but only advised and instructed with love and kindliness. And then he told me something of the sphere on the borderland of which I then was; and of some of its glories; and how the better to sense his presence, as I went about my task to which I should presently return to finish it.

And so he talked, and I felt in very good fettle of

strength and delight, and of greater courage for the way. So did he give me of his larger strength, and of his higher holiness, and I understood a little more than hitherto of man's potential greatness, in humility, to serve his Master the Christ, and God through Him.

He came back with me by way of the valley, with his arm about my shoulder to help me with his power; and we talked all the way down and across, and then, as the ascent of the hill on the other side began, we slowly fell to silence. Instead of words we communed in thought and, when a little way up returning I looked upon him, I noticed that I could hot see him quite so plainly; and began to be sad at that. But he smiled and said, "All is well, my brother. Always it is well between you and me. Remember that."

Still he grew more faint to my sight, and I was minded to turn back again for that reason. But he impelled me gently and, as we ascended, he surely faded away from my sight. I did not see him thus again. But I knew him now as I did not till that time. I felt him in touch with me all the time I lingered on that summit. I turned and looked into the brightness of his sphere across the valley, but I did not see him on the other side.

Just as I was turning to depart, however, I looked again, and I saw a form speeding over the mountain peaks beyond; not a solid form, as his had been, but one almost transparent. Like a ray of sunlight he went away from me visibly, or partly so; and that sight, too, slowly faded. But yet I felt him present with me, felt that he knew of me, and what I thought and did. And I turned to descend with much joy, and greater strength to do my work awhile.

As from that brighter sphere such of blessing is given to me, shall I not in turn hand on some little to those who need it as greatly as I do? And this we do, my charge, through those heavens below our own; and even to you on earth we come and minister with much gladness. For it is very sweet to do to others our brethren what so bountifully is done to us.

I cannot make a bridge for you, as he did for me; for the variance of degree between the earth sphere and this is, at present, too great to be treated so. But there is a Way by which to cross at the appointed time, as

He has said. And His power is greater by far than that of him who made the road for me across the Valley of the Peaks. Of Whom I am a very lowly servant. But what I lack in degree of holiness and wisdom I strive to supply of love, and if we do both serve Him as we are able, He will keep, us in peace, being stayed on Him across the depths from glory to the greater glory which is beyond. #

Monday, December 15, 1913.

I left that spot uplifted for the work I had to do before that time when I should be called hence to be as he is. Oh, the beauty and high peace of that place, and of him who is my guide. If the people of that farther zone are but half so beautiful and so lovely as he, then indeed a blessed race is that to whom I am on my way.

But now, my brother, it is upon me to help you hither on your way.

And this I would, but by little or by much, so I add something to enable you and others on the road I sometime trod myself. Reach me your hand, then, and I will, on my part, what I am able.

246

BOOK II: THE HIGHLANDS OF HEAVEN

I left that place, I say, uplifted, and from that time my own environment was the more plain to me, in that I had viewed it from on high afar to see the outstanding matters in their right proportion, and from time to time I do this now when some problem more vexed than others perplexes my understanding of it. I view it as from the high places nearer that farther sphere, and things resolve themselves more orderly-wise, and become more plain.

This do you, my ward, and life will then appear not quite so much in a tangle; but leading principles will take their place of right, and the Love of our Father be more plainly seen. In order thereto I will continue to describe for you more of this sphere in which my present work is cast.

Descending, I turn to the right hand from the river and, taking a road which bends around the wood some little distance away from it, and through a plain bordered on the right by mountains, I go my way alone in meditation.

Presently I meet a company of those who have their dwelling farther ahead, and these I will describe to you. They are some afoot, and some on horses, and some in wagons, or chariots,—open vehicles they are, of wood, and with gold about them for a binding and bordering, and also devices on their front parts which tell of what realm and order the riders are. The garments of the throng are of many colours, but the dominating one is mauve deepening into purple. There are some three hundred men of them, and I receive and give salutation and inquire whither they are bound, and on what manner of business.

The one I speak to falls out of the line to answer me. He tells me that word has come to his city that a number of those of the Ninth Sphere are about to receive their initiation into this the Tenth, having qualified by their conversation thereto. On hearing this I beg that he will speak to the leader that I accompany them in order to see what is agait yonder, and also that I may add my welcome to their own. On this he smiles, and tells me to walk with him and he will vouch for my acceptance. "For," adds he, "he you call the leader walks side by side with you."

At this I turned and looked on him, greatly surprised; for he wore a purple tunic, truly, but it was without ornament, and the fillet on his head was also a purple band with but one red jewel in it, and no device. Others were much more richly clad, and to look upon more comely and princely. I did not say so much, but he was of development greater than I, as I had already began to suspect, and knew my thoughts without their utterance.

So he smiled again and said, "These new-comers shall see me as I am at this time; for some among them, I am told, are hardly ripe for much display of radiance. So they shall be as glorious as I, and they will not be dazed. Have you not lately had an encounter, my brother, as will serve to show you that too much glory may possibly impede instead of help?"

I confessed this to be the truth, and then he said, "You see I am of that sphere to which your guide belongs, and stay here in order to finish my task: as I myself elect to finish it. So I condition myself in such wise that those our brothers and sisters who come hither shall feel the homeliness of home till they be ripe for the glory of the Court. So come, my brother, and we will overtake those yonder before they reach the river."

We did so and crossed the river with them, swimming it, men and horses and wagons, too, and came to the other side. We left my city on the right, and went on to the pass which goes between the mountains where the scenery is very large and massive. Rocks rear themselves with much stateliness on either hand, like spires and towers and domes, and they are of different colours. Here and there vegetation grows and now a plateau is seen stretching away between the shoulders of two hills, and on it rises the chief city of a colony of happy people, who come and look down on us from aloft, and wave their salutation, and throw flowers to us as lovetokens.

So we pass along and at length emerge into a valley which opens out on either hand, and very beautiful it is here. Groups of trees cluster about fair and stately mansions, and some, of the more homely kind, of timber and stone; and lakes there are and streams falling with sweet music into the river which runs onward from the mountains round which we have come into the distance before us.

BOOK II: THE HIGHLANDS OF HEAVEN

Here the valley closes again, and we see two giant pillars of natural rock through which the road must pass side by side with the river.

We emerge through this Gate, which the Valley people call the "Gate of the Sea," and before us we see the open ocean, into which the river falls from a great height, and is very lovely to see as it falls, like many thousands of kingfishers and humming-birds making their many-coloured flight down the mountainside, flashing and sparkling, into the waters below. We descend by pathways and stand on the shore; but some still remain behind to watch for those who shall come over the sea. We are well timed, for our leader has powers which are of the sphere beyond, and is able to use the forces of this zone with by so much the greater ease. He has so arranged that, but a few moments after we have taken tip our station on the shore, a shout is raised by our watchers above that the company is in sight far out at sea. Then round the bend of shore beyond the river come a company of our ladies who, as I learned when I asked, had their habitation in that district in order that they might join those who came to that shore from distant lands.

Great was the rejoicing of us all to greet them, and theirs to receive and give greeting in return.

Then high upon a rounded summit, below which their home was, we saw their Mother standing. She was robed from head to foot in silver gossamer, and shone through her robe like a beautiful glittering diamond or pearl endowed with life and fresh vitality. She looked intently at the party on the sea, and then began to make a weaving movement with her hands.

Presently we saw a large bouquet of flowers wag taking shape between her hands. And then she changed her movements, and it began to float out and stretch itself into a rope of flowers which went out into the air, high up across the waters, and at length it rested over the people who were on the sea.

Then it drew itself inward, and began to form a flat spiral, and circled above their heads awhile, and then gently settled down upon them, and broke up into a shower of roses and lilies and other kinds of flowers, which fell upon them and about them. As I looked I saw their faces change from inquiring expectation into glad smiles of happiness, for they understood the token they had received, and knew that love and beauty awaited them in this new sphere to which they had journeyed far to come.

Now I was able to see the fashion of their ship. Indeed it was no ship at all, but a raft. How shall I speak of it simply? It was a raft, indeed, but it was no bare structure, for there were upon it couches and beds of soft down, and instruments of music; and of these the chief was an organ on which three men were now beginning to play at one time,—all these and other things of comfort. And at one side I noticed what looked like an altar of offering, but in detail I cannot speak of it, for I do not know the use of it explicitly.

LAUS DEO.

Now the organ begins to sound, and the people afloat break forth into an anthem of praise to the All-Father, to Whom every knee bows in adoration, for from Him only is Life, and all are through Him enabled. The Sun shines forth His life to earth, and the Heavens are as chambers within the Sun for light and warmth of love. To Whom, and to all those Gods Who owe Him birth and due allegiance, be our duty paid in offering of a pure heart and will of loyalty.

Now, these words were of a strange tone to me. But when I heard them, and the music which bore them through the air, I looked once again at the Altar, for I thought to find in it an answer. But this I could not. There was no sign or emblem upon it by which I might interpret this thing. It was but later that I was able to come at the meaning of it.

But you grow towards the end of your powers for this night, my ward.

Therefore we will cease now, and I will take up my theme again tomorrow, if you will. To-night God give you His blessing, as ever. So, good night.. Zabdiel is with you in thought and communion through the day and the night. Remember this and you will understand whence come many thoughts and suggestions. . . . No more now. You begin to tire. Zabdiel. #

BOOK II: THE HIGHLANDS OF HEAVEN
Wednesday, December 17, 1913.

And so we now proceed on to the further account of the coming of those from the far land across the sea. For their voyage had been a long one by way of preparing them against their taking up residence in this their future home.

Now, they had disembarked upon the shore, and all were gathered beneath the high headland which stood above like some giant watch-tower.

Then their leader looked among us for our Chief, and at last espied him, and knew him. For they had met before. So he came to him and the two greeted each one the other with warm love and blessing.

They conversed together for some time, and then our Chief stepped out and spoke to our new brethren, somewhat thus: "My friends and brethren, children with us of the One All-Father, Whom all adore according to that light he has, I bid you welcome to your new home.

"You have come far to seek it, and it will not disappoint you when you explore its beauties. I am but a humble servant here, but as it is to the Colony over which I am set that you will be led to begin your manner of life here, I am sent thus to welcome you.

"As you well know, and have learned by a long course of training, the faith you once held was but one single ray of the whole sunshine of God's great Love and Blessing. In the course of your instruction and development you have come to understand so much as this and more. One item alone of your own peculiar manner of worship have you retained—the Altar I see upon your vessel.

But inasmuch as the distinguishing device has faded from its pedestal, and as I saw no smoke of incense rise as you neared the shore, in offering of thanksgiving and adoration, I think that, as a token and badge, your Altar has lost some, or all, of its meaning to you. It is for you to choose whether you will bring that with you, or leave it aboard to return it to the land from whence you came for the use of others less progressed than yourselves; or whether you will land it, and convey it with you into your new life here.

Will you, of your courtesy, consult together, and tell me?"

251

Then they held a conference, but not for long; and their spokesman said,

"My lord, it is even as you say. There is now little meaning left to us in that which once was of aid to know and worship God our Father. For we have, by much teaching on the part of others, and our own meditation, come to know that all God's children are of one birth and race, as children of the One Father Alone. The time is now when it helps us no more to remember aught which divides, even though it be in love and general tolerance. We would, therefore, send it back; for yonder are those who perhaps remember more of the details of that religion which we have now progressed beyond.

"And now, my lord, we follow you to learn, of your goodness, and that of our brethren who serve under your guidance, what more we may of the Brotherhood of all mankind in the light of this brighter land, and those realms which lie beyond."

"You have very well said it," replied the Chief, "and it shall be so. Had you chosen else it would have pleased me; but this choice pleases me the better. And now, my brothers and sisters, come, and I will lead you into the fields which lie beyond this Gate, and into your Home."

So saying, he mingled with them, and kissed every one upon the brow; and I noticed that, when be did this, their countenances became of a more luminous aspect, like our own; and their clothing became more radiant also.

And the Mother descended from her station aloft, and did as he had done.

They were so happily met with us, and we with them, that we did not hurry to depart. Also their leader came some way with us for company; and we set off through the Gate, while the Mother and her maidens sang a hymn of Glory to the Highest, and to us a welcome and farewell in one. So we took our way inland along the valley.

Now, you will wonder at that Altar, and at the meaning of the speech of our Chief

If I might interrupt you, Zabdiel, why do you avoid telling me his name?

BOOK II: THE HIGHLANDS OF HEAVEN

I will tell you his name as you may put it into these letters, but cannot render it to you in its essential manner. Moreover, that is not permitted me. I will call him Harolen. That has three parts in speaking it, and so has his; and it will serve very well. So, to proceed.

He was much in occupation among the throng until we had passed the valley and river and were well into the country, the aspect of which I have not described to you hereto, for it was beyond that spot where I first met him. Then, when I noticed he had leisure, I approached and asked him who these were, and what worship they and he had spoken of on the shore.

Harolen answered, in effect, that they in the earth life had been worshippers of the God Whose Name was wrapt in the Fire and in the Sun, and Whom the old Persians reverenced.

"ONE LORD, ONE FAITH."

Now, I must add to that, of my own knowledge, this, ensuing. You must know that, when people first come out of the earth life into the first stage of their life eternal on this side, they are as they left the earth. This much you know. They who have any serious religion at all continue their worship and manner of life and conduct according to that religion as to its main and leading principles. But as they progress there is a winnowing, and the chaff is blown away, one fistful after another, as they go on from sphere to sphere. Ye while some shoot ahead, the bulk linger and go more leisurely onward; and those who have left them behind come back to them, from time to time, to instruct them.

So they go on from age to age, and realm to realm, and sphere to sphere; and all the while they approach nearer to the Universal idea of the All-Father. Brethren they still are together; but they learn to welcome, and then to love, brethren of other modes of religious thought and belief; as these others do also. And so there is a constant and increasing intercourse between those of varying creed.

But it is long before most will merge together in absolute unity. These old Persians still retained many of their own peculiar ways of looking at things, and will do so long hence. Nor is it to be wished for otherwise. For every one has a character of his own, and so adds of his own to the commonwealth of all.

But that party had made one more step onward during that voyage on the sea. Nay, rather I would say that during that voyage they had been brought to realize that they had already progressed that one stage in advance. Thus it came to pass that while certain of their phrases, and the way they made their adoration, gave it, to my mind, a distinctive tone and turn, yet that was more of the outer than the inner. And when the test was given them they decided to leave that Altar behind them, and to go onward themselves into the wider Brotherhood of God's Household of the Heavens.

It is thus we leave to float away into the mists behind us one after another of those minor helps which on earth seem so wonderfully important. It is thus we learn here what Love and Brotherhood really mean.

You are troubled, my charge; for I can both see and feel your mind and self at variance. Let it not be so, my brother. For know and be well assured of this: whatsoever is real and good and true will endure. Only what is not as these will fade away. And He Whom you serve is indeed the Truth, but did not reveal to you all truth; which was not possible to be done for those who are subject to the limitations of the life as you live it incarnate on earth. But He said you should be led into all the truth; and that is seen proceeding in the spheres beyond the bounds of earth. Of such I have even now been telling; and this leading continues I know not into what eternities of existence, or into what infinites of expansion in wisdom and love and power sublime.

But this I know—I who, as you, did worship and homage to the Christ of God and of Nazareth, and who pay my reverent devotion now as you are not yet able—this, I say, I know, my ward and fellow-worker in the Kingdom, that He is still on before a long, long way. The light that would blind me is to Him in His holiness as the twilight is to me. Beautiful He is,

I know, for I have seen Him as I am able, but not in His fulness of glory and majesty. Beautiful He is, aye, and lovely as I cannot find words to tell.

BOOK II: THE HIGHLANDS OF HEAVEN

And Him I serve and reverence with glad devotion and great joy. So do you not fear for your own loyalty. You will not take from Him by giving reverence to our brethren of other faiths than ours. For they are all His sheep, if they be not of this fold. Who is, and was, the Son of Man, and so Brother of us all. Amen.

Thursday, December 18, 1913.

The territory through which we passed was hilly but not mountainous, and on every side were green knolls, and here and there a dwelling. As we went Harolen became slowly changed in aspect. He grew brighter of countenance, and his robes began to assume a more luminous appearance.

By the time we had progressed past the woodland on our left hand he was come into his normal beauty and appeared thus. On his head a symbol of light appeared, as it might be a crown of jewels of red and brown, which sparkled and shone forth their rays, and between the rays and about there hovered an emerald radiance. His tunic fell to his knees, leaving bare his arms; and a gold belt he wore about his middle, clasped with a jewel of pearl-like substance, but in colour green and blue. His cap was of like colour, two-tinted, and on his forearms were zones of gold and silver interwoven.

He stood in the wagon, which had two wheels and was very beautiful in wood and metal, and drawn by two horses, white and brown. I noted that brown seemed to be in evidence throughout, but not so much as to give distinction to that colour but, as it might be said, to underlie every device, in a way that its presence was seen, and yet its aspect was subdued.

Symbolism in this land is of much interest and greatly used. I, therefore, seemed to read in this scheme of his colours the fact that he belonged to an order and realm in which brown was distinctive but, serving in this lower sphere, while present of propriety, yet those other colours which are more familiar among us in this sphere were given a place about him who had elected to serve here some time longer than of necessity he might have done.

But as I looked on him, thus so simply garbed and yet so altogether beautiful, I felt his great power. For in his eyes there

255

shone clear holiness, with dignity to command, while his brow, over which his brown hair parted and curled backward about his temples, seemed to woo humility and gentleness as a sister more beloved. Yet he was such as no one of lesser estate might willingly dare in opposition, while none would fear him, so that one be simple in his good intent and loving withal. One he was whom to follow his lead was joy, and in whose protection and guidance implicit trust might well be placed. For he was a Prince, with a prince's power, and wisdom to use it aright in gentleness and love.

So we journeyed on, not much conversing together, but drinking in all the beauty of that place with much gladness of heart, and peace and rest about us. Thus we came at last to the place where the new-comers should pause to stay awhile until they had become familiar with their new environment.

Then they would proceed farther inland to one of the settlements, and perhaps would go some to one and some to another, according as they were the better fitted for this or that in the work and service of this sphere of the Kingdom of God.

Arriving here Harolen called a halt, and asked for silence for a little space, as he had a message to bring to them from his chief city, which lay ahead beyond the rising hills and out of sight.

So we kept silence and, presently, a great flash of light shot through the heavens from some point beyond the hills in front. It struck upon us and we stood all bathed in a flood of brightness; but no one was startled or afraid, for the light had joy in it. But if it clothed us, then about the chariot in which the Prince stood was a very glorious thing to be seen.

He stood there quite still, but the light about him became focussed and concentrated; and he appeared no longer as he had been hereto, but, as it were, transparent and all aflame with glory. How shall I make you to have some small idea of what I wish to tell? Try to picture him made of alabaster, but living and glowing and irradiated through with a beauty of glorious light, itself alive and rejoicing. Every jewel and ornament became suffused with it, and the chariot itself was glowing as with flames of fire.

And all about him were glory and the majesty of life and energy. The horses, also, did not so much absorb as reflect the radiance. And the circlet about his head shone forth with a sevenfold intensity.

Yet he did not rise into the heavens, as well he might have done, so translucent and sublimated had he become in appearance. He stood there still, his eyes looking straight into the light and reading it as a message, as if he saw what we could not see, and that, too, not there but far away ahead over the hills, at the place from which that light was sent.

The next we knew surprised us all greatly. Instead of compelling some wonder or miracle of power, he quietly knelt down in his wagon, and bowed his face into his hands, silent and still. And yet we all felt that he was not afraid, but master, of that light, and of even higher majesty. We knew he bowed to One of greater might and in holiness higher than he. So we, too, knelt and bowed to worship Whom he worshipped, knowing a Power was present, but in whose Person we did not know.

As he knelt thus we presently heard music and voices chanting some very beautiful theme, but in words we none of us could interpret. Still kneeling we looked up and saw that Harolen had decended from his wagon, and stood upon the road in front of us his company. Walking down the road towards him was a Man, clad in white from head to foot. One circle of light crossed His forehead and girded His hair behind. No jewel did He wear, but over His shoulders two bands, which were crossed between His breasts before, and were held in place with a belt. They and it were of silver and red mingled. His face was calm, and with no majesty save that of love and kindness; and He walked with slow and thoughtful step, as if He bore in His heart the weal and woe of some great universe. It was no sadness we saw, but something near akin, and yet I cannot name it, so unfathomable was that quiet all-embracing calm which was about Him.

He came to where Harolen still knelt, and said some word to him in a tongue we did not know; and also His voice was so subdued that we felt He spoke rather than heard Him. The Prince looked up then into His face and smiled; and his smile was lovely, as everything about him was lovely.

Then the Other bent down and folded him in His arms, and raised him up, and stood by his side and held his hand in one of His own. Standing thus

He raised His right hand and, looking on us, He blessed us and spoke words of cheer and encouragement to proceed in our work which lay ahead of us.

He was not eloquent, but rather were His words those of a mother to her children setting forth on A journey. No more than this, and spoken so quietly and so simply, and yet in suchwise that they gave us confidence and joy together, and all fear was taken away. For at the first we were somewhat in awe of Him before Whom our Prince had bent the knee.

Standing thus, the light all gathered itself together and enveloped Him, and while He held the hand of Harolen He became more and more invisible, and then was gone from sight where He had stood. And the light was gone, as if He had absorbed it into Himself, and had taken it with Him when He went.

Once again our Prince knelt down upon the road,

And bowed himself awhile. And then he arose and in silence, waving his hand to beckon us onward. He mounted his wagon in silence, and in silence we followed him round a hill till we came to the place near by where these should abide. #

CHAPTER VII: ZABDIEL'S TOUR OF INSPECTION

At the Children's Home—A lesson in creative faith—At the village of Bepel—Joy and sorrow of the Angels—Into the Highlands—The Highland Watch Tower—How messages are received there—A Horizon of Glory—Walls of light—Motherhood enthroned—The Crimson Glory of the Christ—A colony with a problem.

Friday, December 19, 1913.

"ACCORDING to your faith be it unto you." This stands a promise of power to-day as when first He said it; and it may be claimed with full assurance of fulfilment. Only that faith must be present, and then the present enablement will be manifest, in ways diverse but with no uncertainty of cause and effect.

Now, this is not alone to you, but to us here in these spheres progressed and progressive. It is the acquiring of faith in exercise that we study to compass and, that gotten, we are powerful to help others, and ourselves to enjoy. For it is delight and pleasure to give, more than to receive, as He said.

But do not mistake the nature of faith in the using of it. In the earth life it is of indefinite quality as mostly understood — something between trustfulness and a right understanding of what is truth. But here, where we study all things as to their essence, we know that faith is more than this. It is power capable of scientific analysis, in a measure in correspondence with the progress made by any man.

In order to show you my meaning the better I will tell you of one incident in which this is seen.

I was making a visitation of certain homes at the instance of my Superior, to see how they did who lived in them, and to help by what advice I might, and to report on returning. So I went from one home to another, and came at length to a cottage in a woodland part, where there dwelt a number of children with their guardians. These latter were a man and his wife who had progressed, in the latter period of their ascending, side by side. These had the care of the children, boys and girls, who had been either stillborn, or who had died at birth or soon after. Such are not, as a rule, taken to those Homes in the lower 'spheres, but brought higher for their development. This is because there is little of earth to do out of their natures; and they also need more special care than those who have, even by a little, fought and developed in the earth battle of life.

The guardians greeted me, and the children came, at their beck, to pay me their welcome. But they were very shy at me, and did not easily respond to my talk to them at the first. All these children are very delicate in their beauty who come over here so, and I was much given to loving them, these little lambs of our Father and His Son. So I enticed them, and at length they became easier of manner.

One little man drew near me and began to play with my belt, for its brightness pleased him, and he as inquisitive of its metal. So I sat on a little grass bank, and took him on my knee, and asked him if he would choose what pretty thing the belt should bring him. He was doubtful of my meaning at first and, following, of my ability.

But I repeated my invitation, and he replied, "A dove, please you, Sir."

That was very polite of him, and I told him so, and that when little boys asked in such ways, trusting and believing, then they always got their will, if that will was wise and pleasing to our Father.

This saying, I placed him on his feet before me, and put out my will to the end he desired. And presently the form of a dove was seen in the plate of metal which fastened the belt, and this grew in distinctness, until at length it expanded beyond the plate, and then I took it, and it was a live dove which stood on my hand and cooed, and looked at me, and then at the boy, as if wondering which was the parent of its being. I gave him to the lad, and he took him into his bosom, and ran to show the others what had come to pass.

Now, this was no more than a bait to hook more fish. Surely they came, by one and two, until a little crowd of eager faces looked up into mine, not daring so much as to ask, yet longing to be brave enough to do so. Still I waited and said nought, but only smiled them back their smiles; for I was giving them a lesson in the power of faith, and their acquirement of it demanded some initiative on their part.

It was a little maiden who first braved to titter the wishes of herself and companions. She stepped forward and took the border of my tunic in her little dimpled hand and, looking up to me, said rather tremulously, "If you please, sir—," and then broke off and coloured with confusion. So I hoisted her to my shoulder and told her to ask her will.

She wanted a lamb.

I told her that orders were coming in in some good style, and growing in bulk betimes. A lamb was rather a bigger pet than a dove. Did she believe that I could give her a lamb?

Her reply was very naive. She said, "If you please, sir, the others do."

I laughed heartily, and called them nearer, and they said, Yes, if I could make a dove with feathers, I could make a lamb with wool on it (but they called it fur).

Then I sat down again and spoke to them. I asked them if they loved our Father, and they said, Yes, very much, for He it was Who made all this beautiful land, and showed people how to love them. I told them that those who loved the Father were His true children, and that if they asked Him for anything wise and good, believing

He was present in His life and power, they would be able so to make their wills use that power that the thing desired would come to them. So it was not needful that I should make any more animals for them, as they could make them themselves. But, as this was rather a difficult case to begin with, I would help them.

Then, at my bidding, they all thought of the lamb they wished to, have, and then willed that it should come to them. But nothing came of it apparently; and I restrained my power within certain limitation, of a purpose. After trying awhile I told them to pause.

Then I explained that they were not powerful enough yet, but when they grew bigger they would be able to do even this, if they continued to develop their faith, in prayer and love, and continued, "For you have that power, only it is not yet large enough, except to do small things. And I am going to show you that you have some of that power in you now, so that you will continue to learn your lessons from your good guardians. You have not yet sufficient power to create a living animal, but you have enough to influence one already alive to come to you. Are there any lambs on this estate?"

They said there were none, but there were so—me on an estate rather a long distance away, where they had gone on a visit a short time before.

"And you," I said, "by your faith and power have brought one of these lambs to you."

I pointed behind them and, turning, they saw a little lamb feeding on a path among the trees a little distance away.

They were too much surprised at first to do aught but stare at him. But some of the older ones recovering, broke away and ran, with cries of delight, to the place where he was and, seeing them, he ran sporting and prancing to meet them, seeming as joyous as they to find playmates to sport with.

"It's alive," they cried, and turned to beckon the laggards on; and soon that poor lamb was smothered with fondling and caressing, as he might have been a child of their own begetting. I do think they had for 'him a considerable sense of motherhood and proprietorship.

Now, this may seem more or less casual, according to the bent of him who reads. But it is essentials which matter. And I tell you that the pretty little lesson thus given was the spring of what will eventuate, perhaps long ages hence, in the creation of some cosmos, as it might be that of which your planet is a small member. It is thus the Principalities and Powers began to train for mightier things. What they had seen me do was an act of Creation. What they had themselves done, with some little aid from me, was the beginning of such evolvement, which should lead them on to do what I had done, and then to progress, as we in these spheres do, from power to power greater still as faith is added to, little by little, as we use it in the service of Him Who gives it us to enjoy.

This is faith, and, unseen by you, or not so clearly seen, your faith it is which, sanctified by prayer and high motive, brings to pass its own fulfilment. Use it, then, but with care and circumspection and all reverence, for it is one of the great trusts which He has confided to you—and to us in greater measure—and that is no mean mark of His great love. Whose Name be blessed for the free Bounty of His giving. Amen for ever. #

Monday, December 22, 1913.

Thus far, then, of the children's Home and schooling. And now to other matters of that tour.

I entered a village where some small number of houses were grouped, but each in its own small domain. Here were there several miniature communities of people who had in hand occupations dissimilar in detail only, but in general on the same line of development. The head man of the place came to meet me at a bridge which spanned the stream which wellnigh circled this village and passed onward, eventually emptying its waters into that river of which already I have spoken. Our greetings made, we passed on together. As I went I noticed the neatness of the gardens and dwellings, and remarked on it to my companion.

Could you tell me his name, please?

You may write it down, Bepel. Let us continue.

I came to one, however, which had not so much wealth of aspect, and on this I also remarked, and asked the reason why; for I was not acquainted with what reason it might be which, in this sphere, should arrest the progress of any.

Bepel smiled and replied, "You know the man who lives here, he and his sister. They came over from the Spheres Eight and Nine some good while ago together. Here they progressed and, from time to time have returned to the Fourth Sphere, where they have loved ones and, in especial, their parents. This they have done in order to help them onward. Lately they have come to be some little less at their ease in these surroundings for the love they bear to those behind. It would seem that these are making their progress very slowly, and it will be long before they reach this estate.

These two, therefore, await the coming of some one who has authority to permit them depart to take up their abode with those they wish to help, in order that their more continual presence should be at the disposal of them to enable them onward."

"I will see these two," I replied, and we went within the garden.

Now, you may be interested to know how such a case as this is dealt with here, and so I will proceed, in more or less detail, to describe what followed.

I found the brother in a small coppice to the side of the house and accosted him, inquiring for his sister. She was within, and we went to seek her. We found her there in deep meditation. She was engaged in communion with her parents far away in that other sphere. Rather would I say that she was sending her help and uplifting strength to them, for "communion" implies a mutual action, and the others were little able, if any, to return their thoughts to her.

So I talked with them awhile, and gave them my conclusion after this fashion: "It would seem that the strength required to build up your own progress in this Sphere is being drawn upon by those in the Sphere some degrees behind. You are held back by the love of those who are yonder, and slow to progress. Now, if you go to that Fourth Sphere, and there take up your habitation, you will be able to help them a little, but not much.

For when you are at hand why should they stretch forth to come beyond their own present degree? It is not well, therefore, that you go to them in such manner as that. Yet love is greater than all else, and as it is found both in you and them, it will be of great might to prevail when obstacles which now obstruct have been removed. I would advise that you do not relinquish your degree of this Sphere, but that you come with me to our Chief, and I will ask that he will give you other work to do by which your own progress will be ensured, and that of your loved ones not hindered."

When I departed they came along with me and, after consultation with our Chief Lord, I was glad to find that he, in the main, approved of what was in my mind. So he called them, and gave them words of approof for their great love, and told them that, if they would, they should become of those whose mission it was from time to time to go to the Spheres behind and, there appearing (by conditioning themselves to the environment of the sphere in which they should be), deliver what business he should have to communicate. On such occasions he would request that their parents should be permitted to see and talk with them. By so doing they would be lured onward and upward to join these their two children in those higher realms.

He further counselled great patience, for that this thing might in no wise be forced ahead, but must progress by natural development. To this they assented with much joy and gratitude of heart. So the Chief Lord blessed them in the Name of the Master, and they departed to their new Home well content.

So you will see from this, my friend and ward, that in the higher realms of progress problems arise which feature those of the spheres just ahead of the earth plane. For many there, too, are held back by their love of such on earth who do not so progress that they may come into communion with their spiritual lovers and helpers did these ascend many degrees removed above the state of those incarnate laggards.

But others there are, also incarnate, who, by their own advance, do but by a little, or not at all, hold back their spirit guides, advancing after them by strenuous endeavour, with humility of heart and holy aspiration, that they help the rather, often, and hinder not at all.

Keep this also in your mind with the many other things you have learned. It is possible, nay, inevitable, that you incarnate on earth do help on or pull back your good friends on this side.

In which light think of the Angels of those Seven Churches to whom the Christ sent word by the hand of John. For those each, by the virtues or sinfulness of the Church he had in charge, was judged in person, as through that Church accountable to Him Who assessed each in its exact value, and awarded praise or blame to the Angel-guardian of each Church according as it merited the one or the other. As the Christ, the Son of Man, identified in Himself the character of the children of men, and held Himself accountable for the salvation of His brethren according to the flesh before the Father, so is each Angel-guide accountable for, and identified with, the one, or the community, over which he is placed to serve. He enjoys with them, and suffers with them; he rejoices over them, and mourns over their shortcomings. Remember what He said, for this I have seen, not once, nor two nor three times, but many, "There is joy of Angels before the Presence of God in the Heavens when a sinner repents." And I add to you, my brother,

THE LIFE BEYOND THE VEIL

The bright Angels do not always laugh—though laugh they do, and that in constant. But Angels, too, can weep tears—weep and suffer for your sorrows and sins who fight the fight below. This will not be in tune with the thoughts of us in many minds. Never mind, write it down. For by what reasoning do we joy, if we may not also mourn? #

Tuesday, December 23, 1913

For all that it is so plainly written that men and angels work together in the one service of God, yet men find it hard to believe this to be true. It is because they give too much thought to the things of earth, and too little to the origin of material things. This is not of those forces which come immediately into contact with matter to shape and use it, but beyond, where they use those forces as a potter uses clay to make his jar or vase. This has, in some degree, already been given to you to write down.

Tonight I will tell you some narrative of their doings as we see them at their work from this side the borderline.

Not all are progressed evenly in any one of the spheres, but some are advanced beyond others. Those of whom I last told you were of the least in this Tenth Sphere. I will now tell you of some who have risen to greater life and power. On my way, as I journeyed after leaving the village where the brother and sister dwelt, I paid my visit of inspection to many other settlements.

One of these lay among the mountains towards the zone which marks the beginning of the next Sphere superior to this—not that spot where I met my guide, but at a similar altitude, and some distance away. Hither I ascended by a winding path which led to the high lands among the summits of the mountain range. When I began to ascend the grass was very green and the flowers large and profuse. Birds sang about the velvet path among the leafy trees of forests deep with purple lights and shadows, and many spirits of the woodlands sported or worked with bright smiles as I passed them, giving and receiving, greetings of blessings, and adding joy to beauty by the way.

Then the surroundings began to change, and the trees became more stately and statuesque, the forest less dense and leafy.

BOOK II: THE HIGHLANDS OF HEAVEN

Whereas before glades of flowers and arbours of foliage had been, there now appeared lofty cathedrals of pillars and arches, as the trees stood tip and bent their heads to make them. Deep and lovely still were the lights and shades, but more like those of a sanctuary than of a bower. Of large proportions were the avenues, as I passed them, stretching away on either hand. Here, too, there was a sense of meditation and greater power than away below. And I was aware of spirits in the colonnades who were beautiful with a grander and holier beauty than those I had left behind about the first rises of the hills. This also, as I went, gave place to scenes more awful and inspiring.

Gradually the tree country was left behind, and about the white, gold and red of the summits played lights which told of presences from the higher realm descended on some business, to linger among these heights awhile.

So I came to my destination. I will describe it as I am able. There was a flat space, perhaps a mile in square each way, paved with alabaster stone, which appeared of flame colour, as if it were a floor of glass stretched over a realm of fire whose rays played about it, and glowed through, tinting the air for some hundred yards above. There was no fire of such sort. But this is in what aspect it appeared.

On this level space was one building. It was of ten sides, and each side was diverse in colour and in architecture from all its fellows. Many stories it had, and rose a glittering pillar whose top caught the light which came above the peaks of the mountains, some far, some near—so high was this tower, as it stood there, a sentinel among the mountains of heaven, a very beautiful thing to see. It covered some eighth part of the square, and it had porches on each side. So there were ten ways to enter, and one facing each of ten ways. A sentinel in truth it was; for this is the Watch-tower of the highest regions of that sphere. But it was more than this.

Each side was in touch with one of the first ten spheres; and those who watched there were in constant communication with the Chief Lords of those spheres. There is much business passing between these Heads of the different spheres continually. Here it was gathered up and co-ordinated. If I might descend to earth for a name, I would call it the Central Exchange of that vast region comprised in all those spheres stretching from that which borders on the earth zone, over the continents and oceans and mountains and plains of the second, and then of the third, and so onward to the Tenth.

Needful it is that those who serve here be of very high development and wisdom, and so I found them to be. They were different from the ordinary inhabitant of this sphere. They were always courteous with love and kindness, gentle, and anxious to help and gladden their brethren. But there was a stateliness of absolute calm upon them which never gave place to the slightest agitation whatever news came to them there of the doings and strenuous life they held in direct contact with themselves. They received all reports, information, requests for solution of some perplexity, or for help in other ways, in perfect quietude of mind. When something more tremendous than usual burst upon them, they were unmoved and ready always, quietly confident in strength to cope with their task whatever it might be, and with wisdom to make no mistake. I sat within the porchway of the side which was in communion with the

Sixth Sphere studying some of their records of past events and their concern in them. As I read, a quiet voice whispered over my shoulder, "If you are not too much interested, Zabdiel, in that book, you would perhaps enjoy to see what we do within." I looked round and up at him who spoke, and met his quiet beautiful smile with a nod of assent.

I went within. There was a large hall of triangular shape and, high up, the floor of the next apartment.

We went to the wall, where it met in angle, and there my friend bade me stand awhile and listen. I soon heard voices, and could discern the words they brought. These were being dealt with in a room above us, five stories aloft, and were transmitted downwards, passing through the floor into the ground below, where there were other chambers. I asked the reason of this and he informed me that all messages are received by those who had their station on the roof of the building. These extracted what words they needed for their part of the work, and allowed the residue to proceed downwards into the chamber below them. Here the message was treated in like manner, and again handed on downwards. This was repeated again and again until what was left passed down the walls of this ground-floor room to be once again sifted and the residue passed on below. In each room there was a great multitude of workers, all busy, but without haste, going about their task.

Now, you will think this a strange way to go to work. But the reality was stranger still. For when I say I heard the words, I only tell you half.

They were audible visibly. Now, how shall I put that into your tongue? I can no better than this: As you gazed at the wall (which was treated in different metals and stones, each vitalized by what principle here answers to electricity with you) you saw the message in your brain rather than optically and, when you were sensible of its import, you heard the voice which uttered it in some region far away. In this manner you were aware, in your inner consciousness, of the tone of the speaker's voice, of his aspect and stature and manner of countenance, of his degree and department of service, and other details of help to the exact understanding of the meaning of the message sent.

This dispatch and receipt of messages is brought to high perfection in these spirit realms, and in this Tower of Vigilance to the highest perfection I have encountered. I was not competent to translate what I saw and heard, for the communication had come through the conditions of all those spheres intervening, and had become more complex than I could unravel.

So he explained it to me in simple.

It was to the effect that a party had been sent from the Sixth Sphere into the Third to, help in the construction of some works there proceeding.

Those who had designed them had been of high development, and had included in the apparatus and structure to contain it, a somewhat more advanced scheme than it was possible to construct successfully out of the substance of that sphere. I might put the problem to you thus: If you were to endeavour to build up a machine for the manufacture of ether, and the conversion of it into matter, you would find no substance to your hand on earth of sufficient sublimity to hold the ether, which is of a force greater and more terrific than any force which is imprisoned within what you understand as matter. It was a somewhat similar problem they had to encounter now, and

wanted advice as to how best to proceed in order that the scheme might be carried out to as large an extent as possible. This is one of the simpler problems these high ones are given to solve.

Now, I will tell you more of this at another time. You are spent now and I cannot find words in you to say what I would.

My blessing is upon your life and work. Be assured thereof and go forward bravely. #

Christmas Eve, 1913.

I have spoken of the science of that High Place and it would not be much of help to you were I to continue in that vein; for the wisdom and duties there are of a degree you would understand but little. It would confuse you, and seem not over-wise, what I could give to you. I will, therefore, briefly add what I may, and get on to another theme.

I went up to the storey next above, and found it and the rest full of business, with workers at it in plenty. The walls of these large halls are all utilized in the sifting of messages and other like work. They are not flat walls, such as you know, but all shimmering with vari-coloured radiance, and embossed with devices, and otherwise relieved. All these are instruments of their science, and all are watched, and their effects recorded and considered and handed on to their proper destination, whether to others within that settlement, or to spheres higher or lower, as the business in hand demands.

A HORIZON OF GLORY.

My kind guide took me to the roof of the Tower, and here I was enabled to view the country far afield.

Below me I saw the woodlands by which I had ascended. Further away stretched range on range of high mountains, all bathed in the high celestial light, and glittering like jewels of many colours. About some of those peaks there played a shimmering beauty which reached them from the Eleventh Sphere; and they seemed to be alive and responsive to the presence of high beings whose nature was of a degree so refined that their forms were just beyond the circumference of visibility to one, like myself, of the Tenth Sphere.

Yet I knew that these were come over from their own brighter region, and were on some work of love engaged in this my own. At that I rejoiced very much for the knowledge of the love and power beneficent all about me, and my only speech was silence, which spoke more eloquent than words of mine could do.

At last, when I had feasted long my spirit on this great beauty, my companion gently laid his hand on my shoulder, and said, "Now these, my good brother, are the HIGHLANDS of this HEAVEN. The solitude is such as, in its beauty, fills you with reverence, awe and holy aspiration.

For you now stand at the summit and boundary of your present attainment; and you have here found an environment into which, of your own strength, you are not able to penetrate. But it is given to us, as a sacred trust, and to be used sparingly and with discretion, to unveil the veiled, and look on that which is invisible to our normal sight. Would you that this, for a few moments, be given to you, that you look into what is around you unseen till this present?"

At this I paused, somewhat afraid, for what I saw was as much as I had strength to endure. But, while considering the matter, I resolved that where all was love and wisdom, no harm should be able to strike me. So I entrusted myself into his keeping; and he said it was well.

Then he turned from me and went into, a Sanctuary which was upon the roof of this Tower, and was absent awhile, as I told myself, in prayer.

Presently he came forth, and he was changed greatly; for his robe was not upon him, but he stood naked before me but for a circlet of flashing gems upon his brow. How beautiful he was as he stood there bathed in that soft penetrating light which intensified about him and moved and lived, until his body was like liquid glass and gold and shone forth increasingly till I looked downwards and shaded my eyes from his exceeding brightness.

WALLS OF LIGHT.

Then he spoke to me and told me to stand before him, while he would keep to my rearward, using his power upon me, but not blinding me with his radiance. Thus we stood, his hands upon my shoulders, and the light from him enveloping me also, and, streaming forth on either side of me, it shone far out blending into the distance with those other lights far away about the peaks. Thus a lane appeared in front of me where I stood, its either side bordered with a wall of light, and the space between not dim but of lesser brightness.

I could not penetrate those walls with my vision, as they swept away across the deeps and heights of the mountain-tops, opening out as they went, on either side in suchwise that, while I stood, as it might be, in the angle where the two walls of living flame met just behind me, yet in front it was a space of great breadth between the walls where I could see them far away.

Then he spoke again and told me to watch this space. I did so, and there grew a vision very wonderful upon my gaze, so that I who have beheld many beauties and marvels have never seen aught so entrancing as this.

The two rays struck one on either side a mountain peak which rose into the sky, a sharp needle with lesser spurs about it below. As I looked it began to change, and I saw a large Temple emerge into my view, and about it were a host of high angels in robes of light, moving here and there. There was a high porch and upon it stood a great Angel who held a cross aloft, as if he showed that symbol to some congregation of people in some other far-away sphere. On each arm of the cross stood a child, one in rose-pink garments, the other in green and brown. They sang some song I could not understand, and then, as they ended, each laid his hands upon his breast and bowed his head in worship.

MOTHERHOOD ENTHRONED.

But my guide now turned me about to the right and another vista came into my range of vision. Upon a hillside far away I saw a Throne. It was of light and fire mingled, and there sat upon it a woman who looked in silence into the far, far distance unmoving. She was clad in gossamer which sparkled like silver as her body shone through it; but over her head was a robe of violet-coloured light which fell upon her shoulders and behind her, framing her beauty in suchwise that I thought of a pearl hung against a velvet curtain.

About her, but below her Throne, were her attendants, both men and women. They stood there before the Throne and on either side, silent and waiting. They were all of much more brightness than I, but none was so radiant as she who sat there serene in all her loveliness. I noted her face. It was full of that carefulness which is born of love and pity, but her eyes were dark in their depth of high wisdom and power. She rested her two arms upon the arms of the Throne, and I noted further that all her limbs told of strength, but such strength as is mingled with the gentleness of motherhood.

Then suddenly she stirred, pointed with her hand here, beckoned there, waved to others, as she issued, in no haste, but briskly and incisively, her commands.

All suddenly the crowd was in movement. I saw one party rise and fly off like a flash of lightning into the distance. Another went in other direction. And other troops I saw bring forth horses, mount and ride away into space. Some wore flowing robes, and some were girt with what looked like plated armour. Some parties were of men, others of women, and others of men and women both. In, as it were, a moment's

time, the sky was dotted with diamonds and rubies and emeralds, as these appeared flashing on their heavenly way; and the dominating colour of the group shone back to me, as I stood to gaze in awe and silence.

Thus the lane of light was moved from place to place the whole horizon round and, at each pause, something new to me I saw. Each scene was diverse in character, but of equal beauty with the rest. In such manner I saw some of those who were of higher degree than any I had yet beheld at work in the service of the Father. And when I saw, by the changing light, that my friend had withdrawn once more into the Sanctuary behind me, I sighed for bliss too great, and sank down overcome with the glory of the service of God as I had seen it in operation among those who watched us as we, too, worked, and took account of our needs.

It was thus I came to understand, as never before, how that all the inferior spheres are included within those above, and not lying sharply defined, away each from its fellows. This Tenth Sphere included in itself all those below and was, in its turn, included in those above, together with the others below the Tenth. This is well understood here, up to our own degree. But as we advance, this inclusion of spheres becomes more complex and wonderful, and there are things to understand in it which are unfolded but by little and little. This I have come to see, and am all agape for the further advance when I am ripe for it.

Oh, the wonder and beauty and wisdom of our God!

If what I know be but a little of His scheme of love, then what must the whole be like, and how tremendous!

Veiled are even the lower glories of the Heavenly Lands from mortal eyes, which strain to see them. Brother, be content to go slowly in these things. Such things are veiled in love and mercy. For, could they burst upon you in their fulness, your mind would give way before it all, and you would f or long, long ages fear to go ahead lest worse befall you. I see it now as once I could not. It is wise and good—all wise and altogether good. And He is Love indeed. #

Saturday, December 27, 1913

Now, it was very wonderful that I should thus be permitted to see these wonders of those spheres beyond my estate. I thought upon it afterward, and found I could understand some of the principal intention and motive of what I had seen; but there were many things else I could in nowise fathom unaided. One was in this manner of appearance.

The whole heaven between the two ends of the light-rays, which formed each a wall on either hand of my prospect, was flooded crimson. Deep, deep and intensely deep was the region, on which I gazed, with crimson light. It seemed to be some gigantic volcanic upheaval, for clouds of this luminescence heaved and swayed one upon another, and lifted up great bunks of itself on high, and swept to one hand or other hand, and sank and met other banks of cloud.

All was commotion as of blazing and consuming catastrophic fury. So awful did that red maelstrom seem to my soul that I trembled very much in fear of it.

"Turn me away from it. Of your love, sir, turn aside to some scene less awful. For this is of mystery too terrific for me to uphold myself before its overbearing grandeur."

Thus I besought my friend, who replied, "Rest you awhile, my brother, and you shall see it is not terrific any more. You are now looking toward the onward spheres, the first of these being Sphere Eleven. In what sphere that light shines I cannot tell you, unless I afterward read the record of it, and this is not taken in this College, but in one some distance from here.

'For this you behold is far beyond our duties to deal with. I may be Sphere Thirteen, or even Fifteen, upon which you now look so much afraid. I know not. But this I know—the Christ passes there, and the Crimson Glory you see is the aura of His communion with His loved ones there in love. Look steadfastly upon the sight, for it is not seen so well but rarely, and I will try to enable you to penetrate some of the details therein."

I felt him intensifying his energizing upon me, and strove to raise myself to meet his endeavours. Success did not come, however, for this was beyond me, as I soon found out. All I could see, more than I have told you, were some vague shapes of beauty moving in the midst of the crimson, fiery glory; no more. So I besought him again, rather piteously as I fear, to suffer me to turn away. And this he did. But

I could no more thereafter. I had no heart for aught else. All seemed very pallid as matched against what I had beheld; and I was rather sick at heart awhile that I might not go yonder, and be as they must be who endure so much beauty and yet enjoy to live. By and by I recovered and, when he had come forth of the Sanctuary again, in normal guise and raiment, I could so far as to speak to him in words of thanks for his very large bounty in giving to such as I what he had given.

Now, what may I tell you more of the doings upon that lofty perch? For you will keep in your mind that only a little of our life

275

and actions here are you able to understand, and that only in part. So that I have to choose very carefully what items I show you; which are such that in some degree I may reproduce in your mind and earth phrasing. One more I think I may essay.

A COLONY WITH A PROBLEM.

When the larger visions were ended, we stayed awhile up there upon the roof, and looked upon the country round about us. I noticed, some distance away towards the Ninth Sphere, a large lake bordered with forestland and, here and there, an island, with buildings nestling among trees or peeping above them. Also in the forest ashore was there, now here and now there, a turret to be seen. I asked of my guide what colony was that; for a colony it seemed to be, it hung together so well, and seemed one settlement.

He told me that a long time ago a difficulty arose in dealing with those who arrived in this sphere from other regions, who had not yet progressed in all directions as in some of the branches of heavenly science.—I am not satisfied with that; I will try to make it more clear.

There are some who progress evenly in all the faculties which are theirs; but others do not develop all their faculties equally all along their way of progress. These, none the less, are very highly developed spirits, and come to the Tenth Sphere in due course. But had they developed their neglected powers in the same proportion as the others, they would have arrived here much earlier.

Moreover, arrived here, they are at just such an altitude that what served in spheres behind them will serve no more in future. They must henceforth become more equalized in their faculties, and so of more equal balance.

The problem which gave rise to the establishment of that settlement was no other than this. And there they abide doing their work of help to others, and self-training the while. You may wonder wherein is the difficulty. If you do so wonder, that is by reason of the much more complex perfection of the conditions here prevailing than is the case with you.

It arises from the fact that these people are really of the Tenth Sphere in some portion of their character, and of perhaps the

Eleventh or Twelfth in other portion. And the difficulty is this: They are in some ways too large in power and personality for

their present environment, and yet unable to proceed into the next sphere, where their inferior parts would suffer damage, and catastrophe would ensue which would probably throw them backward many spheres behind, where they would be as ill at ease as ever.

Now, have I made their case clear? If you lift a fish out of the denser water into the rarer air it will have disaster. If you take a mammal from the forest, and plunge him into water, he will die also of the denser element.

An amphibian is able to live if he have both water and dry land. But place him altogether on dry land, and he will sicken. Put him altogether in water, and he will sicken likewise.

Now, these of whom I have been telling are not quite like any of these, yet the analogy will suffice to help you to understand their case. For them to be here is like a bird caged. For them to penetrate higher would be like a moth flying into a flame.

And how is their case dealt with?

They are there to deal with it themselves. I believe they are only in the course of finding the best solution to the problem. When they have done so they will have rendered a service to this sphere which will be carefully recorded for future use. This is continually 'happening in various branches of study. I think they at present have been able to classify themselves according to their leading traits, and are working on a kind of reciprocal system. Each class endeavours to foster in the others that virtue and power which it has and they lack. So does each, and there is a very complicated system of communal education arisen, which is too intricate even for those who dwell in the Highlands to analyze. But something will come of it which will, when finally ripe to be given forth, add to the power and influence of this region, and that, I think, in some very large measure.

Thus it is that mutual service is rendered; and the royal delight of progress is to help others forward in the way, as we go. Is that not so, my friend and ward?

And so, my blessing, and Good-night. #

CHAPTER VIII: COME, YE BLESSED, AND INHERIT

Zabdiel's mission to Fifth Sphere—The Capital City of Sphere Five-Zabdiel's test of the faithful women—The constitution of Sphere Five—The Sixth Sphere—The Initiation in the Sanctuary — Back in the Tenth Sphere—The Temple of the Holy Mount—The King of kings—The Power and the Glory—Zabdiel's farewell.

Monday, December 29, 1913.

OF other things which I saw there I speak not now. It is easier to describe in your earth language the scenes and people and the doings of them which are of those spheres nearer to that of earth. But the higher you go the more of difficulty comes in between, and this sphere is somewhat exalted comparatively; and this that I have but just written is of the Highlands of this sphere. So, as before I told you, I am but able to give a very foreshortened and inadequate view of this land and its glories. So let me to matters of more immediate importance to you, and no less helpful.

ZABDIEL'S MISSION TO THE FIFTH SPHERE.

I come to a time when it was laid upon me by the Chief Angel Lord of this Tenth Sphere to take my journeyings into the Fifth Sphere of a special purpose, which I will now explain.

I was to go to the Capital City of that region and, presenting myself to the Chief, to inquire of the reason for which I had come thither. This he would tell me, having already received word of my coming. Nor was I to go alone, but with me went three brethren for my company.

When we arrived at our destination I found the City very easily, inasmuch as I had known it in that time I was a sojourner in that sphere. But how different it appeared now to me after this long time and my many experiences. Bethink you, friend. This was the first time I had come hither since my advancement from that estate into the Sixth Sphere; and through this and the others I had worked my upward way until the Tenth was reached. Then, after all these stages, and each with its busy life and many incidents to change and develop me, I come back to this sphere wherein, moreover, I had not stayed so long as in any of the others. It was strange, but very familiar, even to detail. The strangeness lay in that when I had first come here from the Fourth Sphere, the glory of it had seemed too great for my apprehension. It dazzled me. But now my eyes had labour to conform to its dimness and want of light.

As we passed through the spheres intervening we conditioned ourselves to each, but went swiftly. When we reached the confines of the Fifth, however, we descended and went afoot slowly from the higher into the lower lands, in order that we might grow into its condition by little and by little. For we should, mayhap, be here for some time, and so would the better be able to endure, and do what work was ours to do.

It was interesting, as an experience, that descent from the mountainous country into the lowlands. There was, as we went down, a continual dimness increasing ever, and yet we were continually accustoming our eyes and bodies to its condition. The sensation was strange and not unpleasant; and to me it was quite new at that time. It exhibited to me the wonderful wisdom which is throughout all and every necessary detail of these realms, this co-adjustment between light and less light, as we went from one onward into the other.

If you understand anything of my narration, then try further to imagine what it means to us when we come through those other less-enlightened realms into your own, to speak thus with you as I do now. Then you will not wonder, I think, that at times we find much to do to get into touch with you, and often altogether fail. Could you see things from this side the Veil you would not marvel at this—the marvel is afoot the other way about.

Now to tell you of the City.

It was on the plain near the middle parts of the region over which the Angel Lord ministered to rule it. It had no walls, as most such cities have; but there were the usual series of Watch Towers, and there were some out on the plain standing solitary, and some within the City, here and there, in carefully chosen positions.

THE LIFE BEYOND THE VEIL

The House of the Chief stood foursquare at the edge of the City, and had a large gate.

Now I will tell you not as it appeared to us who came from a higher place, but as it is in the eyes of those whose normal environment is that same sphere, the inhabitants, that is, of Sphere Five.

The Great Gate of this Palace is of liquid stone. That is quite literally to be read. The stone was not solid, but in flux; and the colours of the gate changed from moment to moment, affected both by what went forward within the House, and also by what was agait upon the Plain before it. It also was affected from the Watch Towers on the Plain; but only by those on this side, not by others on the other side of the City, which were in touch with stations on the other sides of the Palace. It was very beautiful to look at, that gateway, massive on either side and blending into the wall of the main structure, solid above the square arch, and changing in beauty as the colours changed. One part only was constant, and that was the great keystone, in the middle above, which always and ever shone red for love.

We passed within and found many roomy chambers about the gateway, in which were recorders who read the messages and influences coming at the Gate, divided them into their own proper groups, and sent them whither they should go. They had expected our coming, and two youths were waiting in the roadway beyond the Gate to lead us to the Angel Lord.

We passed down the broad street, whereon went people happy of face, as ever people are hereabout. I simply write it down' for you who sometimes and often do not smile for contentment within. For us it is as we should tell you the sky to-day is blue in Egypt in the summertime. Then we came to the chiefest building within the Palace walls, which was the Chief's own quarters.

We ascended the steps before it and passed beneath a porch which ran along its front, and through a door into the Central Hall. It was also square, built with high pillars of liquid stone, like the Gate; and these were also changing continuously in hue, but did not all wear the same tint of colour at any one moment as the Gate did. They were diverse. There were twenty and two of them, and each was different. Seldom were two of them of the same colour at one time; and this give a very pleasant aspect to that hall.

They were also made to blend together their beauties in the large dome of crystal above, and that was a sight even more lovely, and one you must try to imagine, for it is beyond my power to describe.

We were bidden to rest within this hall, and lay on couches near the walls to watch the play of colour. As we did so the effect seemed to invade us and give us a peace and ease which made us feel quite homely at last in this old-new environment.

Presently we saw a light flash out of one of the corridors which gave on to the Hall. And then the Chief came to us and bowed and took my hand, and saluted me very kindly. He was of the Seventh Sphere, and conditioned to the Fifth, as is necessary to rule it.

He was very kind, and did all he could in love to enable us in every way; and then we went to the Presence Room, where was his Chair of Estate, in which he sat me, with my companions about me, and himself near by.

Word was given, and a company of women came into the Hall, and greeted us with courtesy. And then the Chief expounded the nature of my visit to me and to my companions, while the women stood before us in their pretty white and blue robes; but their jewels they had left behind, for this occasion. Yet they were very sweet in their simplicity of attire, whichwas, moreover, becoming to them in the demure demeanour which was upon them in the company of us who were some few spheres removed from them.

It amused me much, and so I asked that he would permit me awhile before he continued. So, descending to the floor, I went and blessed each one, my hand severally upon the head of each, and added kindly words.

Whereupon their shyness was abashed instead of them; and they looked up and smiled at us, and were altogether at their ease.

Now, of the audience which ensued I will tell you when next you sit with me. I have been full in telling what I had to tell, that you might understand the conditions and customs of these parts. So let us leave it there for this time. I blessed them with words and a touch; and they blessed me with their happy smiles. And so we both were blessed, one of the other. That is the way with us. So let it be with you below. It is better thus than otherwise. And so also with blessing I leave you now, my ward, for this time, and asking not your thanks for it. For when we bless it is our Father blesses through us, and His blessing, passing through us, leaves somewhat of its benediction in us in its passage. Remember this also, and you shall know that he who blesses his fellow is blessed himself in the doing of it. #

Tuesday, December 30, 1913.

To continue:

They stood there before me and I tried to find the reason of my coming, but could not. Then I turned to the Angel Lord for guidance in this matter, and he answered me well:

"These our sisters are brought here together, who have worked so, in one band, for these three spheres last past. None of them would go before to leave the others behind; but if one should make her progress faster, then she remained to help those who lingered some little, and together they came on until this place was opened to their entry. Now they have progressed to merit their further advancement, if you should judge it fitting so to be done to them. They await your wisdom to that end, for they have come to know that, were they too soon to go forward into the heaven next ahead, their progress would be the more retarded."

Being thus at length enlightened, it came to me that I too was on my trial. This thing had been withheld from me by my own Ruler in order that, with no premeditation, I should be found face to face with a problem, and my wits be put to hazard in the resolution of it. This added to my joy, for that is the manner with us in these realms, that the harder the task the greater the pleasure, knowing our Leader's confidence that we are able if we will.

ZABDIEL'S TEST OF THE FAITHFUL WOMEN.

So I thought a little space, and rapidly, and this is how I measured it.

There were in all fifteen of these faithful, loving souls, who had so come their long road together. So I divided them by three, and sent five each way into the City. I bade them each bring me a little child, one to each party of five,— and the child should tell me the lesson which they should impart to him, as being what most he should have needed to know.

By and by they returned, and with them were three sunny little children.

Two were boys and one girl.

Now, they came in nearly together, but not quite. By this I knew they had not met with one another by the way, or they would have joined forces, and not parted again, for their love together was very great. So I bade them stand the children before me, and to the first boy I said, "Now, little one, tell me what lesson you have learned from these kind ladies."

To which he replied very nicely, "If it please you, bright sir, I came hither without knowing God's earth, for my mother gave up my spirit into the heavenly land before she gave my body to earth. These lady-sisters, therefore, instructed me, on the way, that I must know that God's earth is the cradle of these brighter spheres. In it are little boys fostered by much rocking to and fro; and no peace is known, as we know it here, until the earth is left behind. Nevertheless, it is of the same Kingdom of our Father's Love, and we must pray for those who are being rocked about unkindly, and for those who rock them too hardly."

And then he added, in perplexity at receiving this one last injunction, "But, my lord, this we do always, for it is a part of our school lessons so to do."

Yes it was a very good lesson, I told him, and one which would bear enforcement at other lips than those of his own teachers; and he was a good boy to have given his answer so well.

Then I called the other little mite, and he came to my feet and touched them with his soft little hand and, looking up to me very sweetly, he said,

"May it please you, kindly-looking sir—" But at this I could forbear no longer. So I stooped down, and caught him up to my lap, and kissed him, tearfully for the joy of love, and he gazing at me in submissive wonder and pleasure mingled. Then I told him to proceed, and he replied he could not with ease and perfection were

I not pleased to set him down on the steps again. This I did, I wondering now, and he continued.

He laid his hand again upon my foot exposed from beneath my robe, and said very solemnly, taking up exactly where I had broken him off so short, "that the feet of an angel are beautiful to the sight and to the touch,—to the sight, because the angel is good, not of head and heart alone, but in the way he goes on the service of our Father; to the touch, for they tread softly ever,—softly where men feel their weight in rebuking for wrongdoing, and softly when he takes up in his arms the sorrowful, to bear him away to these brighter lands of comfort and joy. We shall be angels one day, not little boys any more, but big and strong and bright, and having much wisdom. And then we must remember this, for in that day some one of great degree will send us also to earth to learn and teach at one time; for there are many there who will need us as we do not need who came away so soon. Thus the lady-sisters instructed me, sir angel, and I know it is as they have said since I have seen you here."

Now, the love of little children is always so very sweet to me it unmettles me, in a way, and I do admit to you I lowered awhile my head, and looked within the folds of my lap, while my breast uplifted and sank in its almost painful ecstasy. Then I called all three, and they came—very gladly by their faces, but warily by their feet—and knelt one on either side my thighs, and the little girl before my knees. And I blessed them very earnestly and lovingly, and kissed their sweet bended heads of curls, and then sat the lads on the step beside me and, taking the little maid upon my lap, bade her tell me her story.

"May—it—please—you,—sir," she began, and she said each word so carefully separated from its fellows that I laughed right out; for I knew she had omitted the "kind" or "kindly-looking," or other such endearing adjective, fearing further disaster, and wishing, in her maidenly modesty, to avoid all such.

"Young lady," I said to her, "you are more in wisdom than your years or size, and bid fair to become a very able woman some day, who will govern well where you are set."

She looked at me doubtfully, and then round at the company, who were all enjoying this interview in no common measure. So I bade her, speaking softly, to continue. This she also did, as the boy had done, taking up where she had left off, "that girls are God's dams to nurture His lambs in their bosom, but not until they have grown in love and wisdom, as their bodies grow in stature and in beauty. So we must ever keep in mind the motherhood that is in us, for our Father put it there when we slept in our own mother's womb, before our angel awoke us, and brought us away into these blessed Homes. And our motherhood is very sacred from many causes, and the best cause of all is this: that our Saviour, the Christ Lord (here she crossed her little dimpled hands upon her breast and, with fingers interlaced, bowed very reverently, and straightway continued so), was born of a woman, whom He loved, and she loved Him. When I am grown into a woman I will be told of those who have no mothers as we have here, but know no tender love of mother like ours. And then I shall be asked if I would wish to be mother to some of those not borne by me, but needing some such one as I very sorely. Then I must stand up straight and strong, and answer, 'Send me forth of these bright places into those that are more dim; for I am wishful to suffer with them, if I may perchance help and foster those poor little ones; for they are lambs of our good Shepherd Who loves them; and I will love them for His sake, as also for their own.'"

I was much moved by these three answers. Long before they were complete I had come at several points which showed me that these women must go onward, and together, into higher places; for they were worthy.

So I answered them after this fashion. "My sisters, you have well done in this matter; and your scholars have done well for you. I perceive, among other things, that you have learned what is here to be had for the learning, and that you will be of service in the sphere next beyond. But I have learned also that you will do well to go together as hitherto, for, although you instructed these tiny philosophers each apart from the others, the trend of their answers is the same—love of those in the earth life, and their duty to them. So I see you are of such a concord in purpose that you will be of greater service together than apart." Then I blessed them and told them they should journey back with us when we should be ready to go shortly.

Now, several points I did not note for their instruction then, but kept them back for our journeying together, when I could expound them at my leisure. One was this: so utterly at one were these fifteen loving souls that, in their several instruction of the children, they had fixed on one phase of duty and service alone. All these three children and, by implication, all those who had come over here from stillbirth, were to be sent back to help those on earth by tending and guarding them. They had altogether lost sight of all the other manifold duties allotted to such as these; and the further fact that but a small proportion of those who come hither in the manner they did are ever sent back to do mission work on earth, for the reason that the very refinement of their natures fits them for other work the better.

But I will no further now, so bid you God's Love and blessing, and on your own lambs, too, and their own darn. Believe me, my brother and ward, those of the Kingdom here look with tender eyes on those who keep their sacred charge in love, and fit them the more for this Realm of greatlove when they come hither. Keep this in mind and be glad that it is so, and within the power of every father and mother among you so to do.

Wednesday, December 31, 1913.

Before proceeding further I will describe the City at which these things were done, for the Fifth Sphere, as I know it, has certain points which are peculiar to itself. Most of the spheres, but not all, have one City in Chief; but Sphere Five has three, and there are three Chief Lords who minister there to rule.

The reason of this threefold dominion is found in that this Sphere stands at that altitude, which having attained, a choice has to be made as to the particular way to be followed thereafter. It is a kind of sorting-room, as one should say, wherein are the inhabitants, in the course of their sojourn there, classified into their proper groups, and proceed onward in that special branch of service for which they most properly are fitted.

These three Cities stand each near the borderland of a very large flat continent, and a line drawn through them would form an equilateral triangle. For this reason the broad roads of each City spread out from the largest square, where stands the House, fanlike, through the City and onward in right lines across the open country. These communicate with the other two Chief Cities and the settlements of the plain. But in the middle of the triangle there is a Temple of Worship and Offering, which stands within a large circular glade in the midst of a forest. With this Temple all the roads are linked up by other cross-roads, and hither, at certain times and seasons, come deputies from the Three Cities and settlements under their charge, to combine their worship of God.

Thousands, and tens of thousands, come at one time from all quarters of that sphere, and it is a very wonderful sight to see. They come in parties, and meet together in the glade, which is a large plain of grassland. There they mingle together, and all the different colours of that sphere, mingling also, make a pretty show to behold.

But more lovely than these is the sense of unity in diversity. Some are beginning to progress onward in one direction, and some in another; but over, in and throughout that vast assembly the one vibrant note of deep love pulsates; and all know that this is enduring, and, whatever be their future destination, can enable them to come at one another in whatever part of God's large domain they be forever. So there is no foreboding of coming separation. We know not any such here. For where love is what you know as separation, and its sorrow, cannot come. Even on the earth this' would be so now had 'not man sinned, and so gone away from the right path of development. It will be hard for them to regain this now; but it is possible, for the faculty remains, if it sleep unawakened, except in very few.

Now we must away to the next stage of my journeyings, when I should take my enlarged company into the Sixth Sphere, and there deliver the women to the Chief of that land.

Arrived there we were met, some way from the Capital City, by a company of welcome. For I had sent the message of our coming from the highlands of the borderland of the Fifth Sphere. They came, and among them were some who had known these women, and the friendship was taken up anew with much joy and many benedictions.

THE LIFE BEYOND THE VEIL

When we had arrived at a town where was to be their home for awhile, the citizens came forth in bright attire, both men and women and some few children. They came along the lane, where we were at that time, to meet us.

The trees which grew on either side met overhead in some places and, choosing one such spot, the on-coming company came to a halt and awaited our coming. The scene was very like the inside parts of some cathedral, with leafy roof studded with gems of light; and the people were the choir and worshippers.

They brought garlands of plants and flowers, and beautiful raiment and jewels for their new sisters. These they arrayed them with, and their less radiant garments melted away and vanished before the new robes proper to the Sphere into which they were now come. Then, each amidst her friends, all happy to welcome and be welcomed as to home, they who had come turned about and struck up a sweet marching air, with instruments of melody, and sang as we went forward towards the town. Here the townspeople thronged the walls and towers and gates, and cried greetings of welcome to add joy to joy already great.

Thus it is that initiates are made to know their welcoming, and, when two or three spheres have been passed through, none fear any longer that strangeness of new scenes and faces shall ever mar their progress onward; for all is love, as they very soon come to know.

We went within the gate and into the town, and came to the Sanctuary.

It was a large oval building of very nicely proportioned architecture. The whole, in scheme, was, in significance, that of two circles joined. They symbolized, the one love, and the other knowledge; and the blending of these beneath the central tower within was very nicely and cunningly arranged. Here the light was never still, but ever changing, like that of the Hall of Pillars I lately described. Only there weretwo dominant colours here, the one rose-red and the other violet with green and blue in it. The women were led within, and a large congregation gathered thither.

Then they were taken to a raised place in the very middle of the Sanctuary,and made to stand there awhile. The keepers of the Sanctuary, with their leader, then made their offerings of praise and, when the worshippers joined with them, a cloud of bright mist gathered from them around the women initiates, and bathed them in the conditions of their new sphere, When it passed away from them and floated upward, forming a canopy above, they all stood, in a deep and silent ecstasy, watching the beautiful cloud as it rose and spread out until it covered the space above the other people also. Then came a sound of music, as if it was far away, and yet within the building. It was so sweet and soft, and yet so full of power, that we all felt ourselves to be in the Presence, and bowed in worship, knowing He is ever near.

That music melted away, and yet was with us still; for it seemed to become a part of the cloud of light above us. And, in a way you are not yet able to understand, this is indeed the truth of it. So that cloud of colour and melody of love sank gradually upon us, and was absorbed into our bodies, and made us all one together in the blessedness of holy love.

There was no further Manifestation that they could see at that time. But I, whose faculties have been in longer training, saw what they could not, and knew of those who were present to them unseen; and also from whence the voice came I knew, and the sort of power given in blessing.

But they went away, all very content and very happy together, and the fifteen not the least of them all.

And, Zabdiel, what were you doing all this time?' For I suppose you were the highest in degree there, weren't you?

It ill becomes that I should tell of myself who did but minister in a work of very happy service. The principal of interest were those fifteen. There were three and myself from our own sphere, and none others from any sphere above that one. And to us all the people were very friendly and very kind and loving; and we had much happiness of them by reason of this. Before they would suffer their friends to lead them away to their homes, moreover, those fifteen dear women needs must resist, to come back to us, and thank us, and say very nice words to us in gratitude. We gave them our own in return and promised that we would come again in awhile to inquire of their progress, and perchance give words of counsel.

This at their own desire; in which also they showed wisdom rightly named. For it will be helpful to them, I know, and a help not usually given, because not often asked.

So you see the rule here is, as it is with you, as He said, "To those who ask it shall be given." Which word, my brother and good friend, I leave with you to think upon, with my love and good word of benediction.

Friday, January 2, 1913.

I will that you now come back in your mind to my own Sphere, for there are doings there which I would tell you of. By so much as we progress to learn of God and His ways of wisdom, by so much do we come to understand how simple, and yet how complex, are His forces in operation. This is paradox, yet true nevertheless. Simplicity is found in the unity of forces, and the principle on which they are used.

For instance, love strengthens, and less love weakens, in ratio to its lack, every stream of power which comes from the Supreme Father for our use in His service. They who have come so far as to this sphere are able, by what wisdom they have come at, to absorb into their own personalities, to see the trend of things. We see, as we get towards the Unapproachable Light, that all things are tending towards one central principle, and that is Love. We see Love at the Source of all things. Perplexity is found as from this Source and Centre we proceed outward.

Love still runs onward but has, of necessity, to become adapted, by reason of the lower wisdom of the personalities by whom the service of God is done, and is, therefore, not so clearly seen. When these vibrations of spiritual activity, sent forth by innumerable workers in the one great Scheme, reach the cosmos of matter, the perplexity of adaptation and co-ordination is very much increased. If, then, even on earth, His Love may be discerned by those who themselves are loving, in how much greater degree is it manifest to us.

But yet the wisdom we have before us to attain, if more simple in one sense, is inversely much more intricate, because of the vaster regions over which our view is given to range. As you go from one sphere to another you meet with those whose providence is concerned with ever wider systems of planets and suns and constellations. These you must consult, and from them you must learn ever more widely of the constitution of the Father's widespread realms, and the children of those realms, and His dealings with them, and theirs with Him.

So you will see that we do well to be careful in our stepping forward, that a thoroughness of understanding be had, step by step, for the duties allotted to us become ever wider in their effect, and the consequence of our decisions and actions are fraught with greater solemnity, and have responsibility to wider reaches of space and its inhabitants.

I do not deal, however, with other than your own planet in these messages which I have given you, for the time is not ripe by far for such extended knowledge. What we have now in hand, I and my fellow-workers, is to help the people of earth to a higher wisdom in respect to their duty in love one to another, and unitedly to God, and of our ministry of help to such as, in love and humility, are willing to work with us,—we from this side the Veil, and you on earth being our hands and eyes and ears and the words of our mouth to speak forth, as we help you, that men may know themselves as God made them, glorious potentially and, for the time of the season of their earth sojourn, toilers in a world where the light has been permitted to grow dim.

Now let me tell you of those things of which I spoke.

On a large plain In this Sphere Ten there is a high mountain which stands sheer up from the grassland and dominates its fellow-mountains like a king on his throne among his courtiers. Here and there about the steep ascent, as viewed from the plain, you see buildings. Some are shrines open to the view on every side; some are sanctuaries in which worship is offered, and on the summit the Temple itself, which is over all, and to which all minister and lead. From this Temple, from time to time, Manifestations of the Presence are given to assemblies gathered on the plain below.

Is this the Temple of which you told me before!

No. That was the Temple of the Capital City. This is the Temple of the Holy Mount. It is higher in degree and of different use. It is set here not so much for worship within, but for the uplifting and strengthening and education of worshippers who assemble on the plain. Keepers and officers there are, who worship within the Temple, but these are very high in degree, and few go in with them until they have progressed some spheres onward, and return on some duty to this Tenth Sphere.

It is a Colony of Powers who are advanced beyond this Tenth in their persons, but who visit this High Place on missions of help and judgment from time to time. And there are always some of them there. The Temple is never left without its complement. But I have not been within, and shall not until I have attained to higher power and sublimity in spheres beyond.

On this plain were gathered a very vast number of people, called thither from all parts of this wide Sphere. From some half a mile — as you would say — from the mountain's base they stretched out far across the country, group after group, until they looked like a sea of flowers in gentle movement, their jewels of Order flashing as they moved, and their garments of many hues ever shimmering from one combination of colours into another. High up on the Sacred Mount stood the Temple and, from time to time, they looked that way in expectation.

Presently there emerged upon the roof a company of men whose shining garments told of their high estate. These came and stood upon the Porch of the Temple, above the chief Gate, and one lifted up his hands and blessed the multitude on the plain. Every word he said was clear and loud to the furthest group. They who stood afar both beard and saw with as great ease as those who were nearer. Then he told them the purpose of their coming together. It was in order that certain might be presented before them, who shortly should be advanced onward into the Eleventh Sphere, inasmuch as their progress had been judged to warrant their safe journey on that upward way.

Now, none of us knew who these new initiates were to be — whether oneself or one's neighbour. That was left to be told. So we waited, in some sort of silence, the next that should happen. Those on the Porch stood silent.

Then from the Gate of the Temple came forth a Man, clad in simple white, but radiant and very lovely, On His head was a fillet of gold, and gold sandals upon His feet. About His middle was a belt of red which shone and sent forth rays of crimson here and there as He moved forward.

In His right hand He carried a golden cup. His left hand was upon His girdle, and near His heart. We knew Him at once, the Son of Man, for none else is like to Him Who, in whatever form or Manifestation seen, ever blends two forces perfectly in Himself: Love and Royalty. There is always a simplicity in His grandeur, and a majesty in His simplicity. Both these you feel come into you and blend with your own life whenever He manifests Himself, as now. And when the Manifestation is over, the blessing so received does not pass from you, but remains a part of you always.

He stood there beautiful altogether, and sweet beyond my telling—sweet and lovely, and with just a tincture of sacrificing pity, which did but add to the joyful solemnity of His face. That face was a smile itself, but yet He did not smile in act. And in the smile were tears, not of sorrow but of joy to give of His own to others, in love. His whole aspect, and what His form expressed, was so manifold of powers and graces in combination as to make Him One alone among those others who attended Him there, and to set Him above all as King.

He stood there gazing not at us but beyond us into the realms where we could not follow. And while He stood thus rapt, forth from the Temple, by its several gates, came a long company of attendants, both men and women, whose sublimity was seen in the delicacy of their faces and forms.

One thing I noted, and will tell you as well as I may. Each of those blessed spirits had a well-defined and powerful character written upon the countenance, and in the gait and actions of each. No two had the same virtues in equal parts and combination. Each was a very high Angel in degree and authority, but each a personality in himself or herself, and no two alike. And He stood there, and they on either side, and some on the lower ledge before Him. And in Him, both face and form, were united, in sweet blend and communion, the beauties and qualities and powers of them all. In Him you could see each quality of theirs distinct, yet all blended together. Yes, He was Alone, and His Aloneness lent added majesty to His appearing.

293

Now, think of that scene, and I will tell you more to-morrow, if you find opportunity for my company. Blessing and glory and beauty are where He is, my dear friend and ward, as I have seen, not once nor twice, but many times since I left the earth life. Blessing He brings and leaves with His brethren. Glory is about Him and links Him with the Throne in the High Places of the Heavens of God. Beauty sits upon Him as a robe of light.

And He is with you also, as with us. He comes not in figure but in fact, into the dim earth plane, and brings there also His Blessing and Glory and Beauty. But there they are unseen, except in part and by a few,—unseen by reason of the dark cloud of sin about the world, as we see it, and lack of faith to look, believing. Still, He is with you. Open your heart to Him and you, as we do, shall have what He brings to give you. #

Saturday, January 3, 1914.

Awhile He stood in rapture, silent, still and beautiful altogether to look upon. Meanwhile, in the throng of bright ones about Him a movement began. Slowly, and with no haste, the multitude rose into the air, and took shape until there was an oval of light round behind and on both sides of Him. Those in rear were higher than His head, and those in front were lower than His feet. So a frame was made and, as it took shape, their brightness increased until we scarce discerned the forms of them by reason of the brightness of their glory. They shone golden about Him, but He was more radiant still than all other be, side, as they stood still now, and shining. Only be, fore His feet was there no arc of light, but a breach was made, so that the oval was not complete but gapped at its lowest part.

Then He moved. His left hand He extended and stretched forth towards us in benediction. With His right hand He tilted the chalice towards us, and from its bowl poured forth a thin stream of many-coloured light which fell upon the rock before Him and flowed down the face of the mountain towards the plain. And as it flowed it increased in volume, until it began to lap over the plain towards us, still expanding. It reached us a broad river of light; and in it w ere seen colours in all their hues from deep purple to pale lilac, from deep red to faint pink, from orange-brown to gold. And all these mingled, here and there, in streams of green or other composite hue.

So it came to us, and among us, as we stood there wondering both at the thing done and all the beauty of it. Now it swept onward until it had covered all the ground on which stood that vast multitude of people. But they did not stand in the liquid lake, for it did not rise upon their feet, but formed a sea beneath them, and they stood upon it. Nor could the eye penetrate to see the grassland upon which it rested as upon a sea-bed. It seemed to lie there beneath us very deep, a sea of liquid glass, rainbowtinted, and upon that sea we stood as on firm ground. Yet it was all in motion, here and there in little waves, and here and there in rivulets of red or blue or other colour, flowing among us underfoot, very strange and very pretty to see.

But in awhile it was noticed that it did not serve every one equally.

There was one here, and another at some little distance, and this repeated throughout the throng, who became conscious of a change in them; and this made them to be silent and in very deep meditation. This change also soon became apparent to their near neighbours. For this is what they saw: the flood of light about him who was thus changed ran yellow-gold, and lapped first his ankles, and then, rising like a pillar of liquid glass, all radiant, and bathed his knees, and then still rose until it was about him a pillar of light, and he in the midst of a golden radiance. Then upon his head, in place of jewel, or chaplet, or whatever he wore, there appeared eleven stars. These also were of gold, but of a brilliance greater than the stream, as if it had become concentrated into eleven jewelled stars to crown the chosen one. On each of those so dealt with that fillet of stars rested upon his head near his forehead, and clasped his head on each side behind his ears. Thus it rested, and shone, making the wearer more beautiful, for the light seemed to invade his countenance and all his body, and uplift him above his fellows.

Then the Son of Man tilted back the cup, and the stream ceased to flow.

And the rock became visible once again, where before it had been hidden by the river of light falling. Presently the grassland about the multitude began also to be seen, and at last all the sea of colours had melted away, and we stood on the plain as afore we had done.

Only there remained those who had become enveloped. They were enveloped now no more. But they were changed for aye, and would never be as they had been ever again. Their countenances had become of more ethereal appearance, their bodies also, and their robes were of a brighter hue than those of their fellows, and of another colour. Also the eleven stars remained to crown them with their light. Only the pillar of radiance was no more about them to envelop them.

Now another man came forth of the Temple on the Holy Mount, and cried, with a very strong voice of great sweetness, that those who had the stars should come forth of the crowd and stand before the Mount of Blessing. So they came forth, and I among them — for I was one of those so called — and we stood before the Mountain-foot, and before Him Who stood aloft before the Temple.

While we stood there He spoke to us in this wise, "You have well done, my children very much beloved, in what duty has been given into your hands to do. Not perfectly have you served the Father and Me; but as you were able so you did your work. I ask no more than you do after this manner in the wider sphere of service into which now I call you. Come up to Me, therefore, My beloved, and I will show you the path into that higher place where your houses await you all ready, and many friends to welcome you whom you will find there. Come up to Me."

Then we saw that before us arose a broad stairway whose bottom rested on the plain just before us, and the top at His feet, far above upon the

Mountain-top. So we all went up that long high flight of steps, and we were in number many thousands. Yet when we were well above the plain and I turned to wave my hand in loving farewell to my group of companions who stood looking after us among the multitude below, it seemed that no less number remained than had come thither to the meeting.

BOOK II: THE HIGHLANDS OF HEAVEN

So great was that assembly. When we were all come upon the platform before the Temple He spoke good words of cheer and blessing to those who remained on the plain. If any had been in sorrow that they too were not called along with us, no trace remained upon their faces as I looked upon them then. In the Presence of their Saviour Lord none could sorrow, but only rejoice in His great love and the benediction of His Presence.

Then upon the stairway certain angels descended from the place where we now were, and stood upon the steps, from the topmost until half-way down, or thereabouts. They, being assembled, raised an anthem of Thanksgiving, praising God in High Heavens of His Glory. On the plain the multitude made response in alternation with those on the stairway. So they sank, and made an end.

The choristers once again ascended, and stood with us above. The stairway now had gone away—how I do not know. It was not to be seen there any more. He raised His hands and blessed them, they keeping silence with bowed heads below. So He turned and went within the Temple, and we followed after Him.

ZABDIEL'S FAREWELL

And now, my friend and brother and my ward, I do not say farewell in parting, for I am ever with you to help, to hear and to answer. Count me always near by, for, although my home in proper is far away, as men would reckon far and near, yet, in a way we know to use, I am ever near by you, in touch with you, in what you think, and in what you will, and in what you do. For of these things I have, from time to time, to give account on your behalf. Therefore, if I have been aught to you of friend and helper, remember me in this, that in my reckoning I may have joy of you, as you, if faithful, shall have joy of yourself. Remember the Angels of the Seven Churches, and deal well with me, my ward. Remember, moreover, that one day you also, as I now, will have a charge to keep, and lead, and watch and help, and to answer for his life and how he uses it.

And now my blessing. It may be I shall find means and permission to speak with you again as I have done in these messages. It may be in this way, or it may be in ways more plain even than this. I do not say. Much rests with you in this. But, whatever betides, be strong and patient and in sweet simplicity, with humility, and in prayer. God bless you, my dear ward. I lack the will to bring this to an end. But so it must be. Remember, I am ever near you in the Master's Name and Service. Amen. #

ZABDIEL.

Also Published by Red Pill Press

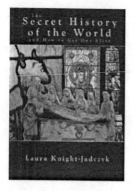

The Secret History of the World and How to Get Out Alive

Laura Knight-Jadzyk's epic work

If you heard the Truth, would you believe it? Ancient civilisations. Hyperdimensional realities. DNA changes. Bible conspiracies. What are the realities? What is disinformation? This is the de nitive book, the real answers, where Truth is more fantastic than ction.

Laura Knight-Jadczyk draws on science and mysticism to pierce the veil of reality. With sparkling humour and wisdom, she shares over thirty years of research to reveal, for the rst time, The Great Work and the esoteric Science of the Ancients in terms accessible to scholar and layperson alike.
ISBN 1-897244-16-9, 786 pages

The High Strangeness of Dimensions, Densities and the Process of Alien Abduction

Anyone who wants to understand the hyperdimensional reality which is the "home" of alleged aliens, should pick up Laura Knight-Jadczyk's *The High Strangeness of Dimensions, Densities and the Process of Alien Abduction.*

With diligent research and a relentless drive for the facts, this book strips away the facade of alien abductions masquerading as mind control and mind control masquerading as alien abductions. Laura then goes on to show how the Evil Elite rulers of the planet have merged, at the highest levels, with the Overlords of the Matrix Control System that underlies the structure of our reality.
ISBN 1-897244-11-8, 431 pages

Visit us at www.qfgpublishing.com for these and other titles, or ask for them at better booksellers.